GROWING UP WITH THE COUNTRY

Growing Up with the Country

Family, Race, and Nation
after the Civil War

KENDRA TAIRA FIELD

Yale

UNIVERSITY PRESS

NEW HAVEN AND LONDON

Portions of this book were previously published, in different form, in "'No Such Thing as Stand Still': Migration and Geopolitics in African-American History," *Journal of American History* 102 (2015): 693–718; "The Chief Sam Movement, a Century Later: Public Histories, Private Stories, and the African Diaspora," with Ebony Coletu, *Transition Magazine* 114 (July 2014); and "'Grandpa Brown Didn't Have No Land': Race, Gender, and an Intruder of Color in Indian Territory," in *Gender and Race in American History*, ed. Alison Parker and Carol Faulkner (Rochester, NY: University of Rochester Press, 2012).

Yale University Press books may be purchased in quantity for educational, business, or promotional use. For information, please e-mail sales.press@yale.edu (U.S. office) or sales@yaleup.co.uk (U.K. office).

Set in Electra type by IDS Infotech, Ltd.
Printed in the United States of America.

Library of Congress Control Number: 2017932063
ISBN 978-0-300-18052-7 (hardcover : alk. paper)

A catalogue record for this book is available from the British Library.

This paper meets the requirements of ANSI/NISO Z39.48-1992 (Permanence of Paper).

10 9 8 7 6 5 4 3 2 1

For my father, Kenyon Brown Field (1946–2004),
my grandmother Odevia Helen Brown Field (1923–2014),
my mother, Susan Ravensdale Field Malis,
and all those whose stories fill these pages and my heart

The relentless search for the purity of origins is a voyage not of discovery but of erasure.

—*Joseph Roach*

CONTENTS

CONTENTS

In New Jersey, our family was black, while back home in rural Oklahoma we were Creek Indian, too. As a child in the 1970s and 1980s, I loved nothing more than listening to my grandmother's stories about growing up African American and Creek Indian in 1920s Oklahoma. In the long wake of the Newark riots, watching Odevia Brown Field plant tomatoes in the patch behind her house, I learned about a time when our family had owned hundreds of acres of land, alongside our Indian and African-descended kin. Grandpa Brown had a place they called Brownsville, she said, where they built a school and a church. I learned, too, about the oil speculators who gradually came to see my (African-American and Creek) great-grandfather; for the occasional lump sum, he worked as a *Mvskoke* translator across Oklahoma, telling them "just where to look for oil." Through my grandmother's stories, I learned about Indian and African-American land loss.

About once a year, my grandmother would pull out the twenty-five-dollar check she had received from Sun Oil Corporation, insisting that I look at it too. I remember how she stared at that check, asking questions, already knowing the answers. In grade school, I memorized occasional facts about slavery and the Trail of Tears, but it was through my grandmother that I learned about the intersection of the two: that some Native Americans had held slaves, that African Americans had participated in Indian "land runs," and that the North American "frontier" was far more complicated than my textbooks let on. During summertime visits to

Oklahoma, I began collecting evidence. Uncle Thurman would take us out to Brownsville, driving red dirt roads for hours, following the perfectly rectangular perimeter of the thousand-acre homeplace. There was no longer a house, but we found the steps to the school, amid a landscape of tall grass, Indian paintbrushes, and oil wells. One year at a YMCA summer camp in the Catskills, when I stumbled across a collection of Indian creation myths nearly identical to the Brer Rabbit folk tales my father occasionally told me as a child, I ran to a pay phone to call him. Was Brer Rabbit Indian, black, or both? These were the wrong questions, but at the time, back east, there was barely language for what I wanted to know. There was, thankfully, the language of family. When I moved away to college, my family's stories stayed with me, quietly highlighting the incompleteness of other historical narratives.

Long before I cared for the discipline of history, my grandmother's stories made me whole, pointing to things I sensed, but for which I had no words. Ronne Hartfield writes, "Our mother's stories have given us the maps by which our tribe locates its journeying, its streams and rivers, its stony places, its sometimes astonishing, more often incredibly affirming twists and turns." E. Frances White attests that her own grandfather's stories were "so wonderful that I began to believe that they could not be true." As she grew older, however, she stopped worrying about whether they were true. "What is important here is that my grandfather *told* me the stories; the stories made sense to me; and, most important, the stories made sense of the world for me." As an adult, I also grew less interested in the veracity of our family stories than in the power and pride we all drew from them.[1]

I hope that this book reminds others of the important place of narratives and storytelling within families and communities. In recent years, psychologists have begun to examine what human beings have long understood, the importance of a strong "intergenerational self": children knowing they "belong to something bigger than themselves." One study revealed that in the face of conflict and uncertainty, "the more children know about their family's history, the stronger their sense of control over their lives, the higher their self esteem." Such findings have particular implications, both urgent and hopeful, for African-American communities.[2]

Forcibly separated from our family members by the first and second Middle Passage, by slavery and the slave trade, we were also separated, in large part, from our family histories. Frederick Douglass opened his 1892 *Life and Times* this way: "The reader must not expect me to say much of my family. Genealogical trees did not flourish among slaves." Rooted in the repetitive social trauma of family separation and "haunted by the need to know," historian Heather Williams writes, in the postemancipation era, descendants searched for "those who were lost through sale or through the negligence of history." When the African-American search extended beyond the history of individuals or individual families, it began "to help construct the history of a people." Just as "enslaved children were stunned when they found out they could be sold," "some people are still stunned by the blow," including the deprivation of family members and family history: "People cannot fathom it, and they want to reestablish and reclaim that history."[3]

And so we have. Dorothy Redford, descendant and genealogist of the North Carolina Somerset Plantation, recalled, "I began as a woman alone, drifting in both time and space," and by the end, she had "a past peopled with links as strong and solid as any family in this nation." As she pieced together the lives of their ancestors and organized a reunion on the grounds, Williams reflects, "All the slaves on the plantation became her people." E. Frances White's family "worked hard to develop strong black egos in its children," and thus sent her to spend a week with her grandfather each summer. He was a follower of Marcus Garvey and "had an impressive library filled with everything he could find on Africa and its diaspora. It did not matter to him whether a book was racist or uplifting; if it was about black people, he would buy it." There she encountered "both a history of the Ku Klux Klan, written by a klansman, and C. L. R. James's *The Black Jacobins*."[4]

My own first copy of *Black Jacobins* came from my granddad. So did Du Bois's *Black Reconstruction*, and every book Joel Augustus Rogers ever wrote. Orphaned as a child in the 1910s, my granddad, William H. Field, was taken in by an unlikely African-American entrepreneur named Charlotte Field. Aunt Charlotte, as he called her, gave him a roof over his head and a job delivering *The Crisis* in Paterson, New Jersey. By the 1950s, following one year at Howard University and several more in the military, he was living in East Orange, New Jersey, and working at the post office in Newark. Around this time, he wrote a letter to Joel Augustus Rogers, the prolific self-trained historian (and onetime Pullman porter) who combatted racist propaganda and popularized black history. In his letter to Rogers, my grandfather lamented the lack of "black books" for his children at the local library, pleading to one of his most cherished authors, for help. Some weeks later, Rogers arrived at the East Orange Public Library with a box of his books. Afterward, my grandmother remembered fixing him dinner—"maybe it was lamb," she recalled—at 74 Stockton Place. Thus while my grandmother shared countless family stories, my granddad, lacking knowledge of his own ancestors, immersed his children in other kinds of stories and another kind of family: the beauty and rigor of the black intellectual tradition. Somehow, I knew, Du Bois and Rogers were "my people," too. How I cherished this extended family. Growing up in a household marked by the insecurities of illness and death, I borrowed their strength.

On July 9, 1977, the *New York Times* published an article about organ transplantation with a photograph of my mother, my father, my grandmother, and me. Having developed kidney failure at nineteen, in 1968, my father received, from my grandmother, an early experimental kidney transplant. The article stated that before the operation, "when Kenyon was so sick that he often 'struggled for breath,'" my grandmother would go down to the basement to be alone. "Everybody would be asleep . . . and I'd just scream, because he was dying before my eyes." When I was born, some years after the surgery, the doctors told my father that he would be lucky to live to see my fifth birthday. But with the help of my mother's fight, my father kept living—eventually becoming a kidney doctor himself, trying to understand this illness and its prevalence within African-American communities—and he carried me well into my twenties.[5]

Over the years, various theories emerged about my father's kidney disease. Somehow they all led back to Okmulgee, Oklahoma, where he spent his first five years in the 1940s. Sometimes my grandmother talked about "greasy creek," the oil-rich creek where they would play, wondering about

1. Photograph from the *New York Times*, July 9, 1977: clockwise from left,
my father, Kenyon; my mother, Susan; my grandmother Odevia;
and me. Courtesy *New York Times*

its effects. Other times she mentioned the day he fell into a gigantic
Oklahoma anthill. The theory that registered with East Coast doctors in
the 1980s amounted to untreated strep throat and a lack of antibiotics during
his early years. The final, unspoken one had to do with leaving Oklahoma.
My father had been raised by his grandparents those first few years of life,
in a country town where he was adored by a large extended family, black,
"mulatto," Indian, and proud; amid a contentious return to his mother and
father in urban Paterson, New Jersey, the separation was traumatic. Thereafter, he would return to Oklahoma each summer, with his younger sister

2. Kenyon Brown Field, left, and Charles Brown, c. 1950.
Author's collection

Beverly, to be with his Momma and Pawpaw, but there was a longing that never quite healed. He seemed to cling to Oklahoma for life.

When my father passed away in 2004, having survived nearly four decades of illness—including a stroke that caused him to lose all of his speech—I stumbled back into history and found his intellectual curiosity and love of life waiting for me there. He loved Oklahoma, and the stories that reside there, more than the many places he had traveled in his fifty-seven miraculous years. Making sense of our unspeakable loss together, my then eighty-five-year-old grandmother accompanied me on nearly every research trip I made to Oklahoma, Mississippi, and Alabama. She was every bit as curious as I, and far more skillful at enlisting others to come along for the ride, as we searched for missing puzzle pieces. In the ten years that followed my father's death and preceded my grandmother's, Odevia Brown Field and I made the unspoken decision to dwell in the past.

I remember clearly the two of us racing back from a morning fact-finding expedition over long and winding roads, hoping to arrive to Sunday buffet at the Sirloin Stockade "in time"—before her eldest sister Marzetta scolded us. We had already missed church. We arrived just in time to find my grandmother's cousin, Clifford Fields. We shared with Clifford what we were up to, and he immediately took me under his wing and proceeded to share with me the decades of scattered genealogy notes he had vigilantly collected. In the years since that serendipitous meeting, Clifford has driven me down hundreds of country roads, knocked on dozens of strangers' doors, and asked nearly every question that no one else dared to ask. While in graduate school, I collected these family stories "on the side." One day, my adviser encouraged me to consider creating scholarship out of them. "Is that allowed?" I asked.

Like many historians, I imagine, I first learned the meaning of change over time, and space, within my own family, as I listened to mythical stories of long-lost black landownership from the vantage point of the post–civil rights era, and as I watched my father decline, a pillar of our family fall, and my world ever so gradually collapse. Surrounded by secrets and the ever-present threat of separation through the passage of time and space, my job—first as a daughter, then as a historian—became putting the pieces back together. I wanted to know how one generation shaped the next, why these stories were repeated, and where the shadows came from. I was drawn, unconsciously, to what memoirist Suzannah Lessard calls the "family architecture." Like Lessard, this architecture taught me "how short time is, how close the generations are, how powerfully lives reverberate down through the structure of family, deeply affecting each other." Because, in our "witting or unwitting" response, "we in turn create the unseen structure in which our children must live."[6] Now, as a mother, I know that most, if not all, of this is beyond my control. But while I cannot change the whole my son has inherited, I can help him to understand the parts: every brick, every blueprint, every unconscious gesture, buried bone, and lost page of our people.[7]

ACKNOWLEDGMENTS

My deepest gratitude is reserved for my extended family—countless storytellers, archivists, genealogists, and family historians—who laid the foundation for this work, and for future work. A number of these individuals shaped the research and writing of this book directly, sharing history, memory, sources, meaning, and analysis. My grandmother Odevia Brown Field (1923–2014) was the first and best storyteller I have ever known, and this project began as hers and mine, in the wake of my father's passing. Several of her oft-repeated family stories formed the foundation of this book. Over time, I brought to these stories a historian's eye, questions about narrative, and an interest in the relationship between history and memory. My grandmother cared about these things too, and her stories changed over time, incorporating new questions and theories. In her last decade of life, Odevia Brown Field accompanied me on multiple research trips to Oklahoma, Mississippi, Alabama, and California, encouraging far-flung family members to join our quest. When I was a child, and again through this project, she taught me how to build and sustain relationships, how to transcend distance and difference, how to be family.

My grandmother's cousin Clifford Fields helped to pull this project back in time, from postwar Indian Territory to the plantation South. Clifford shared decades of notes and family secrets, knocked on dozens of unfamiliar doors across Mississippi and Alabama, and discovered and enlisted new family members we had never known. Alongside Clifford, my grandmother's sister Barbara Player, Clifford's brother Prentiss Fields, and my father's sister Beverly Field Whittington urged me onward. They read and commented on my stories, held up our family networks, trekked through Oklahoma with me, and reminded me all the time why, and to whom, this project mattered. Following my grandmother's passing, Barbara, Clifford, Prentiss, and Beverly made the completion of this book possible, providing names, addresses, stories, photographs, and ideas. Numerous elders and family historians who shaped my research, sharing stories, memories, and genealogical notes, passed away during the course of the project. These include Thurman Brown (1911–2007), Thomas Brown (1905–2007), Jeremiah Fields (1905–2007), Marzetta Brown Wesley (1917–2006), Lillian Brown Greer (1919–2007), Janet Williams (1941–2014), Jeretha Fields Harris (1926–2015), Nathaniel Brown (1931–2016), and Andre Vaughn (1957–2016). Additional family historians and collectors who shaped this journey include Lucille Caldwell, Larry Davis, Philip and Donna Field, Herreece Fields, Norse Gaines, Sarah Wesley Phillips, Velma Howell Brinkley, Kimberly Washington Pierce, Paula Pretlow, Terry Smith, Bill Wilson, and Vernita Woodard. I thank them for sharing their stories, networks, photographs, and years of genealogical research. I thank all the members of the Brown, Coleman, Hunter, Davis, Watkins, Simon, Johnson, Dorman, Scott, Fields, Howell, Evans, and Hightower families. I am blessed to have had such beautiful mentors and collaborators.

This includes family members whom I never met, but who I knew were there with me, having heard versions of the same stories, and asked similar questions, in their own lifetimes. Among these, my utmost respect and gratitude goes to Cecil Cade (1945–1989). In the years preceding his death, Cecil Cade and his partner Mark Phillips carefully collected hundreds of documents, photographs, and stories of Davis and Watkins family history. Perhaps most important, they interviewed and recorded Cecil's beloved aunt Lomie Davis, whose parents—Della Watkins and Elic Davis—are at the heart of this book. Uncannily, Cecil and Mark deposited most of the original materials about Della and Elic's lives in slavery and freedom at the Mississippi Department of Archives and History, a relatively uncommon choice for descendants in the 1980s. I had been to MDAH years before, gathering materials on slaveowning families in this story, but it was not until I came to the end of this project that I realized, thanks to cousin Larry Davis, that a small family "box" had been sitting there all along. Included within the box were the original photographs from which my own photocopies had been made, as well as an audiocassette of a 1986 interview with Lomie Davis (1895–1991).

Some of the most important research for this book happened unwittingly, in the course of family reunions. I thank the many individuals who organized and made possible — booking rooms, planning itineraries, cooking, tracking down far-flung family members, sending airfare, and ultimately returning to Oklahoma — the Brown and Coleman family reunions of 1982, 1997, and 2000, including Marzetta (Brown) Wesley, Herman Brown Sr., Charles Brown, Lillian Brown, James Brown, Nathaniel Brown, Barbara (Brown) Player, and their descendants. More recently, I thank my collaborators on the 2007 reunion and the 2014 memorial gathering of descendants of the Chief Sam back-to-Africa movement, including Julia Brown, Herman Brown Jr., Lyndon Brown, Paula Pretlow, Pamela Pretlow, Teresa Francisco, Andre Vaughn, Bernadette Vaughn-Farley, Kimberly Washington Pierce, Pamela Towns, Beverly Field Whittington, Clifford Fields, and Barbara Brown Player. I am grateful to Norma and K. C. Kemp, Billy and Catherine Brown, Herman Brown Jr., Clifford and Herreece Fields, and Prentiss and Esther Fields for hosting my grandmother and me on our many research adventures over the years. I am grateful for the many family members and kin who have made this project possible in so many ways, seen and unseen.

For my archival research in Oklahoma, I relied upon the Oklahoma Historical Society, the Oklahoma History Center, the Western History Collections at the University of Oklahoma, the Melvin B. Tolson Black Heritage Center at Langston University, and the county clerk offices across eastern Oklahoma. I thank Bruce Fisher, Larry O'Dell, and Kaitlyn Bush at the Oklahoma History Center. I thank especially Shirley Nero of Clearview, as well as Elaine Owens and Henrietta Hicks for connecting me to additional descendants, stories, and source material on the black towns, and for welcoming us all home. I thank Paul Abram for his care and stewardship of the Chief Sam cemetery, and for welcoming descendants to the site; and the Oliphant family for their knowledge of the Brownsville land and cemetery.

For my archival research in Mississippi and Alabama, I am grateful to the Mississippi Department of Archives and History, numerous county clerk offices in northern Mississippi and northwest Alabama, and Coleman, Davis, and Johnson descendants in Mantee, Maben, Montpelier, West Point, Philadelphia, and Mound Bayou, Mississippi, as well as Eutaw, Alabama. Thanks also to the librarians and archivists at the University of California, San Diego, Library, the Library of Congress, and the National Archives. For superb research assistance at the University of California, Riverside, Tufts University, Mississippi State University, and Harvard University, I thank Nicolette Rohr, Rayshauna Gray, Mary Kathryn Menck, Leigha Malone, and Mary McNeil. Their meticulous research, careful organization, and intellectual curiosity were invaluable to the completion of this book.

This book includes a large number of images, maps, and photographs that are central to the narrative. For the majority of photographs of people that follow, I am indebted to an enormous number of descendants who chose, again and again, to document, collect, and archive behind closed doors, amid repeated migrations and displacements, uncertainty, struggle, joy, and loss. For assistance locating additional photographs, images, and maps, I relied upon the Oklahoma History Center, Special Collections, and University Archives at the Oklahoma State University, the *New York Times*, the Mississippi Department of Archives and History, the Rosenberg Library and Galveston and Texas History Center, Special Collections at South Carolina State University, the Schomburg Center, Special Collections and University Archives at the University of Massachusetts at Amherst, Special Collections and Archives at Drew University, Princeton University Libraries, the National Archives, and the Library of Congress. I am grateful to Terry Zinn and Jon May at the Oklahoma History Center; Michael Cassity; Sean McConnell at the Rosenberg Library; Avery Daniels at the Miller F. Whittaker Library, South Carolina State University; and especially John B. Phillips at Oklahoma State University for his vast knowledge of Indian Territory and Oklahoma maps. For the original map included in this book, I thank Patrick Florance, Rayshauna Gray, and the Data Lab at Tufts University.

This project became a book thanks to the example of several extraordinary writers, especially Martha Hodes, Tiya Miles, and David Levering Lewis.

Martha Hodes first encouraged me to consider creating scholarship out of the family stories I was collecting "on the side." Martha taught me how to write with care and how to tell stories that matter. Martha's commitment to family history and storytelling strengthened this book from start to finish. David Levering Lewis gave me the unexpected opportunity to abridge his two-volume biography of W. E. B. Du Bois, and I entered a world that has shaped my life and this book since. I thank David and the late Ruth Ann Stewart for taking me, and this project, into their lives and their home, for their advice on writing and world politics, and for their friendship. As I began this project, the publication in 2005 of Tiya Miles's groundbreaking family history *Ties That Bind* marked, among many historians, the emergence of family history as methodology, as well as an expansive field at the intersection of African-American and Native American scholarship, communities, and struggles, encouraging me on this path. Tiya's example and guidance throughout the writing of this family history has been invaluable.

While completing my dissertation at New York University, I benefited early on from the mentorship, scholarship, and teachings of Walter Johnson, Robin D. G. Kelley, Barbara Krauthamer, and Michele Mitchell, each of whom powerfully shaped my approach to U.S. and African-American history, and the history of North American borderlands. I thank Thomas Bender, Adam Green, Maria Montoya, and Jeffrey Sammons for their wisdom and example. For their long-standing public history, political work, and activism in black and Native communities, I thank Marilyn Vann, Rhonda Grayson, and the Descendants of Freedmen of the Five Civilized Tribes Association. I thank David Chang, Fay Yarbrough, Daniel Littlefield, Celia Naylor, Claudio Saunt, Circe Sturm, Gary Zellar, and especially Barbara Krauthamer for their groundbreaking work in this vein, and for welcoming me into the fold.

Fellow graduate students engaged in historical and political work across the African diaspora made NYU a special place in the mid–2000s. For their support, example, and camaraderie, thanks to Abena Asare, Sarah Cornell, Christian Crouch, Ezra Davidson, Anne Eller, Aisha Finch, Peter Hudson, Tanya Huelett, Kiron Johnson, Rashauna Johnson, Albert Laguna, Priya Lal, Natasha Lightfoot, Seth Markle, Derek Musgrove, Atiba Pertilla, Dawn

Peterson, Sherie Randolph, and Frances Sullivan; and to Valerie Dickerson, Ferentz Lafargue, Yoojin Janice Lee, Zerlina Maxwell, Anim Steel, and Justin Steil. For my first undergraduate teaching experiences at Brooklyn College, which led me to pursue the doctorate, thanks to Saru Jayaraman, Joe Wilson, and Immanuel Ness. For sustaining me with meaningful political work throughout, thanks to Rinku Sen, Alta Starr, Joan Sullivan, and Thomasina Williams.

At Williams College in the 1990s, it was Craig Steven Wilder who first opened my eyes to how and why history matters, and who quietly modeled for me the powerful work of a public historian. Also at Williams, I thank Alex Willingham, Kenda Mutongi, Tom Kohut, Tim Sams, and Anne Katharine Dunlop, who first encouraged me to give history a chance. At the University of Cape Town in 1997, I thank Bill Nasson, Mahmood Mamdani, the Department of History, and the Center for African Studies. At Harvard University's Kennedy School in the early 2000s, I thank Xav Briggs, Marshall Ganz, and Lani Guinier, as well as Neelum Arya, Bernadette Atuahene, Nazanin Samari Ash, Farnaz Golshani, and Trina Vithayathil.

I am deeply grateful to my editors at Yale University Press, Chris Rogers and Adina Berk, for their careful stewardship of this project from beginning to end. Thanks especially to Dan Heaton. Thanks to Erica Hansen, Eva Skewes, Christina Tucker, Robin Charney, and Marilyn Flaig. I am grateful to those who read large portions of this manuscript, including especially Martha Hodes, Khary Jones, Tiya Miles, and the anonymous reviewers. For critical feedback on chapters or pieces of this work at conferences, workshops, and other junctures, thanks to Stephen Aron, Colin Calloway, James Campbell, David Chang, Nathan Connolly, Greg Downs, Eric Foner, Thavolia Glymph, William Hiss, Gerald Horne, Walter Johnson, Martha Jones, Barbara Krauthamer, Tiya Miles, Michele Mitchell, Moses Moore, Celia Naylor, Dawn Peterson, Michael Ralph, Carina Ray, Brenda Stevenson, Melissa Stuckey, Circe Sturm, James Sweet, Deborah Gray White, Francille Wilson, John Witt, and the late Leslie Brown. Thanks to Robert Hill and James Anquandah for their invaluable research in the 1970s on the Chief Sam movement. Thanks to my friend and colleague Ebony Coletu for following Hill's lead to the University of Ghana Legon, for her expansive research on Sam's biography and the public history and memory of the movement in Ghana, and for our collaboration on this for *Transition*.

For funding, I thank the Andrew W. Mellon Foundation, the Ford Foundation, the Huntington Library, the University of California President's Faculty Fellowship in the Humanities, the Organization of American Historians' Huggins-Quarles Award, the Hellman Family Foundation, the Charles Eastman Fellowship at Dartmouth College, and the Neubauer and Bernstein Faculty Fellowships at Tufts. I thank Tufts University, the University of California, Riverside, and New York University. I am grateful to the Mellon Mays Fellowship Program for encouraging me to consider graduate study in the first place, and for supporting me with an expansive, extraordinary intellectual community—including many of the aforementioned scholars—in the two decades since. Most recently, I thank Walter Johnson, Brandon Terry, Kirsten Weld, Shatema Threadcraft, Amy Offner, and all of the 2016–17 fellows at the Charles Warren Center at Harvard University.

Much of this book was written at UC Riverside, at the Huntington Library, and in Los Angeles. Thanks especially to Catherine Allgor, Robin D. G. Kelley, and Brenda Stevenson. Thanks to my UCR community, including Jayna Brown, Erica Edwards, V. P. Franklin, Cathy Gudis, Steve Hackel, Jennifer Hughes, Andrew Jacobs, Molly McGarry, Robin Nelson, Dylan Rodriguez, Dana Simmons, Sterling Stuckey, Jonathan Walton, and Devra Weber. At the University of California, Los Angeles, and the University of Southern California, thanks to Sangeeta Ahluwalia, Stephen Aron, Marne Campbell, Mishuana Goeman, Daniel Lynch, and Francille Wilson. Thanks to the Autry Western History Workshop for support of this project.

This book was completed at Tufts University, where I thank Rachel Applebaum, Ina Baghdiantz-McCabe, Orly Clergé, Heather Curtis, Virginia Drachman, David Ekbladh, Elizabeth Foster, Steph Gauchel, Gabriella Goldstein, Kerri Greenidge, Bruce Hitchner, Matthew Hooley, Ayesha Jalal, Peniel Joseph, Gary Leupp, Lisa Lowe, Kris Manjapra, Beatrice Manz, Steve Marrone, Helen Marrow, Katrina Moore, Adlai Murdoch, Heather Nathans, Monica Ndounou, Jeanne Penvenne, David Proctor, Alisha Rankin, Connie Reik, James Rice, Hugh Roberts, Pearl Robinson, Modhumita Roy, Sarah Sobieraj, Christina Sharpe, Reed Ueda, Sabina Vaught, Peter Winn, Man

Xu, Adriana Zavala, the late Christopher Schmidt-Nowara, and all my colleagues in the Department of History and Africana Studies. Thanks to Danuta Forbes, Lori Piracini, Annette Lazzara, and Cynthia Sanders for extraordinary administrative support, and to the Department of History, Africana Studies, the Gerald Gill fellows and the Center for the Study of Race and Democracy, the Africana Center, Center for the Humanities at Tufts, and the Consortium of Studies in Race, Colonialism, and Diaspora. For intellectual community and collaboration in the Boston area, thanks especially to colleagues Vivek Bald, Adia Benton, Vincent Brown, Laura Cade, Greg Childs, Orly Clergé, Abigail Cooper, Dayna Cunningham, Kerri Greenidge, Brenna Greer, Saida Grundy, Fox Harrell, Elizabeth Hinton, Jasmine Johnson, Rashauna Johnson, Walter Johnson, Tanalis Padilla, Kym Ragusa, Justin Steil, Kaia Stern, Frances Peace Sullivan, Patrick Sylvain, Jalene Tamerat, Sheggai Tamerat, Brandon Terry, Phil Thompson, Sneha Veeragoudar, Cecily Walton, and Jonathan Walton.

I thank my father, who challenged me to ask questions and appreciate beauty, and who believed in me. I thank my mother, who insisted, amid our challenges, that I approach life fearlessly, and showed us how. I thank my aunts and uncles who have stepped in to support us: Barbara Player, Clifford Fields, Beverly Field Whittington, Philip and Donna Field, Tyrone and LaRae Kemp, Bruce Ravensdale, Tony and Kathy Ravensdale, the late Jackie Ravensdale, and Paul and Chantal Ravensdale, as well as cousins Paula Pretlow, Pam Pretlow, Lyndon Brown, Jeretha McKinley, Herman Brown Jr., Penney McCoo, Kay Whittington, Andrea and Ryan Maeck, Michael and Katherine Ravensdale, Chelsea Ravensdale, the late Jesse Ravensdale, Mike Jackson, and Kylah Field. I thank Carol Waters Jones, the late Charles Jones, Gerald Jones, and Jamal Jones for welcoming me, and this project, into their beautiful family. I thank Howard Malis, along with my mother, for countless hours of support. And I thank my son, August Field Jones, for his boundless love, and for giving us all new reasons to tell stories.

While I was writing this book, my father passed away, and I was married and had a child, amid what for me were difficult circumstances. Most days I believe it is a small miracle that I have been able to return to this project. Through each of these changes, and especially becoming a mother, my mind was shattered into a million pieces, and I know it will never be the same. I am grateful for this, too, and for the many friends and loved ones who have helped me through. My final note of thanks is thus reserved for my husband, Khary Saeed Jones. This project drew us together ten summers ago, when I first asked him to join me in Oklahoma to film my grandmother and sixty family members as we crawled through a barbed wire fence and hiked to an overgrown cemetery. Thereafter, as the family history came into focus, our relationship grew on Oklahoma oilfields, and in the shade of the Natchez Trace. Most of all, it grew in the world of ideas, actions, and love. Khary's brilliant attention to narrative and humanity has bolstered this book, and my life, at every turn.

GROWING UP WITH THE COUNTRY

Introduction

Geography is fate.
—*Ralph Ellison*

In 1916, twenty-year-old Lomie Davis lost her father, Elic Davis. Born enslaved on the brink of emancipation in Mississippi, Alexander "Elic" Davis grew up watching men and women of his parents' generation move from plantation to plantation, from country to town, using their newfound "freedom" to find, in Nell Painter's words, "*real* freedom." As an adolescent, Elic Davis witnessed the removal of federal troops from the U.S. South, the brisk evaporation of African-American political and economic opportunities, including the coerced removal of two thousand black legislators and officeholders, and the denial and harassment of African-American personhood across the South. His early life was marked by rising aspirations, deep disappointments, and unfathomable disillusionment. As an adult, he dreamed of Africa and participated in several emigration movements; and when he entered his fifties, he finally made it there "on his own." A few years later, in 1923, he wrote to his daughter, telling her that he was sick and asking for her help in order to return to the United States. Lomie tried, in vain, to obtain a loan in order to retrieve her father. No one heard from Elic again, and Lomie believed he soon passed away in the Gold Coast.[1]

The years leading up to Lomie's quiet loss of her father, from the end of Reconstruction through the rise of Jim Crow, were marked by a steady wave of vibrant emigration that has yet to make a lasting mark on the historiography of the period Rayford Logan termed "the nadir" of African-American experience in the United States, or what Oklahoman John Hope Franklin called "the long dark night." In his lifetime, Lomie's father migrated from northeast Mississippi to the delta hinterlands of the black town of Mound Bayou, from the Mississippi delta to Indian Territory, and from Oklahoma to West Africa. Along the way, he also ventured to New York, Chicago, and possibly Jamaica. Notwithstanding Lomie's memories of her father's unique freedom dreams, Elic Davis was not exceptional. Like thousands of former slaves and their children, Davis and his peers were men of meager means, rural black southerners who time after time "voted with their feet," creating a constant flurry of movement that spanned both "domestic" and "foreign" destinations long before the first steps of the Great Migration. Perhaps no collective response to the demise of Reconstruction has been more seriously neglected—dismissed as demographically insignificant, regionally specific, or otherwise exceptional. By the turn of the twentieth century, a lifetime of experience had convinced freedom's first generation, as Ralph Ellison once put it, that "geography is fate."[2]

Growing Up with the Country illuminates the migration of freedom's first generation out of the South and into the West after the Civil War. A narrative history, this book traces three families of freedpeople and their successive migrations in the half-century after emancipation. Between 1865 and 1915, tens of thousands of former slaves sought freedom through a series of experiments in land ownership, town-building, and emigration that spanned the Mississippi delta, Arkansas, Kansas, Indian Territory, Texas, West Africa, western Canada, Mexico, and beyond. Deepening and widening the roots of the Great Migration, I argue that their lives and choices complicate notions of the quintessential domesticity and "bi-racialism" of the "nadir," revealing instead the deeply transnational and multiracial dimensions of freedom's first generation. First, I show that Indian Territory and early Oklahoma served as one of the first sites of African-American transnational movement in the postemancipation period, decentering the United States in North American history even at the turn of the "American century." Second, I illustrate the gradual emergence of American "bi-racialism" and the painstaking construction of race and nation that undergirded the rise of American economic, political, and cultural power at the turn of the twentieth century. I conclude that the historical erasure of this multiracial, multinational past depended upon the manipulation of family and kinship, or "recruiting 'family' to the discipline of 'race.'"[3]

This is the story of a group of African-American migrants whose lives were defined by the pursuit of freedom. Following in the footsteps of Thomas Jefferson Brown, Monroe Coleman, and Alexander "Elic" Davis—three African-descended, including two so-called "mulatto," men who left Mississippi and Arkansas in a hurry, initially for Indian Territory (present-day Oklahoma)—the story is founded upon the history of sexual slavery and women's reproductive labor, the promise of African-American land ownership, and the emergence of a rigid racial hierarchy in the postemancipation South. So while the rise of black Oklahoma was promoted as "all-black" and self-consciously "domestic," such an image stands in considerable contrast to the racial realities of the period, including the erasure of the multiracial history of the South and West. I maintain that the westward migration of "mulatto" freedpeople, for instance, constituted a telling response to the racial "revolution" that accompanied the demise of Reconstruction. Over the course of their lifetimes, African-descended migrants experienced a constant shifting of racial categories over both time and space. Once in Indian Territory, they gained access to Indian land through purchase and marriage. They simultaneously partook of federal expansion and economic, political, and cultural negotiations over land and space with Indians, freedpeople of the Indian Nations, and white settlers and oil speculators. Freedom was not an uncomplicated claim for African-American migrants.

This complex moment of African-American participation in the expropriation of Indian Territory was tellingly short-lived. Widespread African-American access to Indian land ended abruptly with the advent of Oklahoma statehood, Jim Crow segregation, and oil speculation. After 1907, in the wake of Oklahoma statehood, these migrants and most of their black and Indian counterparts lost their land and the associated mineral rights to white settlers and oil speculators through a combination of legal and extralegal exploitation. Thousands, including Coleman and Davis, joined Chief Alfred Sam's 1914 "back-to-Africa" movement in hopes of claiming lasting freedom once and for all in the Gold Coast, the British colony that later declared independence and established the nation of Ghana. Hundreds of other black, "mulatto," and black Indian Oklahomans migrated in family groups to Canada; still others moved south, over the Mexican border. In the end, a movement that began in the spirit of national expansion ended as a powerful experience of racialized land loss. This moment highlights the role of extractive economies and capitalist expansion in the development of modern America and the emergence of a global color line. At the turn of the twentieth century, the United States was undergoing a seismic shift in self-definition from "nation" to "race," from Indian and American to black and white national projects, revealing the ultimate (though not inevitable) futility, for African Americans, of attempting to distance themselves from racism in the context of an expanding U.S. empire.[4]

By the early twentieth century, "White men's countries rested on the premise that multiracial democracy was an impossibility," and whiteness had emerged as a transnational form of racial identification, "global in its power and personal in its meaning." This was a recent development, however, as the history of Indian Territory and Oklahoma statehood attests. For while color consciousness had a long history, W. E. B. Du Bois noted in 1910, "the discovery of personal whiteness among the world's peoples" was "a very modern thing—a nineteenth and twentieth century matter, indeed," driven by the recognition that colonized peoples were on the move across the globe.[5] As the S.S. *Liberia* pushed off from Galveston Island for the Gold Coast in the summer of 1914—purchased for sixty-nine thousand dollars pooled by hundreds of former slaves in Oklahoma—they most certainly were.

Coleman's and Davis's participation in the Chief Sam back-to-Africa movement constitutes one dramatic climax of this family saga. The movement illustrates an indelible link between continental and overseas movement, challenging the long-standing convention among historians of this period to treat the "western" and "Liberia" movements as "somewhat discrete phenomena" and "largely to discount or ignore the political significance of each," as historian Steven Hahn has put it. That so many westward migrants attempted to move decisively beyond the borders of the United States following Oklahoma statehood underscores my claim that part of what attracted

African Americans to Indian Territory in the first place was its momentary status as a political and economic space on the margins, if not beyond the bounds, of U.S. oversight. Not incidentally, a decade following the Sam movement, many of the families and communities that had sent delegates to West Africa with Sam became ardent Garveyites, producing twenty-eight chapters of the Universal Negro Improvement Association (UNIA) by 1926.[6]

This book bridges stories too often categorized as domestic or international. In fact, the current categories would have been somewhat unfamiliar to turn-of-the-century migrants of the southwest borderlands, a region shaped by competing sovereignties, with no clear path to incorporation into the United States. Building upon the powerful contributions of Michele Mitchell and Steven Hahn on African-American peoplehood and "racial destiny" in the postemancipation era, this book presents turn-of-the-century Indian Territory and Africa as part of a continuum of flight from the late-nineteenth-century South; the forthcoming stories urge readers to view "exodusters" and Garveyites within a single transnational frame, to hear "Liberia" and "Oklahoma" in a single breath. As freedman J. W. Turner wrote in 1892, "The peoples are Greatly stirred up in this country about Oklanhoma [sic] . . . but we are bound for [Liberia]." These stories reimagine the postemancipation period as a series of unbound migrations, deepen the roots of the Great Migration, and highlight the centrality of migration and geopolitics in African-American history.[7]

Challenging the notion of a static and withdrawn African-American political life at the turn of the twentieth century, African-descended peoples led bold political lives in Indian Territory, and when faced with the emergence of statehood and Jim Crow segregation, many refused to acquiesce and chose instead to emigrate. African-American experiences in Indian Territory thus prefigure the emergence of Garveyism, the "New Negro" movement, and the Great Migration. Moreover, this moment informs not only the "firsts" of African-American political life in the postemancipation era but the "lasts" of African-American experiences in Indian country. For at least three centuries, Indian country had served as a space of solace, exploitation, and opportunity for African-descended peoples. At the same time, in turn-of-the-century Indian Territory, Oklahoma, West Africa, and across the globe, African Americans were wittingly and unwittingly immersed in the rise of U.S. domestic and overseas imperialism. As the African-American teacher and orator Alfred M. Green had prophesied four decades earlier, in the midst of the Civil War: "There is no such thing as stand still in this nineteenth century."[8]

History, Memory, Silence

The vast majority of the rural black southerners who dreamed of, and journeyed to, Indian country, West Africa, and beyond, were "men and women whose names and struggles have been lost to history." But not entirely. Frequently, their stories were passed on to children and grandchildren, sometimes distorted along the way. As a child, I often heard my grandmother say, "Grandpa went back to Africa with Garvey." Two decades later, when I learned that Garvey never set foot in Africa, I found Chief Sam—not in Harlem or Chicago, but in the former Creek Nation, the black and Indian borderlands of Oklahoma. Just as the Great Migration had largely displaced the quieter history of black rural emigration at the nadir, so had Garveyism displaced descendants' memories of the Chief Sam movement.[9]

I have located the linkages between these movements by entering each one through the lives that created it. I would not have seen these connections so clearly were it not for the circumstances of my own life. I am a descendant of the three principal actors documented in this book: Thomas Jefferson Brown and Monroe Coleman, both my great-great-grandfathers, and Coleman's first cousin, Alexander Davis. I am also a descendant of Brown's African Creek wife, Julia Simon. Because of these relationships, I have had access to several family letters from the turn of the twentieth century, as well as extensive genealogical detail and family stories, which would have been otherwise unavailable. I have relied on family lore and storytelling as well as archival research.

I have gathered descendants' stories of family migrations, settlements, land ownership, and land loss amid continental expansion and the growth of plantation slavery; the Civil War and Reconstruction; U.S. expansionism,

Jim Crow segregation, and the Great Migration; and the flowering of "racial destiny" and early black nationalism. While I have followed the lead of descendants' stories, I have tested their memories, hypotheses, and speculations about our ancestors' lives against the archival record and the recollections of others who traveled the same routes and faced similar experiences. I have brought much skepticism to family narratives. I have kept my eye on the distance between how the past was remembered and how it may have happened. And while the questions I have pursued have frequently diverged from those that most interest familial descendants, local genealogists, and amateur historians, I have increasingly found ways to appreciate the stakes of these divergent perspectives. History may be "the enemy of memory," as one historian has written, "but there are regions of the past that only memory knows."[10]

Along the way, one of the most persistent patterns I noticed was that the family stories about slavery and freedom I heard at home were largely stories about men—about men my family took pride in as quiet and not so quiet freedom fighters who escaped lynchings, purchased land, built schools, and fought back at white night riders before heading to the Creek nation in the middle of the night. I had probably heard the same prideful story about Grandpa Coleman arriving "by train" to Oklahoma repeated a hundred times before I learned to listen and probe for words about his wives Margaret Johnson Coleman, Belle Johnson Coleman, or Ida Carroll Coleman. I have tried to dig beneath the singular stories about Coleman and his patriarch peers to unearth the faint yet firm footsteps of their mothers, sisters, wives, and daughters. As historians of laboring women know all too well, the women whose stories I sought typically did not write, their names changed more than once, and they died earlier than the men with whom they lived. While some black Indian women owned property in early Oklahoma, most of the African-American women migrants in this story did not.

Yet the keepers of these stories were women. It was the daughters and granddaughters of the men at the center of these narratives who shared them with me as a child. Growing up, I was blessed with many phenomenal women, who talked a great deal about the men in our family. One of these was Marzetta Brown Wesley, my grandmother's eldest sister, who served as one of our family historians for much of the twentieth century. My great-aunt Marzetta Brown Wesley was one of many women who held tightly to particular versions of family stories, serving as gatekeepers and the first line of defense against the constant threat of reputational damage. In 1985, as part of an Okmulgee County history project, Marzetta wrote a short family history entry on the Brown-Coleman clan. There she described Monroe Coleman, her grandfather, as a successful businessman and "upstanding member of the community." Like many of her generation, born in the 1910s in and around the black towns of Oklahoma, Aunt Marzetta tended to tell only the best, or most "respectable," parts of our history and our lives, for reasons that are both tragic and understandable; I have deep wells of empathy for the difficult choices she made each day. Oklahoma's black towns were extraordinary beacons of black respectability. Historian Darlene Clark Hine has powerfully evoked the many dimensions of our past—including sexual violence—that African-American women of this generation "believed better left unknown, unwritten, unspoken except in whispered tones." Reading their "alarm," "fear," and "Victorian sense of modesty," Hine concludes that "those who broke the silence provided grist for detractors' mills and, even more ominously, tore the protective cloaks from their inner selves." Indeed, as I gathered more stories from my grandmother and great aunts over the years, I began to make out another set of footprints, to gather, more specifically, the central role of sexual violence in postemancipation migration. Although the oral sources were typically silent or elusive on the subject, nearly every decision to migrate in this period involved not only the explicit threat of lynching but the veiled threat of sexual violence. Throughout the late nineteenth century, sexual violence against freedwomen and their daughters was the quiet but constant counterpart to southern "lynch law."[11]

These "hidden transcripts" are the roots of the respectability politics that came to dominate African-American lives—and African-American historical narratives—for much of the twentieth century. The oral versions of these stories rang with pride and self-determination, while pointing to a haunting underside of worry, vulnerability, and trauma they attempted to leave behind. In the familial and communal narrative that emerged, Oklahoma was

8

the future, and Mississippi the past. In the context of migration, the past became a place as much as a time, and migration mapped family history and genealogy.[12] Marzetta Wesley rarely entertained questions about our family history before Oklahoma. It was as if our family lineage and history, in fact, began in Oklahoma.

In the wake of the civil rights movement, some of the men, and several younger women, began to push this delicate boundary. In the 1970s, when my grandmother's cousin Clifford Fields used a pay phone in Mississippi to call his mother, Nuna Mae Coleman Fields (in Oklahoma), to tell her he had finally arrived in the community of Mantee, at the plantation where Monroe Coleman had been born, she scolded him, "What are you doing down their stirring up all that mess?" When family genealogist Terry Smith asked his mother about their relatives back in Mississippi, she immediately shut down the conversation. About freedom's first (and second) generation in Oklahoma, Smith later remembered, "After they left Mississippi, they *never* went back—not for funerals, not for anything."[13] And yet these buried secrets and conspicuous silences haunted and shaped the present in Oklahoma.

3. Odevia Helen Brown, front row, second from left, and her siblings, c. 1941. Author's collection

As she grew older, my grandmother Odevia Brown Field began to share memories of her "Aunt Tabby" after the move from Mississippi to Oklahoma. Time after time, she described seeing Tabitha Johnson in the 1920s "all covered up": enveloped in fabric from her neck to fingers to toes, the only skin visible the woman's face. As a child, Odevia always wondered why her aunt did this, why she was this way, and as an adult the image seemed to absorb all other memories of her aunt. To the extent that she wondered what had happened in Mississippi, Odevia found clues in Oklahoma. In the 1920s, while sitting with her four sisters under the shade tree at "713," as they called the home place, they would frequently notice white men circling the house in cars. Watching from the window, their mother would call the girls inside. Rooted in veiled experiences of sexual violence in slavery and freedom, over time these unspoken movements, silences, and whisperings became "the family architecture." To be sure, the "unseen structure" in which my grandmother lived included the haunting memory and continued threat of sexual violence. As Oklahoman Ralph Ellison put it, "Our unknown history doesn't stop having consequences even though we ignore them."[14] This "unknown history" includes countless stories of sexual violence, terror, and vulnerability; stories erased or obscured by segregation, shame, and silence; stories that fail to conform to exceptionalist narratives of racial uplift; and stories that were not built to invoke pride. Shards and slices of lives, many of them were not stories at all.

Racism, Solidarity, and Humanity: The Writing of Black Lives

This book is about the complications of freedom. In his stunning conclusion to *Black Reconstruction* (1935), W. E. B. Du Bois wrote, "Three-fourths of the testimony against the Negro in Reconstruction is on the unsupported evidence of men who hated and despised Negroes and regarded it as loyalty to blood, patriotism to country, and filial tribute to the fathers to lie, steal or kill in order to discredit these black folk." For Du Bois, however, "what is inconceivable is that another generation . . . should regard this testimony as scientific truth, when it is contradicted by logic and by fact." Here Du Bois captured the state of American historiography in the first half of the twentieth century, driven as it was by the mainline racism of the Jim Crow era. A small number of midcentury African-American historians, however, began to tell another story. Nell Painter wrote in 1977 that for much of the twentieth century an unceasing discourse of racial inferiority "prompted Black historians to disprove these charges with concrete examples." Mirroring Marzetta Wesley's impeccable posture, the earliest generations of black historians "emphasized respectable individuals, 'credits to the race,' who have made 'contributions' to American life in general." Veering toward "considering isolated individuals in a vacuum," this understandable focus on "heroes" in African-American history nevertheless obscured the vast history of a people. The Jim Crow era has enjoyed a long afterlife in American historiography.[15]

Responding to a racist and exclusionary historiography that had alternately vilified, omitted, pitied, and pathologized African Americans in slavery and in freedom, in the wake of the civil rights movement a younger generation of American historians, amid gradual integration of the profession, began to cohere around narratives of "agency" and resistance that sustained significant scholarship of the 1970s, 1980s, and 1990s. This intellectual movement was accompanied by increasing contestation of the myth of "objectivity," and a growing set of historians whose lives transcended historical boundaries between scholarship and activism, subject and object, and whose scholarship often emerged in solidarity with social movement.[16]

In the past decade, scholars of slavery and other subjects have begun to lament scholarly attention to "agency." Scholars' preoccupation with "agency," several historians have argued, is a problem, in part, because "all human subjects have agency." Practically, historian Walter Johnson has shown, the overuse of the concept has meant that enslaved people's actions were "emptied" of other meanings: "personal meaning, political meaning, and cultural meaning, and metaphysical meaning." In short, the well-intentioned, politically compelling "trope" of the new social history had narrowed historians' field of vision. This trend was exacerbated by the "binary of free and unfree labor." In fact, Du Bois anticipated this debate when he titled his first chapter of *Black Reconstruction*, "The Black Worker." More recently, historians of the Civil War era have begun asking related questions about the role of racism in narrowing historical imagination. The tendency to "imply that freedpeople were all-but-unsinkable political actors," historian Jim Downs writes, was "not only a reaction to specific, if long dead, schools of thought but is also part of a, usually unspoken, political agenda that seeks for laudable reasons to counter present-day racism." While many historians seem "tangled in this mess," novelists and playwrights from Hurston to Hansberry and Morrison, Downs observes, "reveal black characters who make mistakes, take the 'wrong path,' or are not candidates for sainthood."[17]

That there has been so little room in African-American historiography for this basic range of humanity should stop us all in our tracks. It should urge writers away from "sweeping accounts" in favor of "details that often find little place in historical narratives hell-bent on seeing freedpeople as heroes." It should remind us that such characters may in fact have the most to teach us about freedom. As W. E. B. Du Bois asked in *Black Reconstruction*, "What is the object of writing the history of Reconstruction? Is it to wipe out the disgrace of a people which fought to make slaves of Negroes? Is it to show that the North had higher motives than freeing black men? Is it to prove that Negroes were black angels? No, it is simply to establish the Truth, on which Right in the future may be built."[18]

In many ways, the subject of this book was not my choice. In accepting the subject as my own, however, I have made two important choices. First, I have steered wide and clear of the seduction of ready-made stories about race and power that might have obvious heroes and villains, choosing instead settings whose dynamics of race and power are admittedly complex and rarely obvious; for instance, Indian Territory in the late nineteenth century had relatively few white residents at the outset, but many African Americans, Native Americans, and black Indians. Writing about race, power, and white racial nationalism in this context was intriguing to me. Born in the Deep South—a region built by the marriage of slavery and early American imperialism—in the postemancipation era African-American migrants participated in the latest iteration of U.S. empire—the settlement of Indian Territory and the "closing of the frontier"—in nuanced and important ways. This book treats African Americans and Native Americans as complex actors on the North American "frontier" by paying attention to the presence of

Native Americans as slaveowners, and African Americans as settlers on Indian land.[19] Here I offer stories about linked vulnerabilities that reflect the overlapping and interconnected struggles humans have always faced, and continue to face today.

In this sense, *Growing Up with the Country* is a study of how people, in the face of adversity, make freedom "real." I show that people make freedom with the stuff that surrounds them. In the late-nineteenth-century United States, this included the rise of racial nationalism, settler expansion, and domestic and overseas imperialism, as well as the continuing influence of what came before—knowledge and experiences of migration, land, freedom, and privilege rooted in the antebellum period. By placing the somewhat more familiar stories of struggles for political and economic opportunity, family, community, and institution building against this backdrop, I offer nuanced portraits of both African-American freedom and American expansion. Especially in the wake of massive nineteenth-century migrations and the global demise of racial slavery, "white men's countries" were grappling with racial and national crises and becoming "cramped for land." In 1910, Du Bois commented on the centrality of property ownership to the propaganda of whiteness. "But what on earth is whiteness . . . that one should so desire it?" he asked. "Whiteness is *the ownership of the earth* forever and ever, Amen!"[20] For a brief and sudden moment in turn-of-the-century Indian Territory, settlers of color dabbled in this elusive power with some of the same racial, national, and religious fervor that they witnessed among their white neighbors. The stories uncovered contribute to a more complicated and complete history of African-American freedom and American expansion in a crucial era of world history.

Second, I turn to the "proudly small." I enter broad narratives of African-American migration and American expansion through the window of a small number of "ordinary" lives; in this sense, my approach is microhistorical. Microhistory "observes historical change up close," and challenges conventional narratives by revealing how individual lives meet, shape, and upend broader historical patterns. The emergence of African-American family histories—in spite of vast silences and disparities within the archive—raises new possibilities for microhistorical approaches to the African-American past. "African American history may be one of the last fields to receive a mi-crohistorical treatment," one historian writes. Nineteenth-century African-American history has been dominated instead by powerful, "sweeping accounts of the black experience," from John Blassingame's *The Slave Com-munity* to Ira Berlin's *Many Thousands Gone.* Notwithstanding the contribu-tions of smaller regional and thematic studies, on balance, "scarce records, especially the lack of firsthand accounts for many aspects of black life, make microhistory's tight focus on the 'proudly small' difficult to achieve." Difficult, but not impossible. The 1990s and 2000s first saw the flowering of North American and U.S. family histories and microhistories—from Laurel Ulrich's *A Midwife's Tale* and John Demos's *The Unredeemed Captive* to Martha Hodes's *The Sea Captain's Wife.* Building upon the groundbreaking scholarship of Adele Logan Alexander and Nell Irvin Painter, in the past decade, from Tiya Miles's *Ties That Bind* to Mary Frances Berry's *We Are Who We Say We Are,* I have had the additional good fortune of developing my own work amid the scholarly emergence of African-American and diasporic family histories and other microhistorical approaches to nineteenth-century African-American and diasporic lives.[21] This capacity of the historical profession to accept and reward small stories about "ordinary" black people is not disconnected from the heretofore limited capacity of the film industry to accept a diversity of narratives about black individuals, or from the capacity of local, state, and federal governments to affirm that all black lives matter.

The late Clement Price once noted that "belief in American exception-alism (writ white) had encouraged the analogous belief in African American exceptionalism." Here I am writing against exceptionalism of both sorts, in the spirit of what Du Bois called "essential humanity." I illus-trate that microhistorical approaches offer unique gifts to the study of African-American history, allowing scholars to sidestep now threadbare, if not "long dead," binaries of agency versus domination, slavery versus free-dom, heroism and the usual reification of race, contributing instead to a more complex historiography of African-descended peoples in slavery and in freedom.[22] What stories did enslaved and freedpeople tell themselves and one another in the midst of the repetitive trauma of separation and sexual violence? What sense did they make of their lives in a world in which the twin passages of birth and death were controlled, indeed owned, by others? And in the violent aftermath of such a world? What kinds of catharsis have family history, folklore, and storytelling—largely below and beyond the radar of professional scholarship—offered to enslaved men and women and their descendants?

These are the kinds of complex questions about human survival that family history and microhistory, alongside autobiography and memoir, offer to African-American historiography. If the lauded historical recovery of "agency" was accompanied by the "eclipse of institutions," as one historian has worried, then microhistory may offer a viable third way. Perhaps the lasting legacy of the new social history lies not in "slaves' agency" or freedpeople's resistance, but in the growing recognition that enslaved (and freed) people's stories and collective insights about their own experiences matter in great ways. Indeed, their voices can illuminate the political and economic structures that constrained their own lives, how they interpreted the meaning of freedom, and contributed to black intellectual traditions and the public history of slavery and freedom. To this end, I follow the lead of my own family members—their heroes, their villains, but most of all the majority who were neither, and vastly more interesting. I am committed to representing this full range of humanity that I have always known as a granddaughter at the table of family history, but have only rarely known as a professional historian. I would like to let "the scraps of evidence" determine "the argument and the arc."[23]

Family and Family History

Family mattered in special ways to freedom's first generation. If slavery was defined, at least in part, by a lack of control over one's family life, so was the idea of freedom entwined with the pursuit and control of family and kinship. Carrying recent memories of the domestic slave trade and the separation of parent and child, husband and wife, for many freedpeople, the vision of an emancipated future rested gravely on the sanctity of one's family life. During the Civil War, for instance, Annie Davis mingled family and freedom in her

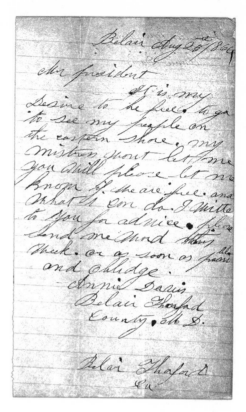

4. Letter from Annie Davis to Abraham Lincoln, August 25, 1864. National Archives

August 1864 letter to President Lincoln: "Mr. President It is my Desire to be free. To go to see my people on the eastern shore. My mistress wont let me you will please let me know if we are free. And what I can do."[24]

In the aftermath of the war, freedpeople like William Robinson "wrote letters to churches, and . . . got on the road, traveling to towns where he had promising reports that his mother might be." In fact, for many, historian Heather Williams has beautifully illustrated, the very meaning of freedom lay in the freedom to "move about" and, ultimately, the possibility of reuniting with family. For the largely rural people that composed freedom's first generation, family and kinship networks—with their attendant economic value—were necessary to make freedom "real." In this respect, surely they exchanged ideas about kinship with their Indian and black Indian kin. In many African and indigenous societies, one historian notes, "the opposite of slavery" was not freedom but kinship. Rooted in the repetitive social trauma of family separation and "haunted by the need to know," as the nineteenth century came to a close, Williams reveals, descendants searched for "those who were lost through sale or through the negligence of history." This African-American search necessarily extended beyond the history of individuals or individual families; "it is also meant to help construct the history of a people."[25]

Against this backdrop, it should go without saying that when I write about family I am not writing about biology, "blood," or DNA, but about kinship and attachment. One of my rituals has been to write and rewrite into this narrative the names of nonbiological relations who were not "nonetheless" family, but *necessarily* family, as well as the names of biological relations— including children born outside of legal marriages, and the children of second, and sometimes hidden, families—about whom others dared not speak. In so doing, I attempt to fill the space between the "official" truth of lineage and property inheritance and the "unofficial" truth of who people parented, comforted, and struggled alongside. In other words, I am interested in the constructed nature of family history, lineage, and pedigree, and the largely unsung diversity of sexual, marital, familial, and household relations upon which African-American and U.S. history have proceeded and depended. This includes those who did not adhere to contemporary dictates of nation, gender, sexuality, class, and especially race, and have been systematically misremembered, obscured, or omitted from written records and oral tradition.[26]

Moreover, in the "unofficial" truth of who parented whom, who comforted whom, and who struggled with whom sits the profound importance of individual subjectivity. Nell Painter writes: "I remain convinced that historians should keep in sight the fundamental lessons of psychology and psychoanalysis: that all people, even people who describe themselves primarily as raced or gendered, are individuals; that individual subjects develop within families; that families need not be related biologically; that attachment does not necessarily connote positive feeling; that attachment and grief do not stop at social barriers of color or class."[27] Every time I read these words to myself, or teach them to my students, I am struck by how radical they are, and how ordinary they ought to be. I wonder how different the world would have to be for these words to be ordinary.

Growing Up with the Country is a family history because these narratives have lived and will continue to live, first and foremost, within family and kin networks, where they belong to storytellers and listeners alike. I am interested in how and why certain stories were retold and remembered, and others buried. "The stories that we refuse to tell . . . do matter," writes E. Frances White. I hope this book encourages historians, descendants, and historian-descendants of African-American families, to greet such stories with open arms and ears; to put aside narrow arguments, long-held secrets, and taboo subjects in favor of rich and layered, spectacular, ordinary, and beautiful stories of a diverse people. "American history is longer, larger, more various, more beautiful, and more terrible," James Baldwin once wrote, "than anything anyone has ever said about it."[28]

"A Century of Negro Migration"

The following chapters trace the families of migrants Thomas Jefferson Brown, Monroe Coleman, and Alexander Davis. In Chapter 1 I narrate the life of Thomas Jefferson Brown, the son of an African-American father and Irish mother, who migrated from Arkansas to Indian Territory in the 1870s. There Brown was married twice to black Indian descendants of the Creek and Seminole nations; in the period of Dawes allotment, this "white-looking" father was able to secure more than a thousand acres of land, a school, church, and post office, founding "Brownsville," a black and Creek settlement in Indian Territory. I use Brown's story to illustrate how early African-American settlers initially bolstered their claims to freedom in the postemancipation era by attaching themselves to American expansion, Native Americans, and the acquisition of Indian land. In so doing, they mingled with white settlers who were also crafting new identities for themselves in Indian Territory. By the time Monroe Coleman, two decades Brown's junior, bought the plot adjacent to Brownsville, he was participating in a much larger emigration movement. Born in northeastern Mississippi in 1869 to a freedwoman and, perhaps, her former slaveowner, Coleman migrated at the turn of the twentieth century in the fervor of racial uplift and prideful black town building and purchased a plot of land in Indian Territory from a Creek freedman. In order to reconstruct the complex origins of "all-black" Oklahoma, in Chapter 2 I explore Coleman's decision to participate in this racially self-conscious movement within the context of his early life as a "mulatto" child in Reconstruction-era Mississippi, rumors of white parentage, and the emergence of twentieth-century "biracialism." Throughout this "revolution" of color and kinship, class remained; to this end, Chapter 3 traces the migratory life of Alexander "Elic" Davis, the "country preacher" and "huckster" who led his cousin, Monroe Coleman, to Indian Territory. Here I highlight their divergent experiences and reconsider the nadir in African-American history through the lens of black emigration, in relation to the rise of sharecropping and early black nationalism. Finally, in Chapter 4 I explore Coleman's and Davis's responses to the political and economic constraints of Oklahoma statehood, Jim Crow segregation, and oil speculation, including their participation in the 1913–15 Chief Sam back-to-Africa movement.[29]

W. E. B. Du Bois aptly described the decades that followed general emancipation: "The slave went free; stood a brief moment in the sun; then moved back again toward slavery. The whole weight of America was thrown to color caste. . . . A new slavery arose." Against this backdrop, part of what attracted African-American migrants like Brown, Coleman, and Davis to Indian Territory was its image, migrant George Coleman put it decades later, "as a place near the border of civilization." "In the spring of 1885," this white migrant recalled, "a neighbor and I decided to take Greeley's advice to go west and grow up with the country." A decade later, the *Christian Recorder* invoked Greeley's "long ago advice" to summon "the unsettled but ambitious Afro-American youth, 'Go West, young man.'" In the middle of the American continent, in this lingering transnational space, these men pursued their claims to freedom via American expansion and the acquisition of Indian land, only to lose this land and its attendant mineral rights to white settlers and oil speculators. Landless migrants like Davis, who moved and fought for political rights instead of land, lost just as much ground in the transition to Oklahoma statehood. In the end, economic opportunity and political rights proved equally elusive. In the spirit of "racial destiny," African Americans of diverse backgrounds and disparate means increasingly "fastened in the colored group," and began to look again beyond the U.S. nation-state.[30]

The new state of Oklahoma developed into a hotbed of African-American emigration due to widespread economic and political exclusion, the emerging discourse of "racial destiny," and the extraordinary mingling of racial and national identifications that characterized the region. Many black Oklahomans abandoned the Territory for West Africa, Canada, and Mexico, highlighting more explicit transnational and diasporic dimensions of African-American emigration after emancipation. Coleman and Davis helped to build the Chief Sam back-to-Africa movement in hopes of claiming lasting freedom once and for all. The Chief Sam movement began in Oklahoma, an American borderland at the turn of the twentieth century, and ended on the western coast of Africa during the First World War. Its roots, however, stretched across the American South and back to the transatlantic slave trade. This book reveals that this movement was not only prelude to Garveyism and the Great Migration but also capstone to what Carter Woodson once called "a century of negro migration" within and beyond North America.[31]

Today the Indian allotments that Coleman and Brown family members once lived upon remain largely untouched, save a couple of dirt oil roads that wind through the land. While their old wooden houses no longer stand, when I started this project, my great uncle Thurman could still tell me exactly when to turn and where to look for the old homeplace and gravesite, forty-five stones overrun by trees and brush, and barely legible. "Every inhabited landscape is a palimpsest," novelist Jonathan Raban has written, "its original parchment nearly blackened with the cross-hatching of successive generations of authors, claiming this place as their own and imposing their designs on it, as if their temporary interpretations would stand forever."[32] Due to a steady decline in population and economic development since the Great Depression, and a few committed folks who tend to this land and its stories, many "temporary interpretations" have in fact survived.

Thurman Brown was raised on this land by his grandfather, Thomas Jefferson Brown, who is buried there along with Monroe's wife, Belle, and all those relations who passed before the land was lost in the 1910s. Not incidentally, Creek Freedman Washington "Wash" Bruner, who sold Monroe his family's land, is buried there too. Uncle Thurman spent the better part of the twentieth century as one of the only black cattle ranchers around. The few newer residents, white, and in some cases part Indian, who now live on the land, have also become invaluable to my family and to me, by knowing the land intimately and following signs like "the tall birch tree," and "lilies," which "always tell you where the old homeplace was." Significantly, these families consistently spoke of the family gravesite as "the old Indian cemetery," revealing just how thorough has been the erasure of the history of African-American land and freedom in Oklahoma. As Du Bois despaired at the turn of the twentieth century, the "ownership of the earth" had become central to the construction of a new racial order and "the discovery of personal whiteness." But this order was indeed, in Du Bois's words, "a very modern thing."[33]

I hope these stories will encourage renewed appreciation of the centrality of land and displacement to U.S., Native American, and African-American history. To this end, I borrow French historian Pierre Nora's concept of *lieux de mémoire,* or sites of memory, documenting places that continue to mark a will to remember against a growing loss of memory. This work has been shaped by the myriad return journeys that descendants have made especially within the past three decades, searching out the gravesites, homeplaces, and land that were once so central to their ancestors' ideas of freedom. This book documents not only what is remembered but the will to remember as a subject in its own right, and those countless "'black and unknown bards,' historians without portfolio, who inscribed their world with landmarks made significant because men and women remembered them so complexly and so well that somehow the traces of their memory survived to become history."[34]

Beginning in the Brownsville settlement with my family, I have spent much of my time throughout this project at gravesites across Mississippi, Alabama, Oklahoma, and Texas, searching for the resting places of any possible ancestors, whether designated Creek, black, white, or not at all. These are stories of peoples forced or coerced to "leave behind" their ancestors.

They recall earlier stories about the meaning of death and dying for the first generations of enslaved Africans in seventeenth- and eighteenth-century North America. Removed from their ancestral homelands, one historian suggests, "the African born" could claim no belonging to a portion of the earth. Instead, "she was born and she would die without a home," her "rootlessness" exposed, her soul and descendants divorced from African-born relatives, "condemned to dwell in troubled terrain."[35] Again in the nineteenth century, forced migration was the rule, this time for Creek and African Americans alike—from the southeast seaboard to the Mississippi Valley in the "second Middle Passage," and from Georgia to Indian Territory through forced removal. Finally, in the wake of the Civil War, many, perhaps most, freedpeople—some whose kin had been buried in the same plot as their slaveowners—had to pick up and go elsewhere yet again.

Places have long served human beings "as durable symbols of distant events," yet it is often only when we find ourselves "literally *dislocated*" that our sense of place asserts itself most powerfully.[36] One of the most profound aspects of African-American and Indian history lies in the unwitting abandonment of one's homeplace, one's spiritual markers, and the remains of one's ancestors. As the stories I offer here unearth often anonymous cycles of movement and displacement, I hope they are meaningful not only in their capacity to transform and reimagine the current state of Native American, African-American, and U.S. history, but in their capacity to nurture an appreciation of our physical environment, our place in time and in space, and our relationship to our ancestors and heirs across the globe.

ONE

"Intruder of Color"

Freedom, Sovereignty, and Kinship in Indian Territory

When Thomas Jefferson Brown finally decided to make his home in Indian Territory in 1870, he had been there many times before. For months he had been going in on day trips from Arkansas, his grandson mused more than a century later, learning the Muskogean languages and becoming familiar with the land, people, and opportunities for economic gain. In spite of national boundaries, promises of federal "protection," and claims to Indian tribal sovereignty, the borders between the nineteenth-century United States and Indian Territory grew increasingly porous, especially following the Civil War. American settlers in and around the Territory were scrambling for more and more land, and soon economic and familial relationships across these boundaries began to flourish. During the late nineteenth century, settlement by "non-natives" was perceived as the greatest threat to sovereignty in the Territory.[1]

While most early American settlers in post–Civil War Indian Territory were identified in government records as white, some were recorded as black or "mulatto," the latter a category still prominent on the federal censuses of this period. One such settler, Thomas Jefferson Brown, was born in 1850s Arkansas to an African-American man and an Irish woman. In the course of the late nineteenth century, Brown married twice to African-American descendants of the Creek and Seminole nations. One hundred and sixty acres of land was allotted to each of his eight children due to their mothers' presence on the U.S. federal Dawes rolls specifying tribal membership and land allotments for Cherokee, Choctaw, Creek, Chickasaw, and Seminole citizens and freedpeople. This "white-looking" father secured

23

more than a thousand acres of land, a school, church, and post office—a black and Creek settlement in Indian Territory, known as Brownsville. In so doing, he followed in the footsteps of African-American men who for centuries made their livelihood in Indian country, often by marrying and linking their fate to Indian and black Indian women, communities, and land. In this way, a degree of freedom could be achieved by distancing associations to southern slavery, by illustrating one's proximity to Indian-ness, or by legitimizing one's relationship to American national expansion and land.[2]

While Brownsville is remembered by descendants today as a black settle-ment, perceptions of Brown when he first arrived in Indian Territory, in the 1870s, were less about his racial identification than they were about his na-tional (or *non*national) identification; indeed, Brown was initially catego-rized in Creek national records as a "non-native" or an "intruder." Brown's experiences in Indian Territory and Oklahoma reveal that at the turn of the twentieth century, the United States was undergoing a seismic shift of self-definition from "nation" to "race," and from Indian and American national projects to black and white national projects. Native American and black Indian women played critical roles in this transformation.

Brown's migration to Indian Territory after the Civil War embodied an attempt to escape racism and claim freedom and American citizenship through the acquisition of land, and through relationships with Indians, especially Indian women, as a means to acquire that land. In this context, migration involved some African Americans distancing themselves from blackness and connecting themselves instead to the project of American national expansion. This chapter details the various meanings of Brown's acquisition of Indian land through marriages to two African-descended Creek and Seminole women, and especially the significance of his "non-native" or "intruder" status in the Territory. For a time, Brown's position in Indian Territory afforded him myriad privileges associated with American expansion and proximity to Creek national belonging. Brown's African Creek wife, Julia Simon, and her children, could still be Creek, and racial constructions had not yet negated African-American and black Indian claims in the Creek nation.

Three decades after he arrived, however, circumstances had changed dramatically. Responding to growing pressure from land-hungry American settlers within and beyond Indian Territory, the federal government intervened in the name of tribal "protection." By the early 1900s, all collectively held Indian lands had been individually allotted by the federal Dawes Commission, as in the case of Brown's wife and children; in turn, many of these Indian (and black Indian) allotments were quickly sold or ceded to white and some newer black settlers. In addition, the government deemed the remaining lands "surplus" and available for sale to incoming settlers. In 1907, the state of Oklahoma was officially founded on most of the same terms of racial segregation and disfranchisement that had driven many African Americans out of the South in the first place. In the 1910s, Brown—like many African-descended and Creek landowners forced or coerced to abandon their land—lost his family's property to the explosion of land and oil speculation, developments aggressively underwritten by a system of racial classification newly enforced by white settlers, and state and federal governments alike. Brown's dream of linking his family to nation came to a halt as racism obscured the possibility of citizenship within a sovereign territory.

While the experience of land acquisition for settlers like Brown functioned as a national project, the experience of land loss decades later was principally a racialized one. As Indian sovereignty was dissolved and notions of racial purity and "blood" acquired growing significance, "race" ultimately eclipsed "nation" as a guarantor of rights and resources in the Territory. The emergence of a rigid black-white dichotomy thoroughly obscured the more nuanced possibilities of the preceding period in Indian Territory. As a result, the area where Brown settled has been remembered by descendants as a "black" settlement (connected to Oklahoma's "all-black" town movement), revealing just how complete the twentieth-century erasure of black Indian kinship and property ownership has been. By the 1920s, in spite of the powerful history of African-descended Creeks, Brown's grandchildren were still attempting, in vain, to distance themselves from freedpeople and slavery, in favor of their Creek lineage. Brown's story illuminates an evolving racial hierarchy within the context of an expanding U.S. empire.

"Half-Irishman" in Arkansas

Born free on the border of Arkansas and Missouri around 1851, Thomas Jefferson Brown was known as Jeff or T.J. His father, John Brown, was perhaps one of thirty free African Americans working in the border town of Fort Smith before the war, and, as Brown's grandson recalled, "His mommy was a full-blooded Irishman." Perhaps Brown heard stories from his mother of a Scots-Irish family's journey over the Appalachian ridge, or else a more recent migration to the United States. Between 1840 and 1850, in response to devastating famine, Irish immigrants were arriving at American port cities like New Orleans in tremendous numbers, and many settled in the Deep South. Arkansas's Irish population nearly tripled over the course of the decade, and the vast majority lived in the cities of Fort Smith, Little Rock, and Helena.[3]

During the same period, Brown's father would have been subjected to "confusing and troublesome" constraints. Of the free African American in antebellum Arkansas, one historian has noted: "In some respects he was treated like a white person, and in others like a slave." Given descendants' claims that Jeff looked like "a white man," his father may have been categorized as "mulatto" and perhaps manumitted by his owner, a relatively common practice in Arkansas at the time. Sixty-seven percent of the free African-American population in Arkansas was listed in 1850 as "mulatto," compared to sixteen percent of the enslaved population. Given the shared surname and the small number of large slaveholders in Arkansas, John Brown's former slaveowner could have been a man also by the name of John Brown who, in 1854, sold his long-standing Dallas County plantation and several of the women and men he owned, moved into insurance and law in Camden, Arkansas, and began hiring out some of his slaves. This is one path by which John Brown may have first arrived at Fort Smith.[4]

When she met John Brown, Jeff's mother may have been working as a domestic or seamstress, selling produce or other wares, or perhaps operating a tavern or boardinghouse. John Brown's relationship with an Irish woman in Fort Smith, Arkansas, suggests that he was already, by this time, free. The "frontier village" of Fort Smith, Arkansas, was one of only two cities in the state with any significant concentration of free African Americans before the war, and the census of 1860 lists no slaves in Fort Smith. Indeed, slavery was primarily a rural institution in Arkansas. As a free person of color before the war, John Brown may have worked as one of a small number of African-American artisans in Fort Smith, at least until 1859. If the relationship between Jeff Brown's parents was made possible by the unique circumstance of Fort Smith, the family would have nevertheless been among hundreds forced over the Missouri border at the time of the 1859 expulsion of all free African Americans from Arkansas. In February of that year, the Arkansas legislature passed a law requiring all free African Americans to leave the state by year's end. Those who remained could be impounded by the county and hired out for twelve months, effectively reenslaved. As a result, the number of free African Americans living in Arkansas fell from 682 to 144 in the year immediately following this expulsion.[5]

Brown's father fought and died in the Civil War; five thousand African Americans organized within several years of expulsion into four regiments of Arkansas Volunteers of African Descent. Soon after the war, mother and son returned to Fort Smith. After the war, paramilitary violence continued, especially along the Missouri border. For several years after the war, "the Ku Klux hunted the militia and the militia hunted the Ku Klux." At the same time, the state government passed Arkansas's short-lived black codes, prohibiting, for instance, any "negro or mulatto" from attending the state's existing public schools. But by 1869, as Radical Reconstruction gained national momentum, federal resources provided some protection to the freedpeople of Arkansas. While political violence mellowed, however, economic prospects across the Deep South, especially in neighboring Mississippi and Louisiana, were dim. As sharecropping took hold, poor white and black southerners alike scrambled for a way out of these states. In the early 1870s, Arkansas's Reconstruction government created the Office of Commissioner of State Lands and Immigration, recruiting not only "fair-skinned foreigners" but also freedpeople of the Deep South; the office circulated literature portraying the state as "a new Africa."[6]

This may have been a hard sell for ten-year-old Jeff Brown, described by his grandson as "half Irishman and half black"; general emancipation probably had mixed results for Brown. Having lost his father to the war and returned to Fort Smith, he witnessed, alongside his mother, the beginnings of freedpeople's migration into Arkansas and perhaps wondered what it could mean for him and the life he had known or imagined. As he followed his mother around town, surely he noted white southerners' growing obsession with color. In "the year of freedom," agents of the Freedmen's Bureau in Arkansas immediately displayed a "keen awareness of color," inscribing in marriage records the "color" of the bride, groom, and parents: "I have this day united in matrimony Henry B. Smith of County D____ and Mamala Johnston of Pine Bluff Arkansas age of man twenty-one years color Brown and of his father Brown and of his mother Yellow age of woman twenty years color Yellow and of her father Yellow and of her mother Yellow." In Pine Bluff, agents recorded hues as "black, dark, brown, light, white, medium, and yellow." General Sprague, head of the Freedman's Bureau, voided "all marriages of white persons with negroes or mulattoes." And freedmen Washington and Alvin Lewis, allegedly living with two white women near Lewisburg, were confronted by the Ku Klux Klan for this "sexual violation." Washington was killed, and Alvin Lewis escaped.[7]

As he came of age in the "frontier village" of Fort Smith, perhaps Brown noted that in the absence of "slave" and "free," color seemed to matter more and more to white southerners, particularly in domestic matters. Martha Hodes has noted the striking absence of violence across *antebellum* cases of interracial marriage, adultery, and bastardy; by contrast, after the war, she writes, "freedmen who consorted with white women (or who were accused of such behavior) became transgressive in a way they had never been under the oppressive regime of slavery."[8] In the late 1860s, as Jeff witnessed the death of his father and his only brother, one wonders how his relationship with his Irish mother may have changed as he came of age in this new world.

While freedpeople "tested their freedom" in many ways—assuming new names, searching for lost family members, creating their own histories and myths—so too did freeborn, manumitted, and "other" African Americans of myriad backgrounds; they often attempted to distinguish themselves—as did many immigrants in the postemancipation era—from the masses of newly emancipated freedpeople so readily disparaged by white southerners and northerners during this period. Antifreedmen sentiment proliferated among Americans of diverse backgrounds, gradually shifting into antiblack racism, paralleling the rise of American biracialism. James Oliver was an African American who had escaped from slavery and migrated to Santo Domingo before the war; after the war, he returned to Arkansas but "adamantly refused to be labeled a freedman." One historian has noted that some African-American barbers in Fort Smith cringed at the prospect of cutting other African Americans' hair and what this could mean for their own social and economic standing, which had been built upon service to elite white southerners. African Americans continually debated what to call themselves, and individual freedpeople alternately accepted, challenged, or ignored the myriad understandings of race and color that circulated in the aftermath of the Civil War. Nineteenth-century nomenclature that one scholar has catalogued included "African, Ethiopian, Free African, Colored, Negro, Children of Africa, Sons of Africa, Colored American, people of color, free people of color, blacks, Anglo-African, Afric, African-American, Afro-American, Afmerican, Aframerican, Africo-American, and Afro-Saxon."9

Perhaps Brown considered what to call himself. His granddaughter remembered few details about him, except that "he was very fair, very fair." His own son, Tom Brown, recalled, "Well I just know he was my daddy and I never knew nothing about his folks." When asked whether he resembled him, he replied, "No, my father, he looked like a white man," and Brown's granddaughter immediately echoed, "That's all I remember." Thomas Jefferson Brown was classified by census takers as "mulatto" and seems to have been able to "pass" for white (and, later, Indian) in some settings, a fact not incidental to life in postemancipation Arkansas. Indeed, color significantly shaped one's material circumstances and opportunities in the postemancipation South and the Southwest. As former slave Mary Peters of Little Rock, whose father was white, recalled her childhood years, "They didn't like my mother and me—on account of my color. . . . They tell their children that when I got big enough, I would think I was good as they was. I couldn't help my color. My mother couldn't either." Between 1850 and 1860 the "mulatto" population in Arkansas doubled, "increasing the color spectrum and complicating the task of those engaged in fashioning new identities."[10]

As Brown carved a place in this changing world, in the absence of his father or an extended kin network, his "frontier village" of Fort Smith began to play an increasingly critical political and economic role in Indian Territory; in turn, Indian Territory shaped life in Fort Smith. Supplies moved in and out of Fort Smith, now a venue of trade for the eastern part of the Territory as well as western Arkansas, and from there federal court officials pursued and prosecuted Indian Territory "outlaws." Coming of age in this growing city, Brown would have heard many stories about life in Indian Territory; when he was ready to strike out on his own, he headed there. While trade markets in Indian Territory were certainly attractive to "non-citizens" (that is, non-Indians) such as Brown, he may have had more personal reasons to leave Arkansas. Brown appears to have met and married his future wife, Creek freedwoman Aurelia Bruner, while still living in Fort Smith. Whether or not his marriage to Aurelia was preceded by another marriage in Fort Smith, Brown appears to have been "on the run." Indeed, when asked when and how his father came to Indian Territory, Tom Brown, Brown's then 103-year-old son, hinted at a hurried migration: "He came in here from Missouri (by way of Fort Smith). . . . But that was before statehood. He was on the run, my daddy was." Many prospective settlers had begun to view Indian Territory as a place where one could escape American law; local papers frequently called Indian Territory a "haven" for "divorce-seekers" and other fugitives.[11]

"Growing Up with the Country"

Around the time of his sixteenth birthday, Brown "got on his own and he came to Cherokee Nation." Probably with Aurelia Bruner's help, "he learned how to speak the language," his grandson recalled, "and that's how he interpreted." Brown was a "non-citizen" or an "intruder" in the eyes of the Indian Nations. The Creek, Cherokee, Chickasaw, Choctaw, and Seminole nations allowed noncitizens to live and work within the Territory

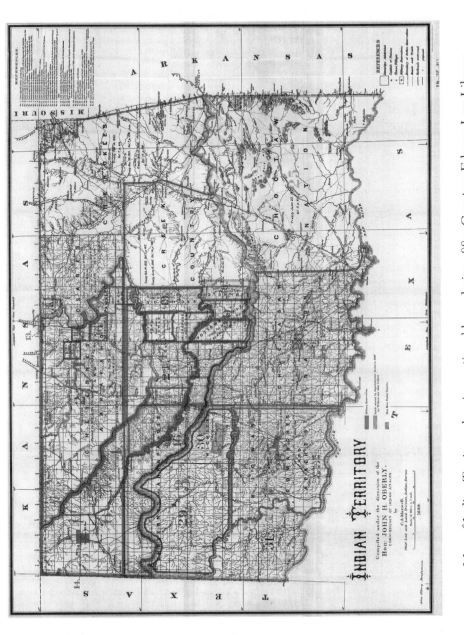

5. Map of Indian Territory showing national boundaries, 1889. Courtesy Edmon Low Library, Oklahoma State University, Oklahoma Digital Maps Collection

under a permit system that required the payment of taxes and other fees, under supervision of the U.S. government. Despite mounting complaints by the Nations, however, the rules regarding noncitizens were only loosely enforced, if at all, and the challenge of identifying and removing "intruders" was common knowledge.[12]

In the face of few restrictions, American settlers of all backgrounds were rapidly launching new lives for themselves in the Territory throughout the 1860s and 1870s, and many depended upon their relationships with Indians for survival. E. L. Fisher, who migrated in 1878 and settled near Thomas Jefferson Brown, noted that the Territory was still "a very rugged and wild country," including "a great many Indians . . . though not so many white people." Moreover, he claimed, "almost all the white people who were here were refugees from some state who had come into the Territory to escape punishment on account of felony which they had committed. Everyone carried a pistol and a Winchester." The country, Fisher added, was "full of wild game and also full of what were called wild Indians though if a white person could gain the friendship of the Indians there were no better friends to be had."[13] Fisher's description of this "rugged" and increasingly tumultuous setting implies that "friends" were essential to the settlement process.

Indeed, friendship, in this context, could mean economic survival. For his part, when Fisher settled near Brown's eventual homeplace, he "took a lease on some land there from an Indian woman, Sookie McCarty, a widow, and cleared out some of the land, built a log house of hewed logs and planted a small crop of corn." Fred Brown, who came in from Texas in 1886, put it more bluntly: "I ran about seven thousand head of cattle. Of course, it was under an Indian for everyone who held cattle had to be under an Indian. In fact everything was under Indian control at that time. Hick Harrison was our Indian. He claimed all land or had charge of it." The contention that all cattle ranchers "had to be under an Indian" indicates that American settlers, by the 1880s, had learned how to navigate many of the economic and legal obstacles they perceived with regard to the enforcement of Indian Territory borders and sovereignty. The notion of "our Indian," moreover, indicates that in spite of formal "Indian control," at least some of these American men perceived *themselves* to be in control. Brown's grandson Thurman recalled that he started out making fireplaces in the Cherokee and then Creek nations. Perhaps he relied on other settlers, white and black, for various components of this trade. Oklahoman Nancy Towery recalled that her father and uncle, who had "the intention of farming" when they settled, ended up working as brick masons. At first, they "put up a brick kiln" and made three kilns' capacity of brick—"molded by hand and . . . cooked for fifteen days"—for men "planning to build some stores."[14] Brown's success in this rapidly changing environment depended not only on skills learned in Fort Smith but on networks built in Indian Territory.

When Brown married the twenty-something Aurelia Bruner, the African Creek daughter of Tecumseh Bruner, he did so aware of the myriad benefits of citizenship in Indian society. While outside settlers were rarely granted citizenship, many, like Brown, married Indian or black Indian women. "She was a Creek freedman," said Aurelia Bruner's cousin, Paro Bruner, in an 1899 Dawes Commission interview, for she was born in Indian Territory and living there "when the treaty was ratified and her father enrolled her," one year after the close of the Civil War. Before the war, Aurelia Bruner's mother had been enslaved, he added. At the time of the interview, Paro Bruner was the seventy-five-year-old *micco* (town king or chief) of Canadian Colored Town and had served in the Creek National Council in the House of Kings or House of Warriors since 1870. His parents had been enslaved by a Creek slaveowner, and Paro had experienced Indian removal as a child in the 1830s. When, in 1899, the Dawes Commission interviewed Paro and other family members to determine the validity of Aurelia Bruner's claim (and thus her daughter Chaney's) to Creek citizenship, Commissioner Bixby asked him directly, "She was not a slave of an Indian was she?" To this, Paro Bruner indicated that Aurelia Bruner had been owned by "a white man by the name of Capt. Spring." Apparently, after moving to Arkansas during the war, Aurelia's father brought her to the Territory to enroll her in 1866, after which "she went back to Ft. Smith, and then she came back here the wife of . . . Jeff Brown." About fifteen years old at the close of the Civil War, Aurelia Bruner appears to have "separated" from a Freedman named Bud Dean before marrying Brown. Chaney Wallace's response to the Dawes Commission about her father's origins illustrates the salience of national categories at the close of the nineteenth century. When asked whether her father, Jeff Brown, was a Creek, Wallace replied, "No sir." The commissioner continued, "What is he?" to which Chaney Wallace replied, "A United States man."[15]

In the 1870s, the marriage between this "United States man" and Aurelia Bruner meant, for Brown, access to new land and markets, as well as a share of government funds designated for Creek and Seminole citizens and families struggling in the wake of war. Moreover, connection to Tecumseh Bruner, Aurelia's Creek father, who during this period was a Lighthorseman (a member of the mounted police force in the Territory), may have exempted Brown from rigid law enforcement and eased his incorporation into the Territory. Throughout the history of the southeastern United States, American men frequently gained access to Indian markets and land through marriage to Native American women, who played powerful economic, cultural, and political roles in historically matrilineal societies such as the Cherokee, Creek, Seminole, Chickasaw, and Choctaw nations. During the eighteenth and nineteenth centuries, property, including land, was inherited through the matrilineal line, though the U.S. government ultimately encouraged patrilineal inheritance, due to widespread intermarriage between property-holding American men and Indian women. Similarly, in the nineteenth-century United States—Mexico borderlands, historian Andrés Reséndez has noted the "inescapable economic dimension" of such transnational unions. As in nearby northern Mexico, marital ties facilitated citizenship and land acquisition in the Territory.[16]

Indeed, Brown's marital status and children were of paramount importance for the duration of his life in Indian Territory. When Brown married Aurelia Bruner in the early 1870s, around the time of the birth of their first child, Rena, he married into the long, rich history of the Bruner family and the Creek and Seminole nations, including African-descended members of these nations. The Bruner family had migrated from Alabama in the early 1830s as part of Indian removal. They were among the Upper Creek families, who were consistently opposed to removal; following forced removal, they settled together in the "new" Indian Territory, near the Canadian River. Not incidentally, settlement of these "immigrant nations" in the "new" Indian Territory encroached upon the lands and markets of the eastern

Comanche. Creek freedman William M. Bruner was told that when his Bruner grandparents came from Alabama in 1835, they traveled in ox wagons along with several families of Creek Indians. William Bruner was one of hundreds of men and women known as *Estelvste*—the Creek word invoked to refer to African-descended people of the Creek nation. They had lived among the Creeks, one historian has noted, "since the first Spanish entradas through the Creek lands" of the Southeast during the early sixteenth century. They shared a language, food, worldviews, and kinship ties with the Creeks; and, by the early nineteenth century, as a portion of the southeastern Indians adopted the agricultural practices of southern planters, many African-descended Creeks ultimately provided slave labor and contributed to the wealth of leading Creek families.[17]

Slavery within the Indian Nations was distinct from slavery in much of the U.S. South in important ways. Operating without an overseer, and often supporting themselves with clothing and food by tending to their own "squaw patches," many enslaved men and women of the Creek nation experienced a different sort of enslavement. For much of Native American history, one historian has argued, "captivity operated on a continuum." Moreover, before and after emancipation, African-descended Creeks—enslaved and free—also served as cultural brokers, ministers, warriors, interpreters, and negotiators as Creek Indians contended with tribal divisions, Indian removal, and the Civil War. The historical record reveals instances of slaveowners borrowing money from enslaved men and women (though this was not necessarily unheard of in the plantation South). Bolstered by the promise of citizenship and an equal share of tribal funds following emancipation, African-descended Creeks established themselves as subsistence farmers, as well as traders, merchants, and cattle ranchers, in Creek country.[18]

Included in this class was Aurelia Bruner's cousin, the aforementioned Paro Bruner. Creek Joe Bruner recalled that the first time he met Paro was in 1898, until which time he had known "very little of my father's people": "I was a member of the House of Kings in Okmulgee, and there met an old ex-slave named Payro. He was a member from one of the three negro towns of the Creek Nation. When he heard my name called he came over and told me that he had been my grandfather's slave and had come to this country with him. Payro said my grandfather's name was George and that they had been landed people in Alabama." Paro played a prominent role within the Creek nation and among African-descended Creeks, serving in the 1870s in the House of Warriors and as town chief of the black town known as Canadian Colored. Thomas Jefferson Brown's children referred to Paro as "Uncle Parrow Bruner." Their maternal grandfather, Tecumseh Bruner, was Paro's uncle.[19]

6. Paro Bruner, c. 1900. Paro Bruner was town micco (chief) of the African Creek town known as Canadian Colored. Courtesy Oklahoma Historical Society

7. Paro Bruner, c. 1900. Courtesy Oklahoma Historical Society

But by the time Paro shared this family history with Joe Bruner in 1898, much had changed for Estelvste—increasingly referred to as "colored" or "Negro" citizens of the Creek nation—just as it had for Joe, his fellow Creeks, and Indians across the Territory. While the treaty of 1866 had granted freedpeople of the Indian Nations citizenship "by adoption" and promised equal protection, this promise held far less weight at the close of the century. In 1890, when Mary Carrer, "a colored citizen of the Cherokee Nation," was accused of assaulting another Cherokee citizen, a local paper reported: "An able argument was made to the point that citizens by adoption were entitled to the same rights under the treaty of '66 as Indians by blood, but the court held that while Indians by blood have the right under that treaty to be tried by their own courts only[,] yet negro citizens are subject to this court also."[20] This verdict reflects a transitional moment in which freedpeople of the Indian Nations—many of whom were of Native American, as well as African, ancestry—were subject to two sets of laws (in this case, U.S. and Cherokee) and were prohibited from sharing the same rights and protections as "full-blood" Indians.

Such distinctions were indicative of a broader transformation under way in the Territory as a whole. Longtime resident E. L. Fisher noted that around 1890, "the Territory began to be developed very rapidly, people came fast; homes were built; farms cleared and broken out; railroads were being built; townsites were laid out and there was one continual thing following another for the Territory was fast becoming an agricultural country from what was once the best grazing country known to men." At the same time, amid the racially complex history of the Indian Nations and the sudden influx of African-American and white settlers, a distinctly multiracial society was fast evolving in this borderland, and politicians and reformers alike increasingly viewed the region as a threat to civilization and Indian "progress." Responding to land-hungry settlers within and beyond Indian Territory—as well as to benevolent rhetoric about private property as the cornerstone of "progress" and Indian assimilation—in 1887 Congress passed the Dawes General Allotment Act. By the early 1900s, all collectively held Indian lands had been individually allotted by the federal Dawes Commission; in turn, many of these Indian (and black Indian) allotments were quickly sold or ceded to white and some newer black settlers. Moreover, the government offered the remaining "surplus" lands to new settlers.[21]

Acre by acre, the Dawes Act depleted the American Indian land base, forced American Indians into capitalist land markets, and, in turn, imposed patrilineal nuclear households in place of long-standing matrilineal societies. While the Creek, Cherokee, Choctaw, Chickasaw, and Seminole nations were initially exempted from this act, a decade later the federal government coerced their compliance with the Curtis Act of 1898, paving the way for statehood. What underwrote and yet complicated this staggering decision by the federal government was the presence of so many nonnative settlers in Indian Territory, and the related problem of identifying and removing intruders. By 1900, there were more than three times as many nonnative residents as Native Americans in Indian Territory.[22]

"Blood" Sovereignty

Beyond the central violation of Indian national sovereignty by then under way, the most immediate consequence of the Dawes Act in Indian Territory related to enrollment. Before alloting land, the federal government aimed to determine tribal membership, and past attempts at producing rolls of citizenship had largely failed. The commissioners argued that Dunn's roll of Creek Freedmen, a census taken in 1867 in order to distribute proceeds due from the sale of the Creeks' western lands to the United States, was a reasonably authentic beginning for identifying freedpeople of the Creek nation; however, Paro Bruner and other Creeks disagreed, having lived through the earlier enrollment process. Moreover, since the 1866 citizenship agreement, "one of the issues that created both worry and anger," among Creeks more broadly "was the enrollment of former slaves as freedmen. There was a great deal of resentment over the federal government's forcing the tribe to grant citizenship, and there was disagreement about who was eligible." Perhaps as a result of this "disagreement," Bruner believed the Dunn rolls had "omitted" many African Creeks with legitimate claim to citizenship and "failed to get the names right" of those they did count.[23]

In the context of the subsequent Dawes Commission, enrolling the Creeks proved to be especially challenging, in part because they functioned as a confederation of forty-four bands, with members living in separate towns, each with a town micco responsible for keeping track of its citizens. Furthermore, many people operated without surnames, or with multiple names, and there were no official records of vital statistics. Congress required that the Dawes rolls be "descriptive" in order to ensure positive identifications when assigning allotments; the census card included the applicant's age, sex, and "degree of Indian blood." But many people were known by more than one name and often changed names. Commissioners noted, "Surnames are changed overnight. . . . In some cases two or more children are given identically the same name." Although the commission was meant to be guided by legal standards, one historian notes that its decisions on citizenship were more often led by "the facts known by the Old Settlers" than by written records.[24]

The contested citizenship of Aurelia Bruner, Brown's first wife, offers a case in point. By 1899, when the Dawes Commission launched the aforementioned investigation into her daughter Chaney's Creek citizenship, Aurelia had already died. Thus the commission asked Paro Bruner, "Do you know the old people?" Bruner replied, "Yes, pretty well." Regarding Aurelia's registration on the 1867 Dunn roll (frequently the basis of Dawes enrollment), Bruner noted that although "her father enrolled her" back in 1866, ultimately "she was not on the roll; she was on some omitted roll as many was omitted." He added, "I have been writing to the council time and again." Among the individuals they interrogated was Chaney's father, Thomas Jefferson Brown. The forty-eight-year-old man insisted that Aurelia was a citizen of the Creek nation, that her name was on the Dunn roll, and that the citizenship of his daughter Chaney "has never been contested as I learned before this Commission." As to why Chaney had not received the twenty-nine-dollar remittance, he added, "I suppose it must have been in the neglect of the officers; they got a list of a whole lot of them wrong. I didn't find out until after wards that she was not enrolled."[25]

Because of this "omission," throughout 1899, 1900, and 1901, the children of Thomas Jefferson Brown and Aurelia Bruner worked vigilantly to prove their Indian "freedmen" lineage, and to obtain land allotments for all the children. The Dawes Commission first summoned Chaney to its Muskogee office for an interview in 1899, followed by Paro Bruner, Thomas Jefferson Brown, and several other relatives. By this time, the Muskogee office, at least a day's travel from Brownsville, had become a locus for people of all backgrounds eager to make or improve their lives in Indian Territory. Although the office assigned numbered tickets to control the crowds, some developed the practice of selling these tickets to the highest bidder. When Chaney Wallace finally approached the desk of enrolling clerk Phillip B. Hopkins, she was sworn in and her testimony recorded by the commission's stenographer, D. W. Yancey. There, if it was not yet clear, it emerged that the Commission was contesting Chaney's claim to Creek citizenship, in part due to the time her mother spent in Arkansas, where she had met Brown. Others, whose claims were not contested but were authenticated by previous rolls, were issued citizenship certificates and sent on to another office to select land for allotment. Chaney was sent home, only to be called to testify once again in March 1901.[26]

Two days after returning to Brownsville, Chaney Wallace sat down to write an urgent letter to her elder sister, Rena (Brown) McNack. In this letter between Brown and Aurelia's two eldest daughters—passed down to Brown's grandson, who cherished it for the rest of his life (1911–2007) in a worn leather envelope—Chaney desperately urged Rena to register "at Wonce," in order to ensure Creek land allotments for all family members. Painfully illustrating the importance of specificity and consistency in the process of substantiating their birthright to the Dawes Commission, Chaney wrote:

> I just want to tell you to go and file right away and when you go you must call for eally Brun [er?] and you must tell them about your grandfather name and uncles an aunt name that is on the Dun roll and they will ask you about your Sister and your Brother and you must tell them and you must tell the age of them. So you must tell them that I am 28 year old that you are about 25 or 26 and fred is about 21 or 22 years old and you must tell them Sil is about 18 or 19 years old and you must tell them that Lemmie is about 16 or 17 years old and you must talk one thing. Don't make no mistake in your talking and you must tell them about my children ages and that Washington is 7 years old last October the 24 Day and tell them that Fredonia was 5 years old last august the 30 day and you must tell them Bennie was 3 year old last febuary the 19 Day. So Papa say that you must try and get 25 Dollar this fall for to pay uncle Parrow Bruner for his truble with us to prane our right up and PaPa Say that you must tell Aran to go and file right away at Wonce and Don't Delay for (in fall they . . .?), So give my love to all And Try to go right away and file at Wonce and be done with it So you must Do What I tell you for I just got back on the 27 So I will close my short letter from your truly sister, Chaney Wallas[27]

Here Chaney references their ancestors' presence on the "Dun roll" of 1867, indicating their historic designation as "Creek freedmen."

41

Chaney also references in this letter "uncle" Paro Bruner's "truble with us," hinting at the powerful role town micco Paro Bruner played within the Dawes allotment process, particularly for African Creeks. Paro had initially warned others in 1894 that "nothing good would come from a division of common property," predicting that the Creeks would be driven from their land and homes. When allotment began, however, Paro was one of several African Creeks who participated in the work of the Dawes Commission, "seeking out bona fide citizens" and making sure they were "properly en-rolled." At the time, some of Thomas Jefferson Brown's fellow African-American "intruders" were being accused of trying to "pass" as Creek freedmen in order to gain access to land. Amid rampant suspicion, Brown paid twenty-five dollars to "uncle" Paro, probably in order to defend his children's claims to Creek citizenship. Two years later, in January 1902, the

8. Dawes Commission enrolling Freedpeople at Fort Gibson, c. 1900.
Courtesy Oklahoma Historical Society

Dawes Commission reached its conclusion "that Chaney Wallace, who is 28 years of age, is a daughter of Aurelia Bruner whose name appears upon the Dunn roll of Creek freedmen, and that the names of Chaney Wallace, Washington Bruner and Fredonia Willis appear on the 1895 authenticated Creek roll and that Bennie Sango was born after that roll was made. The commission is therefore of the opinion that the parties named should be enrolled as Creek citizens."[28] Aurelia Bruner's children would have been grateful for Paro Bruner's influence throughout this process.

One of the most glaring flaws in this deeply problematic allotment process in Indian Territory lay in the Dawes Commission's emphasis on "blood quantum" and the distinction drawn, or made, between Creeks and freedpeople of the Creek nation, who made up as much as one-third of the Creek population. African Creeks constituted thirty-two percent of the Creek population, according to the census of 1895. The distinction between freedpeople and African Creeks, however, further complicates this calculation. Rolls taken before 1896, by the Indian Nations themselves, had not included a "blood quantum"; a few noted whether an individual was "full-blood" or "mixed blood"—"the only distinction most tribes considered important at the time." Even G. W. Stidham and other Creeks who adamantly opposed the political influence of African Creeks had nevertheless long acknowledged that African Creeks with "Creek blood" were, for all purposes, Creek. But determining "quantum of blood" for purposes of allotting land was hardly straightforward. Silas Jefferson testified in 1895, when asked whether he knew any former slaves who were also descendants of Indians, "I have seen many a one." Jefferson testified further that in Creek country it was impossible to tell whether someone was Indian or black or white by appearances. Determining an applicant's "degree of Indian blood" was an impossible challenge that turned to controversy when property restrictions and eligibility for benefits were made contingent upon this very percentage.[29] The federal government's intervention in the shape of the Dawes Commission accounted, in part, for the turn-of-the-century inflation in the value of "blood" in Indian Territory; but so, too, did the federal government's lack of intervention, especially in relation to illegal settlement of the Territory prior to allotment. In this sense U.S. federal intervention and nonintervention into the activities of settlers conspired in the destruction of Indian sovereignty, and the rise of racism therein.

In short, the focus on "full-blood" status and notions of racial purity expanded exponentially as more and more white and black "non-natives" began to settle the Territory, carrying with them experiences of the Deep South. And when Oklahoma became a state in 1907, it did so on the promise of adopting Jim Crow legislation similar to that which then governed Arkansas and the other southern states. While "blood" had mattered to privileges within the Nation, "blood" identities were now officially sanctioned by the U.S. federal government; "full-blood" status was now linked to the dominant racial categories of an expanding U.S. empire.[30]

Many Creeks, including both Indians and freedmen, strongly opposed the idea of allotment overall, believing it meant the end of their way of life and their right to govern their own territory. Some of Brown's neighbors resisted allotment, actively participating in what became known as the Crazy Snake Rebellion in 1909. In a brief article on the rebellion, the *New York Times* revealed the racialization and national dismissal of Indian and black Indian resistance in this moment: "After all, though Crazy Snake is a Creek Indian, his murderous band is largely composed of half-breeds and lawless negroes, and though the Creeks have had a grievance since their lands were thrown open to settlers, most of the others are merely cattle thieves whom the Sheriff has been pursuing. The romance of the red Indian is dead and probably Crazy Snake and his lieutenants soon will be in the same safe condition." Notwithstanding the use of "blood" in this dismissal, Joseph Bruner recalled the actual reason behind the rebellion was that the Snake Indians did not want individual allotments but wanted the Creek nation to "share equally" in the gas, oil, and pasture leases.[31]

Prior to allotment, Creeks of various backgrounds had shared in many resources, including education. As Thurman Brown recalled stories of his father's childhood, a century later: "Well you see . . . Poppa and them went to school right in here, in Wewoka, a place here called Mekasukey. Creek Indian and black folks went to school together in Mekasukey." In spite of this shared history, the advent of statehood and allotment gradually fractured such communities. Built in 1891 for the education of Creek and

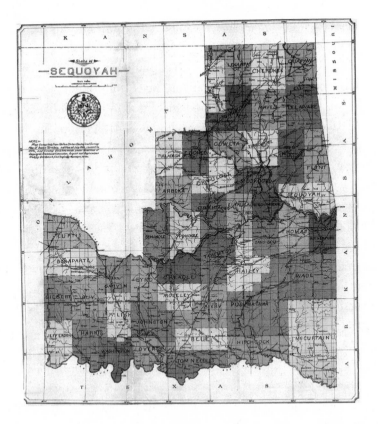

9. Map of Proposed State of Sequoyah, a 1905 bid to secure statehood under Native governance. Courtesy Edmon Low Library, Oklahoma State University

Seminole boys, Mekasukey Academy initially enrolled freedmen. By 1910, however, a number of them "were 'Jim-Crowed' out of the academy."[32] While many Native Americans resisted allotment and Oklahoma statehood to the bitter end—eventually advocating, unsuccessfully, an Indian State of Sequoyah in 1905, in order to retain control of their land—most African-descended residents were excluded from both the construction of, and Native resistance to, Oklahoma statehood.

African-descended residents were not represented in the Sequoyah Convention of 1905, nor in the Single Statehood Convention that same year, instead organizing a separate convention of their own. Launching the Negro

Protective League of Oklahoma and Indian Territories in August 1905 "for the purpose of arousing our people in the two territories to the importance of safeguarding our political and civic rights," hundreds of African Americans ultimately condemned the segregationist state constitution. At the same time, Brown, like many of those residents versed in the economics of individualized land ownership, urged his children's participation in the allotment process. Many African Creeks, freedpeople of the Creek nation, and African-American "intruders," tried to negotiate the best deal they could within the new system of allotment and the racial hierarchy codified therein.[33]

Brown's marriages to Aurelia Bruner and Julia Simon—descendants of "full-blood" Creek and Seminole grandparents—became the basis of his own family's land acquisition. His wife Aurelia Bruner appears to have been descended from both categories of enrollment offered by the Dawes Commission; that is, although her children were placed on the "freedmen" rolls, her ancestors included "freedmen" of the Indian nations as well as Indians "by Blood." Following Aurelia Bruner's death in the 1880s, Brown married Julia Simon, Aurelia's niece, who appears to have shared this joint lineage on her father's side. However, Julia Simon's children were able to claim Creek "by Blood" ancestry because their "full-blood" ancestry was on Julia Simon's *mother's* side, and the Commission had decided to "observe the usages and customs of each tribe," in this case that citizenship would follow the mother's status. As Brown's grandson Thurman recalled: "See, if your momma was a Creek and your daddy was a Seminole, you was a Creek. If your momma's a Chickasaw and your daddy's a Seminole, he had to live where your momma was. . . . Two miles up from Crumwell, in Seminole County, they call it Sandy Creek, with Seminoles on one side and Creek on the other. All the mommas was born in Creek County, their kids had to be on the Creek side. . . . And they had to follow their mommas."[34]

Within the first two years of the twentieth century, at least eight of Brown's twelve children by Julia were allotted the promised 160 acres each, due to their maternal enrollment as "Creek, by Blood" on the Dawes rolls. The Brownsville allotments rested exclusively upon Brown's children proving their connection to "full-blood" ancestors, which they could prove only through Julia Simon's mother's family. As the family transitioned from

Creek to American citizenship, this process probably involved *not* mentioning the possibility of "freedman" relatives and ancestors, such as those clearly present within Julia's *father's* (and thus Aurelia's) family. Certainly Brown's children by Julia would have avoided mention of these ancestors by name in the testimony they delivered to the Dawes Commissioners in Muskogee in 1901, emphasizing instead their "full-blood" lineage; color and appearance powerfully shaped this process.[35]

Decades later, Brown's grandchildren remembered Thomas Jefferson Brown as having "some training and education and many trips to Muskogee," and as someone who "saw to it that each child's allotment was joining—so the township was established 'Brownsville' using the family name." According to Brown's granddaughter Marzetta Wesley, "There in this community of Browns was the Post Office, General Store, School and Church." Brown's ability to direct the placement of these individual allotments (an uncommon feat for many allottees), his maneuvering of "Creek by blood" status, and the success, however temporary, of the Brownsville settlement may have raised suspicions for his African Creek in-laws about the motivations of this "non-native." In the years leading up to allotment, Brown and Julia had twelve children, at least eight of whom received allotments before the cutoff in 1907. Julia's last children were born "too late" to receive allotments. As her son, the 103-year-old allottee Tom Brown recalled in 2007, "Now, my brother Oscar, the baby boy, he was born too late. See he come in nineteen seven, when Territory went into a state."[36]

Soon after the 1907 allotment cutoff, Brown and Simon's last child was born. They named her Ella Mae. Two years later, thirty-something Julia Simon died of unknown causes; a month later, so, too, did two-year-old Ella Mae. At 103 years old, Jeff's son Tom Brown recalled, "I had a sister, a baby sister, her name was Ella Mae. . . . One of the Simons choked her to death. Our daddy, and [his son] Ellwood went out to kill him, kill him, but they couldn't find him." When asked about the source of this conflict, Odevia Field answered, "What she [Julia Simon] probably did wrong was marrying my grandfather for some reason. Maybe. All I could remember them saying was he married her because of the land and the money. And the more children he had I guess they'd acquire that. It could be all related to

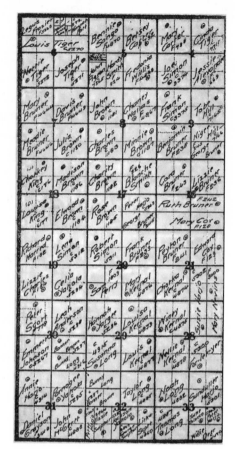

10. Allotments of Julia Simon Brown and eight of her children, forming Brownsville community, c. 1907. E. Hastain, *Hastain's Township Plats of the Creek Nation* (Muskogee, OK: Model Printing, 1910). Courtesy Oklahoma Historical Society

land."[37] Land was certainly a frequent point of contention, and Jeff's marriages into the Bruner-Simon clan seem to have attracted scrutiny.

Despite tribal resistance, internal conflict, and bureaucratic challenges, the Creek nation's land was ultimately allotted to those individuals who could prove Creek national membership or that they were freedpeople of the Creek nation, ultimately folding individual allottees into the capitalist land market, releasing the collective "surplus"—and a great portion of the future state of Oklahoma—to the U.S. government and incoming settlers. Since some allottees were assumed to have little experience with private land ownership, the law provided that individual allottees should be protected against land loss by making "sufficient land for a good home for each citizen . . . inalienable for twenty-five years," at which point, the commissioners speculated, allottees might be more accustomed to individual landholding. Dawes agreements with each of the five nations contained provisions to protect a limited (forty-acre) portion, known as the "homestead," against alienation, while the remainder, known as the (individual) "surplus," would soon "pass freely" in and out of Indian control, as Angie Debo first noted in 1940. Feeding on what Debo called the "wild, speculative, active spirit of the oil field," oilmen pushed for the lifting of even these restrictions, and in 1908, Congress acquiesced.[38]

But they did not do so evenhandedly. Instead, they passed legislation that removed nearly all restrictions on the "surplus" of all Creeks, except "full-bloods," as designated by the Dawes rolls. Because many "mixed blood" allottees—who were in some cases simply children of one Creek and one Seminole parent and were in other cases freedpeople of the Indian Nations—had lived all of their lives among the Indians, in this case among the Creeks and Seminoles, many also shared their experience of collective land ownership. Within months, most had lost their land to white grafters and oil speculators. With this single piece of legislation, more than 1.5 million acres were suddenly available for purchase by speculators near and far, and the majority of these acres belonged to freedpeople and "mixed blood" members of the Indian Nations and their children, such as those residing at Brownsville.[39]

Race and Land Loss

Surely Brown worried as he watched African Creeks—still faintly recalled as Estelvste—being divested of their land and socially and politically segregated from Creeks and white settlers alike through a violent combination of federal allotment policy, state and local Jim Crow policies, and rampant land and oil speculation. The rights of Creek freedpeople were increasingly neglected, as a new wave of African-American settlers and intermarriage further blurred the boundaries of these populations. In short, "race" superseded national or nonnational status as the leading indicator of rights and resources in Indian Territory; one's "race" (and *not* one's historical membership within the Indian Nations)—as designated by the Dawes Commission—now determined whether or not one's allotment would be "protected" from the rampant speculation, taxation, debt, and foreclosure that immediately transpired. In response to segregation and mounting discrimination, the emergence of the "all-black" towns also helped to obscure the once distinct position of Creek freedpeople in Indian Territory and thus the Creek origins of such communities. The intensifying Jim Crow "order" and the advent of oil speculation intertwined to muddle the possibility and relevance of black Indian identities. As one historian posits, the story of the Estelvste "tells of the nation choosing a future with no place within it for truly multiracial societies." In this sense, the choice echoed broader dynamics, within and beyond the aftermath of U.S. Reconstruction; at the turn of the twentieth century, historians Marilyn Lake and Henry Reynolds note, "White men's countries rested on the premise that multiracial democracy was an impossibility."[40]

Against this backdrop, Thomas Jefferson Brown's grandchildren were taught, again and again, about their roots, namely their Creek family history. Especially following Oklahoma statehood and the death of their Creek mother, Thomas Jefferson Brown insisted that they know their exact status in the Creek nation in terms that nevertheless reflected the growing significance of race and "blood" in Indian Territory. His son, Charles Brown, passed this on to his own children in the 1920s. Marzetta Wesley recalled, "Pawpaw always told me, *you are not a freedman*. Others may say they are, but you are not. You are Ceasar Simon's great-great-granddaughter. And Charity Simon."[41] The statement reveals Charles Brown's, and Thomas Jefferson Brown's, investment in distancing their children, when possible, from slavery and claiming, in its place, Creek lineage. In this way, Brown attempted to link his children's fate not to race but to nation, and in this case the Creek nation; American national citizenship was no longer the hopeful claim it may have seemed for many African Americans at the time of Brown's initial migration.

As the Bruner family history reveals, however, Creek and enslaved lineage were not mutually exclusive, and many Creek freedpeople had been both slaves and relatives of their Indian slaveowners. Indeed, both of Brown's wives may have been descended from both slaves and slave owners. Brown's

11. Charles Augustus Brown (son of Thomas Jefferson Brown), left,
c. 1900. Author's collection

insistence on his children's heritage reflects the fact that even those who
could prove "Creek by blood" background along with African ancestry were
losing traction during this period, particularly in the aftermath of allotment,
the massive influx of white and African-American migrants from the Deep
South to the new state of Oklahoma, and the emergence of Jim Crow and
oil speculation. Ironically, turn-of-the-century proclamations in local papers
about African Creek participation on equal footing in the Territory had encouraged this influx to the so-called Promised Land; in 1904, in the Muskogee *Cimeter*, Paro Bruner himself still described Creek country, relative to
the brutality of the surrounding region, as "an island surrounded by land."
But by the end of the first decade following Oklahoma statehood, the rights
of all African-descended peoples in the Territory were systematically de-
nied. Echoing the Mississippi State Black Codes of 1865 that prohibited African Americans from purchasing or leasing land, white Oklahomans
began to limit African-American access to land. In 1911, white farmers of
Okfuskee County (immediately north of the Brownsville allotments) signed
oaths pledging to "never rent, lease, or sell any land in Okfuskee County to

any person or persons of Negro blood, or agent of theirs; unless the land be located more than one mile from a white or Indian resident."[42]

By such tactics, distinctions between Creek freedpeople and the recent wave of "state" migrants—that is, between black Indians and more recent black settlers—were quickly flattened, effectively racializing the whole, allowing black Indians fewer and fewer opportunities to claim national membership within the Indian Nations. For the most part, Creek freedpeople faced the same discrimination imposed upon all African Americans of early Oklahoma, and in some cases they expressed resentment toward the newcomers. Their complaints, however, had hardly a place to register, as their particular "freedman" status held decreasing significance within the new state; there were few opportunities to assign meaning to their singular history within the Creek nation. Where there had once been social sanctions against a Creek freedman's marriage to "state Negroes," these quickly broke down in the face of white and Indian hostility toward all people of any African descent.[43]

Within a year or two of statehood, as the Brownsville land was pursued by oil speculators, Brown began urging his children to move away from their rural settlement, closer to the then burgeoning city of Okmulgee, where, in the spirit of racial uplift, African-American education, employment, and sheer safety were more easily achieved. His eldest daughter, Rena, moved first, and her siblings soon followed from the Brownsville settlement. Soon a new wave of black migration—to northern cities and beyond the United States—would further obscure the multiracial, multinational origins of this family and community.

For the Browns and other black and black Indian families facing racism and dispossession across rural Oklahoma, the quest for land shifted to a hunt for jobs and education. Along the way, settlements like Brownsville were leased, mortgaged, and sold to white settlers, speculators, and banks. Before the value of petroleum beneath much of the black and Indian land holdings of Oklahoma was known, and before the state of Oklahoma was ten years old, the Brown family was already largely gone from the land. Following in the footsteps of his Estelvste ancestors who served as negotiators and translators, Brown's son Charles ultimately made part of his living, however unreliable, by

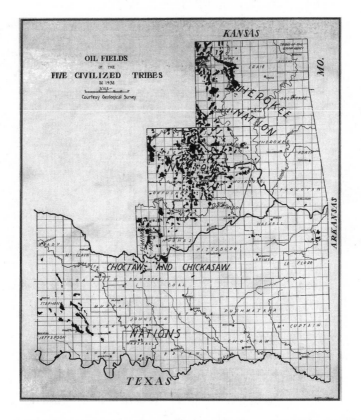

12. "Oil Fields of the Five Civilized Tribes." This map may have been
adapted by Angie Debo from a 1932 U.S. Geological Survey Map. Courtesy
Angie Debo Papers, Special Collections, Oklahoma State University

translating the Muskogee language for white oil speculators and directing them
to oil-rich lands throughout the Creek nation. Three decades later, in 1949,
Brown and several of his peers, including the famed *Black Dispatch* editor
Roscoe Dunjee, pitched to Oklahoma City lawyers a "stock-selling" enterprise:
the black-owned Southwestern Oil and Gas Company of Boley, Oklahoma.
In their prospectus to potential investors, company officers included a photograph of black Oklahoman Forest Anderson, with the caption "Oklahoma's
richest Negro." The company was short-lived, but Charles Brown continued
to make a living through oil and gas leases for several decades thereafter.

13. Charles Augustus Brown et al. proposed the black-owned Southwestern
Oil and Gas Company, c. 1949. Courtesy Barbara (Brown) Player

"Seems he instinctively knew the 'ripe' locations to set up wells and invest," his daughter, Barbara (Brown) Player, recollected. "He gambled on some and lost some, etc.; sold some land when he was lucky and/or needed cash (for too little in exchange, probably). Also sold sections of leases to make it for another day. This seemed to have been his struggle." Player added, "I often look back with some regret that I didn't stick around OK longer to help Pawpaw achieve his dreams."[44]

In 1870, when Brown first settled in Indian Territory, perceptions of him were less about his racial identification than they were about his national (or *non*national) identification; recall that Brown was initially categorized on Creek national records as a "non-native" or "intruder." Brown bolstered his claims to freedom and American citizenship in the postemancipation era by attaching himself to American expansion, American Indians, and the acquisition of Indian land. In this context, migration for African-American men like Brown involved distancing themselves from blackness and connecting themselves, instead, to the project of American national expansion. For a time, Brown's place in Indian Territory was somewhat unusual and afforded him myriad privileges associated with American expansion and proximity to Creek national belonging.

By 1904, however, when a Mississippi freedman purchased the allotment belonging to Chaney Wallace's son, Washington "Wash" Bruner, the emerging opposition instead lay largely between black and white national projects. Soon the experience of land loss in relation to Jim Crow and the rise of oil speculation in early statehood Oklahoma bound together black and black Indian families, gradually processing their newly linked fate within the state of Oklahoma. Race and color had so significantly shaped access to resources in the Territory that by the second decade of the twentieth century, the reverse was also true: resources could shape perceptions of one's racial and national origins. "When you get as much money as Johnny (a freedman)," one Creek freedman posited, "you're an Indian not a Negro."[45]

As Indian sovereignty was dissolved and notions of racial purity and "blood" acquired growing significance, "race" ultimately eclipsed "nation" as a guarantor of rights and resources in the Territory. Two generations later, in the 1920s, in spite of the rich history of African-descended Creeks, Brown's grandchildren were still attempting to distance themselves from freedpeople and slavery, in favor of their Creek lineage. In the end, as much as the experience of land acquisition for settlers like Brown had functioned as a national project, the experience of land loss decades later was deeply racialized. The emergence of a rigid black-white dichotomy thoroughly obscured the more nuanced possibilities of the preceding period in Indian Territory. At the turn of the century, Brown's experiences reveal, the United States' self-definition shifted decisively from "nation" to "race," from Indian- and American-ness to blackness and whiteness.

Brownsville was remembered by twentieth-century descendants as Thomas Jefferson Brown's land, not Julia Simon's or Aurelia Bruner's, and as a black settlement, not an Indian or black Indian one. This is partly because Thomas Jefferson Brown, listed as "mulatto" on the census, appeared in most twentieth-century recollections as the patriarch of the family; because it was he, descendants thought, who arranged the placement of the allotments adjacent to one another, applied for and received the post office, set up the schoolhouse and church; because he outlived both Aurelia Bruner

14. Luerenda Hunter Brown, c. 1910. Her marriage to Charles Brown linked the Brown and Coleman families and land. Author's collection

and Julia Simon; and because, in the twentieth century, his third wife was a "non-native" African-American woman. But it is also because of much broader changes afoot in Indian Territory and Oklahoma in the early 1900s. Most important, the value of "blood" emerged paramount in turn-of-the-century Indian Territory, beginning with the Dawes Commission's attempt to distinguish between "Indians by blood" and "Creek freedmen," when so many residents were in fact connected to both groups. The resulting rolls codified a hierarchy within which "full-blood" Indians were entitled to more land and "protected" from fraud. This shift was soon bolstered by a Jim Crow state that, for purposes of segregation, classified nonblack Creeks as "white" and African Creeks as "black," and distributed resources accordingly.

At the age of ninety-six, Thurman Brown was one descendant who, having grown up in Brownsville and having been raised by Brown, remembered it the way it actually was. While examining an allotment map of the area, I said to him, "This would have been Grandpa Brown's land." He looked up from the map abruptly and said, "You mean Grandma Brown. *Grandpa Brown didn't have no land.*" Having witnessed the first century of Oklahoma statehood, Thurman knew better than most the historical relationship between land and identity. Willfully tying the land to his black Indian grandmother Julia (Simon) Brown, Thurman highlighted the origins of this land as a nineteenth-century Creek allotment, at a time—before widespread African-American settlement of Indian Territory and the rise of Jim Crow—when African Americans could still *be* Creek.[46] The story of Thomas Jefferson Brown's migration narrates the construction of a new racial order in Indian Territory, and, ultimately, the limits of North American escape.

As he relayed this story, Thurman did not bother to mention that "Grandma Julie" Simon—the grandmother who raised him when he was a young child, following the death of his parents—was categorized Creek "by blood," whereas his father's mother, Aurelia Bruner, was designated a "freedman." Thurman knew the subtleties of African Creek history, having been raised by Julia Simon and Thomas Jefferson Brown, a Bruner in a house full of Simons, the only Creek "freedman" in a house full of Creeks "by blood." He responded suspiciously when, as a teenager, I first started asking him questions about the supposed differences between these populations. A few years later, I caught up with him, and as our conversations evolved, we both quietly acknowledged what had happened to our history. Shortly before he passed away in 2007, in the midst of the national controversy over Cherokee membership, he told me, "You know, the Cherokees want 'full-blood' only now," and that the Creeks might follow suit. Then he turned quiet.[47]

TWO

Passing for Black

White Kinfolk, "Mulatto" Freedpeople, and Westward Migration

The thirty-something man of color who purchased the Creek allotment adjacent to Brownsville around 1908 was known to some descendants as Grandpa Coleman, or Monroe, and, occasionally, to census takers, as James Monroe Coleman. Born not long after the Civil War, he experienced relative prosperity during Reconstruction, prosperity rooted in a privileged relationship to the Coleman planter family and a legacy of his mother's antebellum labor. Years later, amid the violent reversals of southern "redemption," however, Monroe Coleman and his family left Mississippi and migrated to Indian Territory. Responding to contemporary popular literature of Indian Territory as a "Paradise," Monroe Coleman was drawn, like his neighbor Thomas Jefferson Brown, to the freedom that the Territory seemed to offer. While Brown's father was not a planter, both Brown and Coleman were sometimes described as "white-looking" men, classified by census takers during Reconstruction as "mulatto." Both bolstered their claims to freedom in the postemancipation era by distancing themselves, literally and symbolically, from plantation slavery and ultimately attaching themselves to Indian country and the acquisition of western lands.[1]

But while Brown had migrated largely on his own in the 1870s, like numerous nineteenth-century "pioneers," by the time Monroe Coleman migrated in 1904, he was participating in a movement far larger than his own. By the turn of the twentieth century, elaborate notions of racial destiny, peoplehood, uplift, and nationalism were on the rise across the South, and these ideas pushed and accompanied black and "mulatto" settlers like Coleman as they picked up, this time in collections of family groups, and headed to Indian Territory in wagons, on foot, and by train. This Oklahoma "fever" among black and "mulatto" southerners culminated between 1890 and 1910 with the migration of more than 100,000 African-descended southerners to Indian Territory and Oklahoma. Like the settlement of white migrants that preceded and outlasted this movement, African-American settlement was made possible by federal expansion and the dissolution of Indian Territory that began with the Civil War and ended with the Dawes Commission's allotment of collectively held Indian lands. But this turn-of-the-century movement of African-descended southerners constituted a strategic, collective response by freedpeople and their families to the stunning violence and exclusion of the post-Reconstruction South.[2]

In their overlapping efforts to establish a black state, and ultimately black towns and settlements, in the Territory participants trumpeted a promising racial future in the West at a decibel intended to drown out the rhetoric of racial inferiority and the reality of racial violence that dominated the South. Journalists and town boosters (often one and the same) focused on the "all-black" towns as prideful experiments in racial self-determination and domestic black enterprise. Unlike the Kansas "exodusters" who had migrated in the 1870s, by the close of the century Oklahoma's migrants (some of whom had participated in the Kansas exodus) had the advantage of a burgeoning black press in which to publicize their actions; in this sense, the movement exemplified historian Benedict Anderson's characterization of the press as a hallmark of nation-building, readying the ground for the growth of twentieth-century black nationalism; yet migration itself also bolstered the "imagined community." By the mid-twentieth century, while African Americans were entering the segregated historical profession in some numbers, most of the towns were in steep decline, and the black town movement (and newspaper archive) was ripe for public history and memorialization. In the years after towns like Boley and Clearview were nearly emptied of their people by the Great Depression, the Dust Bowl, the world wars, and the Great Migration, African-American citizens continued to use the story of the black towns to prove—as the towns were, in some sense, created to prove, a half-century earlier—the potential of "the race" for "civilization" and greatness.[3]

While drowning out the rhetoric of racial inferiority, however, this destinarian message also drowned out the complexities of freedpeople's lives in ways that shaped contemporary headlines, the archive, and subsequent scholarship. Closer attention to early Oklahoma reveals, among other things, story after story of a westward "escape" of planters' sons whose origins straddled the color line. Monroe Coleman and his family "came by train," his grandchildren repeatedly boasted, hinting at their grandfather's relative status, financial wealth, and diverse ancestry. Yet the postemancipation presence of such "new people" was no secret among southerners. The history of racial slavery in the American South included constant intervention in the sexual and reproductive lives of many enslaved women and families that continued in new forms after emancipation. But it was after the Civil War, amid cries of "racial amalgamation" and "race war," that the visibility of "mulatto" offspring of such interventions became a heightened source of anxiety to white planters. At the end of the Civil War, historian Joel Williamson notes, "whites had invented the term 'miscegenation' to cover the whole phenomenon of mixing black and white." Every bit an invention, "it was a term that carried dire implications." The racial revolution—the "rising rage for identity" and violent replacement of slave and free with increasingly rigid categories of black and white—wrought by the Civil War era had particular "dire implications" for families that were "losing the color line." In many ways, the growing impossibility of this visible and sometimes prosperous population was a harbinger for the racialization of southern class structure that would ultimately shape the lives of all freedpeople after Reconstruction.[4]

In an effort to reconstruct the complex origins of "all-black" Oklahoma, in this chapter I explore Monroe Coleman's decision to participate in this racially self-conscious movement against the backdrop of his early life as a "mulatto" child in Reconstruction-era Mississippi, amid rumors of white parentage. In so doing, I also illuminate the relationship between migration and the construction of racial categories. Reading Coleman's life alongside the lives of others who left a few more written records, I suggest that the westward migration of "mulatto" freedpeople constituted a telling response to the racial "revolution" that accompanied the demise of Reconstruction. While the rise of black Oklahoma was promoted, narrated, memorialized, and ultimately historicized as "all-black" and self-consciously "domestic," such an image stands in contrast to the racial realities of the period. Coleman's migration not only brings to life the erasure of racial complexity in the West, as the previous chapter reveals. It also demonstrates how "the relentless search for the purity of origins" has produced a thoroughgoing, painstaking erasure of the multiracial South.[5]

This chapter delves more deeply into stories of several of my ancestor's contemporaries — including the life paths of Ransom Edmondson (a Fisk University classmate of W. E. B. Du Bois) and Jackson Townsend, among others. Like Coleman, both Edmondson and Townsend were "mulatto" men born to southern white planters in the 1860s, and both moved westward following the foreclosure of Reconstruction. I incorporate their stories, among others, in order to question, illuminate, and bolster my claims about Monroe Coleman, about whom I hold fewer direct sources. In my exploration of Thomas Jefferson Brown, the subject of the previous chapter, I had the benefit of more abundant sources through Brown's African Creek kin network and oft-repeated family stories about his life. In the case of Alexander "Elic" Davis, the subject of the subsequent chapter, I had the benefit of the oral testimony of his daughter, Lomie Davis, which drove my archival research. While Coleman may have had greater financial resources than both Brown and Davis, like many "mulatto" freedpeople, he lived relatively quietly in the countryside for much of his life, choosing autonomy if not exile; in spite of his relative wealth — in many family histories a reliable indicator of a deeper paper trail — Coleman's ideas and thinking about his times have remained more elusive.

The subject of "mulatto" freedpeople has only rarely been studied in such terms. For many important reasons, recent historians of the era have focused our attention on continuities within the experiences of freedpeople; the ubiquity of the slavery-freedom binary, however, has obscured not only the ways in which freedom often looked like slavery, but the tremendous diversity within the experiences of freedpeople. At the same time, pressing twentieth- and twenty-first-century concerns about class, color, privilege, and racism, and the perceived political and cultural need for racial solidarity, have discouraged intellectual curiosity about this diversity as chauvinism, submerging critical truths about the roots of contemporary "racial" thought.[6]

"New People" in the Civil War Era

Monroe Coleman was born three years after the war. Even as Kaziah pushed her son into the postemancipation world in Mississippi, she worried for his future, imagining what his free life might hold. When the census taker looked in on Kaziah's household a year later, the notes he chose to make—"Mu" and "Coleman"—acknowledged baby Monroe's color and the surname of his mother's slaveowner but betrayed no specific knowledge of a white father. Remembering Monroe Coleman years after his death, his grandchildren recalled that he could "pass" for white, or sometimes American Indian, when selling his corn, tomatoes, and melons in Okmulgee, Oklahoma, in the 1920s. He was identified on all but one federal census as "mulatto," until the category disappeared in 1920. Notwithstanding the frequent conflation of color and parentage—Monroe's white ancestry may have derived from a previous generation—several grandchildren remembered that Coleman's relative privilege came from his connection to a white father. "Documentation of sex," historian Martha Hodes writes, "is almost always a casualty in the pruning of family papers."[7]

At the time of Monroe Coleman's birth, his mother, Kaziah, may have been working within the Coleman home as what some planters called a "house servant." Antebellum domestic service has been described by historian Anthony Kaye as "a family trust." In the wealthier Natchez district, "slaves and owners agreed house service was rightly the province of families with long-standing ties to master, mistress, or their kin." Amos Wright "recalled how the lot of a 'house boy' fell to him from the boughs of three family trees. He and both his parents, Joe and Rebecca Eddins, belonged to the Powers family until they were bequeathed to their owner's granddaughter, Delia Wright." By the time Amos entered the Wright household, family

connections extended three generations, "and he gave the tie its due by taking the Wrights' name." While it is painfully difficult to reconstruct precise
kinship connections among enslaved members of the Coleman plantation,
across generations Coleman planters had maintained close relationships
to a few enslaved men, women, and children. These may have included
Kaziah.[8]

As a young girl on the Coleman place, perhaps Kaziah heard stories about
her slaveowner's family extending back to Robert Coleman, who had migrated in 1652 from Wales to Virginia, and settled where the Appomattox
meets the James River. A century later, after a stint in North Carolina—long
enough to commingle with the local Cherokees—Coleman descendants
migrated to Fairfield County, South Carolina, on land granted from King
George; five decades later, overcome by "Alabama fever," they moved on to
the Old Southwest, settling on both sides (Alabama and Mississippi) of the
Tombigbee River in the 1820s. As domestic cotton cultivation and global de-
mand took off after Alabama statehood and, ultimately, Indian removal,
thousands of planters moved southwest from the Carolinas to what was then
Indian country and the "southern frontier." The Colemans were early participants in this movement. Settlers were especially drawn to the banks of the
Tombigbee and its potential for transporting cotton and other goods, via Mo-
bile, into the Gulf of Mexico. When Alexander Donelson returned from
scouting lands on the Tombigbee River in 1811, he wrote to his uncle, Andrew Jackson, "I am much pleased with a great proportion of that country,"
describing it as "the most desireable country I have ever seen, if settled by
civilized people." During this same period, Israel Pickens purchased more
than a thousand acres of land for a cotton plantation, worked by enslaved
men and women on the Tombigbee.[9]

The communities the Coleman planters settled in these American borderlands had long been shaped "by indigenous migrations, successive waves
of French, Spanish, and British colonists, and the introduction of people of
African descent." When they first ventured into the Mississippi Territory in
1799, William and John Coleman had been "granted passports" to go through
the Creek nation to the Tombigbee, and return. Two decades later, when
their South Carolina kin moved south on the heels of Alabama statehood

and expanding pressure toward Cherokee expulsion, they needed no such documents. One branch of the Coleman family settled in an area they called Mesopotamia, "the place between the rivers." Instead of the Tigris and Euphrates, it was the Black Warrior and Tombigbee Rivers; as with the nearby French settlement of Demopolis, settlers' choice of names invoked centers of ancient culture of the venerated Mediterranean world. Just before their arrival, in 1819, Greene County had been created by the first Alabama state legislature; the county was named for Revolutionary War General Nathaniel Greene. Israel Pickens participated in drafting Alabama's first state constitution and in 1821 became governor. Gradually the indigenous and European place names that had long peppered this region of imperial contest were replaced with American ones. The cultural dimensions of this settlement process help explain the invention of the "New World." "Newness enacts a kind of surrogation" scholar Joseph Roach writes, that "conceptually erases indigenous populations, contributing to a mentality conducive to the practical implementation of the American Holocaust." Within a decade, the federal policy and political violence of Indian removal expelled Muskogean peoples and communities that found themselves within the new boundaries of the new state of Alabama.[10]

At the same time, the idea and rhetoric of the "frontier" during this period bolstered the myth that white Americans could get out from under the bounded economic and social obligations and constraints of the southeast seaboard—creating an "empire for liberty." Such rhetoric reinforced the fiction of the independent white frontiersman. The nineteenth-century "frontier"—including the increasingly profitable "Old Southwest"—was presented time after time as a "solution" to "racial" problems; through frontier expansion, both staunchly pro-slavery planters and antislavery advocates of "free labor" ideology imagined that their personal and political interests could be protected. Yet here and elsewhere, pro-slavery interests won out.[11]

The development of this region ultimately depended upon the work of millions of enslaved African Americans, clearing fields and supporting the myriad needs of white families during migration and settlement—creating an "empire for slavery." At each stage of migration, African-descended Colemans may have cleared forests, constructed buildings, built tools, forded rivers, and planted cotton. Before he died in South Carolina in 1795, for instance, planter Robert Coleman conveyed to his son Thomas "a Negro boy named Moses," and the name Moses appears to have lived on among African-American Colemans after emancipation. When John Coleman first settled in Alabama Territory in 1818, he was accompanied by an African-American man known as Trim. Trim waited for nearly a year on the uncleared land while John returned to the upper South to retrieve his family. Wiley and David Coleman were born in the new state of Alabama at the height of southern expansion. While not large slaveowners, one of these brothers may have inherited Kaziah, or her mother, from their father in the early 1850s. A few years later, he forded the Tombigbee with Kaziah; a decade later, he may have fathered Monroe.[12]

Witnessing the war from the western banks of the Tombigbee, Kaziah was busy learning how to survive as an adolescent girl under slavery when it ended. Kaziah knew that African-descended people were not everywhere enslaved; before leaving South Carolina, she had heard whispered stories, perhaps from her grandmother, of a free childhood in Senegambia, of black independence in Haiti. Perhaps she wondered why not here, in Mississippi. Why not her mother, or one day her son? Yet when freedom finally came, Kaziah, like many freedpeople, was worried. She could not have experienced the jubilation of emancipation without its haunting underside of vulnerability and anxiety, drawn from the acknowledgment that former slaveowners continued to control the vast majority of land and labor, and thus black lives—but this time, without an economic stake in their physical survival, let alone their well-being. In the immediate aftermath of emancipation, amid the brutalities of the black codes, special investigator to Andrew Johnson General Carl Schurz traveled through Mississippi and found: "Some planters held back their former slaves on their plantations by brute force. . . . Men who are honorable in their dealings with their white neighbors will cheat a Negro without feeling a single twinge of their honor. To kill a Negro, they do not deem murder; to debauch a Negro woman, they do not think fornication; to take property away from a Negro, they do not consider robbery." Two years later, in 1868, Kaziah watched as Reconstruction sped into action, with Union forces stationed throughout the state.

Shortly before Christmas, Kaziah was, for at least one long, haunting moment, at the will of her former slaveowner; whether or not he forced the act, by exiling Kaziah from her familial world as a child, controlling her food, shelter, and sustenance ever since, he coerced—visibly and invisibly—her adolescent intimacy. This, too, was freedom. Kaziah's lifelong connection to this man and his family raised endless, unanswerable questions about the right way forward in the postemancipation era.[13]

Monroe Coleman grew up working on the Coleman plantation, managing day-to-day activities on the white planter's farm, evidenced, according to his grandchildren, by the superior agricultural and business skills he later carried with him to Indian Territory. It would be easy to assume that Monroe Coleman, like tens of thousands of formerly enslaved children, was a victim of "apprenticeship," and that Kaziah had little choice in the matter of her son's employment.[14] This may have been true. More likely, however, Kaziah wielded some power, as she weighed the costs and benefits of keeping her son in the Coleman household during Reconstruction. Amid the violent backlash to the war's end and the early days of Reconstruction, Kaziah, like many freedpeople, used her antebellum kinship networks in an attempt to protect her child.

Fifteen years after Coleman's birth, when his contemporary William Du Bois arrived at Fisk, one hundred miles north, in the mid-1880s, he noted the significant presence of "mulattoes," most about Coleman's age, with stories not entirely disconnected from his own. Du Bois recalled in his autobiography, "Lots and lots of mulattoes of that sort, some of whom were financed by their fathers, and some of them were financed by the fact that as mulattoes they got the better jobs." Du Bois was impressed by this particular class of confident, "modishly dressed," men and women, writes David Levering Lewis. "The sons and daughters of slaves and slave masters, few of them displayed servile traits because, to the extent advantages flowed from it, they were beneficiaries of the slave system." So while "conditions close to poverty" marked the origins of the majority of Du Bois's classmates, it was these "affluent sons and daughters" who "set the tone and defined the institutional character" of Fisk a generation after emancipation. One such classmate was Ransom Edmondson. In his autobiography, Du Bois recalled Edmondson as "a handsome man, tall and thin, olive-skinned with a mass of brown hair, wearing spectacles and curiously dignified. He was five or six years older than I and acted as assistant librarian under Professor Morgan who taught Latin. He and a younger brother were sons of a rich white planter." To the Massachusetts-born William come South, Lewis writes, "mulattoes seemed to be everywhere." While he lacked the wealth and mobility of the most affluent, this was Monroe Coleman's generation, and these were some of his circumstances, too. They were, in Lewis's words, "walking indictments of the concupiscence, hypocrisy, and paradox at the core of all master-slave societies."[15] The postemancipation presence of such "new people," was, however, no secret.

Before the war, white and black observers had anxiously noted the rapid growth of the "mulatto" population. The majority of this growth derived from the domestic slave trade—including the "fancy girl trade," in which "mulatto" women were explicitly sold for sexual slavery, concubinage, and prostitution. "What, after all, could be more valuable," historian Brenda Stevenson notes, "than a woman of 'white' complexion who could be bought as one's private 'sex slave'?" This trade expanded exponentially on the nineteenth-century "southern frontier." Ex-slave and blacksmith James Pennington recalled that "the finest specimens of coloured females" were often "raised for the express purpose of supplying the market of a class of economical Louisan and Mississippi gentlemen, who do not wish to incur the expense of rearing legitimate families," and, in other cases, were "exposed to the most shameful degradation, by the young masters in the families where it is claimed they are so well off." Thus, like most southerners identified as "mulatto" in the 1850s, Mary (Edmondson)—Ransom Edmondson's mother—was enslaved; at that time, in Mississippi, "not one mulatto in twenty" was free.[16] Those liaisons involving the planter elite were particularly politically consequential. "It seems that in almost every community in the slave South," Joel Williamson notes, "there existed at least one slave woman whose distinctly lighter-colored children testified to a falling from racial grace by one or more white men." In short, sexual slavery and the domestic slave trade produced a diverse set of offspring—some whose fathers were enslaved men, others whose fathers were white planters—who together populated the category of "mulatto" in the Civil War era. And while planter families often attributed such children to "casual connections" with poor white inhabitants, many were the children of slaveowners.[17]

Such liaisons sometimes resulted in white planter fathers providing for the "upbringing, education, and economic security" of their enslaved children; some manumitted and bequeathed property—occasionally including other slaves—to their free and enslaved African-descended offspring. In 1856, in Madison County, Alabama, white planter Samuel Townsend died and freed in his will fifty of his slaves, leaving these fifty women and men an estate of more than $200,000, including other women and men who remained enslaved. In accordance with his will, several of Townsend's "mulatto" children attended Wilberforce Academy. The planter family, "perhaps for two generations or more," Williamson notes, "became inextricably mixed with several of its own slave families." While these were "set aside and freed," the estate administrator "bought and sold other blacks for their benefit." In such places, on the eve of the Civil War, "whole settlements were losing the color line in a welter of browns, yellows, and reds." Because of the size of the estate and execution of Samuel's will, "the Townsends left a clear trace of their mulatto progeny." Such faithful execution of large bequests to "mulatto" offspring was unusual, partly because potential white heirs so often successfully challenged these wills in southern courts.[18]

Many more planters left less of a "clear trace," yet were no less active in sexual liaisons across the color line in the Civil War era. Occasionally, in lieu of property bequests, such men left startling traces on the federal census, judiciously claiming all of their children, leading or allowing census takers to delineate some "mulatto" and others "white." Ransom Edmondson's father, Thomas J. (T. J.) Edmondson, was one such planter in Carroll County, Mississippi. A year into the war, when fourteen-year-old Mary Edmondson, an enslaved woman, bore Henry, the first of four "mulatto" boys within the household of T. J. Edmondson, she may have had little confidence in his future "upbringing, education, and economic security." At the time, Mary was living and working in the household of T. J. Edmondson, his wife, Elizabeth, and their four-year-old son; she was reportedly working

as a cook. Into this family, Du Bois's future classmates — Ransom and John —
were born to Mary (Edmondson) in 1863 and 1865, followed by a fourth
child, William, just after the war. At the time, the value of T. J. Edmondson's cotton proceeds was $3,888 (the rough equivalent of $60,000 in 2017),
unusually high for the surrounding community. The constitution of their
household might recall the widespread practice of concubinage, exemplified by Mary Boykin Chesnut's troubling description of her neighbor's
"black harem with its consequences under the same roof with his lovely
white wife." Within a decade, both women — wife Elizabeth Edmondson
and formerly enslaved Mary Edmondson — were gone from the household
(probably deceased), and in 1880 fifty-six-year-old T. J. Edmondson appears
to have been living as a widower with one white and three "mulatto" sons.
While the white son was farming alongside his father, the three "mulatto"
sons were recorded as students.[19]

The Edmondson family was not exceptional. Across the lower South
in the antebellum era, in nearly every community, "there were mulattoes of
recognized and respectable white parentage." On the eve of the Civil War,
however, a "rising rage for identity" among white southerners left less and
less room for such open relations, and "a civilization on the make took great
pains to blind itself to the whiteness of its mulatto children." So while multiple tensions were rising in the 1850s — "between masters and slaves, between plain folk and patricians, between free Negroes and whites, and
between slaveholders and their wives, daughters, and mothers" — "probably
nowhere was the social order more visibly fractured . . . than by the presence
of increasing numbers of mulattoes in the homes of leading Southerners."
The specter of secession catalyzed the forced erasure of this multiracial past.
In the lead-up to southern secession, and throughout the war, white southern politicians began using, like never before, racism and the language of
racial purity, mobilizing the emerging politics of white privilege among the
many to preserve the long-standing profits of racial slavery for the few. White
Americans, North and South, came to fix upon "race mixing as a clear and
present problem." In their efforts to unify southern Whigs and Democrats,
white slaveowners and nonslaveowners, southern secessionists characterized the Union with images of "race war" and "racial amalgamation,"

disavowing notions of equality in favor of scientific racism. In fact, these symbolic threats of "racial amalgamation" drew their power from the history of American racial and sexual slavery.[20]

If Monroe traveled to Carrollton with his father in the mid-1870s, he may have traveled the length of Choctaw County, forty-five miles, by wagon, from his homeplace. Along the way, perhaps Monroe and his father crossed paths with Ransom and his father, whose homeplace was in the nearby community called Duck Hill. Observing Ransom, this "mulatto" youngster with planter T. J. Edmondson, perhaps he exchanged a glance with him. Maybe the two wandered off for a moment, before being reprimanded with a stern word or physical force. Perhaps Monroe looked up from the ground when Ransom addressed his father, as such, in public. More likely, they both knew better.

Monroe Coleman was barely six years old, and these were heady times. The Reconstruction years of Coleman's childhood were marked by high hopes and deep disappointments. Politically, freedpeople fought for black men's citizenship and voting and participated in an unprecedented experiment in multiracial democracy, including the election to office of nearly two thousand African Americans, the vast majority of them former slaves. As a young child, perhaps Coleman witnessed aunts and uncles participating in the promise of the new Freedman's Bank, or the South's first public education system. He learned that a former slave from a neighboring county had been elected to the U.S. Senate. This story of Reconstruction is profoundly important, but also woefully incomplete. Looking at what it actually meant on the ground to be enslaved children at the time of emancipation, coming of age suddenly legally "free"—with little to no material resources to make freedom "real"—reveals the problem of an all-too-neat narrative of slavery vs. freedom.[21]

Like most southerners, and especially those of freedom's first generation, Monroe Coleman's hope was to own his own plot, grow his own food, and live independently. But after the Civil War, abandoned and reclaimed lands were returned to former slaveowners, and most former slaves were required to sign annual labor contracts with former owners. Vagrancy statutes made it a crime to be found in public without a contract; once arrested for such "crimes," freedpeople were assigned for decades, often life, to convict labor camps some called "worse than slavery." This was both old and new: old-fashioned control of black labor rooted in slavery, and a newfound criminalization of black bodies that had everything to do with the question of black freedom. At the same time, the violent backlash to Reconstruction expanded. The Ku Klux Klan had begun the year after emancipation, using violence to terrorize freedpeople, Republicans, and laborers, targeting individuals as well as black churches, schools, and Mississippi courts. In Meridian, for instance, during an 1871 trial of two freedpeople, Klansmen had opened fire in the courtroom, killing the two defendants and the Republican judge, launching a riot and the murder of thirty or more black men. In the 1870s, following a brief suppression of the Klan, in coordinated efforts, some white southerners, rich and poor, launched a wave of racial violence that targeted political participation and any semblance of economic prosperity and ultimately put an end to black voting.[22]

In the 1880s, as Monroe entered adulthood, many of the racist laws established in the aftermath of emancipation, and repealed during Reconstruction, were being enacted once again. At the same time, vast numbers of freedpeople became increasingly indebted to planters, unable to repay debt, change employers, or receive a wage. The result was the virtual immobilization of many black laborers in the rural South. Moreover, lacking the value assigned by the slave market, freedpeople were considered replaceable and "suffered gross mistreatment up to and including murder at the hands of plantation owners." Many of the same ex-slaveowners brutally dominated the landscape and lives of black laborers, once again with the approbation of the state and the increasingly blind eye of the nation. Black men and women would be picked up for trivial violations, charged with enormous fines, and forced into labor camps, where they served local industry and the state. And while the violent reinstatement of an immobilized, black agricultural labor force fulfilled the economic desires of many white planters in the wake of Reconstruction, so did the use of poll taxes, literacy tests, and electoral violence fulfill their political ambitions and secure the new racial "order."[23]

The rise of this "order" in the post-Reconstruction South had consequences for all African-descended southerners, including a number of
freedpeople who had prospered and were not yet indebted to white planters,
or dependent upon them for a wage. Ironically, the growing symbolic violence of the post-Reconstruction era—public lynching—was increasingly
reserved not for supposed black dependence or destitution, but for the offense of black independence and visible prosperity. While lynching was not
entirely new, the practice burgeoned during Reconstruction, as African
Americans began to participate in electoral politics and to establish their
own businesses, communities, and towns. Around this time, in the mid-
1880s, Ransom Edmondson and his younger brother were sent away. They
enrolled at Fisk, in Nashville, a day's trip to the north, where Ransom
appeared, to a young William Du Bois, "curiously dignified."[24]

Although Monroe Coleman would stay physically put in Mississippi for
another decade, his self-presentation was increasingly in flux by the mid-
1880s. A few years earlier, his mother, Kaziah, took the surname Miller (perhaps having married a freedman); her children were listed by census takers as
Millers instead of Colemans. That year, they were also recorded as "B" instead
of "Mu." Moreover, as head of household, Kaziah was economically and
physically vulnerable. A decade after emancipation, she chose to present her
sons as Millers even though Miller was either dead, absent, or nonexistent;
while the change may have been a statement of self-determination or economic convenience, the will of the census taker, or happenstance, it may
have also provided some cover to the reality of concubinage that spanned slavery and freedom in Mississippi. Perhaps as a result of these circumstances,
Monroe Coleman was recorded twice on the 1880 census; once as Kaziah's
"Black" son on June 15th, 1880, and the next day as a "Mulatto" laborer and
boarder in the house of Jackson and Easter Barton. This was not unusual. The
"mulatto" sons of white planters are scattered across the federal censuses of
this period, frequently the lone "mulatto" boarder in an otherwise "black"
household, or else the lone "mulatto" laborer in an otherwise "white" household; these children and adolescents are often recorded twice within the same
community. Together, such findings reflect the extraordinary ambiguities of
race and kinship that accompanied the transition from slavery to freedom.[25]

Some years later, as Monroe reached adulthood, he chose to use the Coleman surname, while his mother maintained Miller. Monroe's grandchildren recall that Monroe was closely connected to the Coleman planter family, and that he may have benefited from the connection in the aftermath of emancipation. Coleman's first cousin Lomie Davis remembered two linked families—the Colemans and the Griffins—that were wealthy, compared to the Davises. About the Griffins, she recalled, "Some of my relatives . . . in Mississippi . . . Oh they were very wealthy. They didn't pay attention to the rest of us. I don't know how they got that way, but they was . . ." She described the Colemans similarly: "They seem to have gotten up in the world." Having been kept on to run the farm on behalf of his owner's wife, his use of the Coleman name may have reflected this circumstance. But as he grew into adulthood and Reconstruction came to a halt, political and economic opportunities for freedpeople quickly evaporated, and Monroe considered leaving the Coleman plantation to make his own way in a post-Reconstruction world. In the face of political and economic exclusion and widespread racial violence and harassment, any advantage previously ascribed to "mulatto" men and women, including the children of former slaveowners, disappeared too. Still, financial support sometimes accompanied

15. Monroe Coleman, center, and sons. Author's collection

those who quietly moved away from their white fathers during this tumultuous period.[26]

"Turn Our Faces to the West": Racial Violence and Disappearing Homeplaces

Indeed, in 1886, had Ransom Edmondson planned to return from Fisk
to his homeplace in Carroll County the summer after sophomore year,
he may have reconsidered. The news probably came to Margaret and
Monroe Coleman in Mississippi first, before traveling north to Edmondson
and his Fisk classmates. On the seventeenth day of March, the Carrollton
Massacre took place in Edmondson's Mississippi homeplace, not far
from Duck Hill. An armed force of one hundred white Mississippians on
horseback "moved on the court house, surrounded it, and opened . . . fire"
on a group of "peaceable, unarmed" African Americans who "had shown
their respect for the law by going to the court house" to attend a trial.
Like thousands of former slaves during this time, they were killed for
attempting to participate in the democratic process—that is, for appearing
to be citizens, for appearing to be free. The next night, in Memphis, Ida
Wells wrote in her journal, "O God, when will these massacres stop?" A
few weeks later, Frederick Douglass spoke out. "In any other country such
a frightful crime as the Carrolton massacre—in any other country than
this," Douglass wrote, "a scream would have gone up from all quarters of the
land for the arrest and punishment of these cold-blooded murderers. But
alas! Nothing like this has happened here. We are used to the shedding of
innocent blood, and the heart of this nation is torpid, if not dead, to the
natural claims of justice and humanity where the victims are of the
colored race."[27]

The association of race and criminality was so complete by the close of
the nineteenth century that a curious trend had emerged. In a speech delivered on the anniversary of emancipation in Washington, D.C., Douglass declared "that much of the crime attributed to colored people, and for which
they were held responsible, imprisoned, and murdered, was, in fact, committed by white men disguised as Negroes." The "presumptions in courts of

law and in the community" were so opposed to African Americans that "color was the safest disguise a white man could assume in which to commit crime"; indeed, "all he had to do to commit the worst crimes with impunity was to blacken his face and take on the similitude of a Negro." But "even this disguise sometimes fails," Douglass continued, citing a case of "Mr. J. H. Justice, an eminent citizen of Granger county, Tenn.," who had attempted a robbery and to fix his offense "upon a Negro." "All worked well till a bullet brought him to the ground and a little soap and water was applied to his face, when he was found to be no Negro at all, but a very respectable white citizen."[28]

A few years later the 1890 census appeared, marking "twenty-five years of freedom" and "a much-anticipated data source for assessing blacks' status in a post-slavery era." Out of this data, "new statistical and racial identities" emerged. Reflecting the emerging impact of discriminatory laws, southern labor camps, "everyday racial surveillance," and the emerging prison industrial complex, the 1890 census showed African Americans at twelve percent of the nation's population but constituting thirty percent of the prison population. In spite of discriminatory laws and punishment, "white social scientists presented the new crime data as objective, color-blind, and incontrovertible." Neither "the dark color of southern chain gangs nor the pale hue of northern police mattered to the truth of black crime statistics." From this moment forward, blackness was "refashioned" and "became a more stable racial category," in opposition to whiteness, through crime statistics and racial criminalization.[29]

Thus one of the most important consequences of the betrayal of Reconstruction was this violent replacement of slave and free with increasingly rigid categories of black and white, including the criminalization of blackness. In some cases, for some white planters, this meant hiding, distancing, and variously rejecting the black and "mulatto" kin that they had occasionally supported, if not fathered, in the antebellum and postemancipation era, as the translucent cover of slavemastery gave way to the sunlight of general emancipation. "If you ask an African American where she gets her last name from, and if she has heard tales," historian Thulani Davis writes, "at least in my experience, she will talk not about a one-time slaveholder but a white biological forebear." By the 1890s, amid continuing cries of "amalgama-tion," the visibility of such "mulatto" offspring of white planters became a growing source of anxiety to white planters, and acknowledgment of such children was on the decline.[30]

For such children, education offered one critical path. Just as Samuel Townsend's "mulatto" children were sent to Wilberforce in the wake of his 1850s death and their manumission, many were sent away in the posteman-cipation period, especially amid the violent backlash to Reconstruction. So it was that Du Bois first met Ransom Edmondson at Fisk in the 1880s. Per-haps the turn of events in Mississippi explains Edmondson's mature age at Fisk; he was in his twenties, five years older than Du Bois, though both were members of the class of 1888. Alongside Edmondson at Fisk was "the un-named relative of a future U.S. president, chauffeured to campus daily; . . . studious Thomas J. Calloway, a Washingtonian who carried himself like a senator and became a lifelong friend; [and] the high-strutting Frank Smith, much older and madly popular with the coeds." Indeed, by the 1880s, as cir-cumstances deteriorated for freedpeople across the South, institutions like Fisk, and Talladega College in Alabama, begun in the 1860s, held singular appeal for those with a stake in the future of this class. But Edmondson's elite education—"dancing off a pinhead of privilege"—was by no means typical for these sons of white men. Monroe Coleman's privileges on the homeplace and few years of rural schooling were more commonplace.[31]

What Edmondson did share with Coleman, however—and with tens of thousands living in the South at the close of the nineteenth century—was the pressure to get out. In July 1886, four months after the massacre in his hometown, the *Fisk Herald* reported that Edmondson was sticking close to Nashville for much of the summer break: "R. C. Edmondson is in the city now and expects to remain here the rest of the summer." In February 1888, several months before his expected graduation, the paper reported that Ed-mondson was "called away by urgent duties at home." Immediately after graduating from Fisk in absentia, perhaps following an advertisement for teaching posts placed in the *Fisk Herald*, Edmondson headed to central Texas, where "I got a taste (only a taste) of western life." By 1890, when he wrote a letter to the class of 1888, care of class president Du Bois, he was

16. Monroe Coleman, c. 1900. Author's collection

"rattling around in Galveston," having lived in six Texas towns and three boarding houses. "What am I doing in Galveston? A rather delicate question when no evasion will be accepted. Strange to say the profession of teaching is not held in high esteem by the populace hereabouts. And yet this is my occupation." Lifting the "curtain of my private life," Edmondson revealed, "I am 28 years old, not married; not engaged and not improving in personal attractiveness, that is to say if wrinkles are unsightly." He noted that he had tried to take a course in law, "but being bowed down with debts and wanting of means for personal needs, I gave up the idea for the time." Right now, he added, "the only aim I may be said to have is to get together some property."

Edmondson's humble letter to his classmates, dusted with "debts" and "wanting of means," does not suggest any significant bequest from T. J. Edmondson, who appears to have died by this time.[32]

Unlike educated white sons of the South, for Edmondson and thousands of well-educated African-American and "mulatto" sons and daughters, there was not only little to no employment available but no homeplace to which to return. By the close of the nineteenth century, when Margaret Coleman was bearing her first child in Mississippi, she and Monroe had witnessed

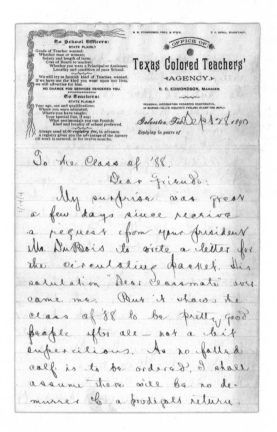

17. Letter from Ransom Edmondson, Galveston, Texas, to
W. E. B. Du Bois and Fisk classmates. Courtesy Special Collections and
University Archives, University of Massachusetts at Amherst

dismissal of the aforementioned two thousand black officeholders. They witnessed the nullification of Monroe's right to vote, the effective reenslavement of tens of thousands, the criminalization of black mobility and prosperity, and, finally, the proliferation of public lynchings of black and "mulatto" men, women, and children.

During this time, freedpeople worked vigilantly to protect black and "mulatto" children from the kinds of sexual violence that had produced such "color hierarchies within families" in the first place. Thus the act of protecting or insulating one's children was itself deeply racialized and entwined in the emergence of full-fledged segregation at the turn of the twentieth century; it was both a response to and an ingredient in the emerging racial hierarchy. Oklahoma native Ralph Ellison called it "an example of the rapidity of historical change." "Within thirteen years Afro-Americans were swept from slavery to a brief period of freedom, to a condition of second-class citizenship," Ellison wrote. "And from a condition of faint hope, through a period of euphoric optimism, to a condition of despair. The familiar world of slavery was gone, but now they faced a world of ambiguity in which their access to even the most fundamental of life's necessities was regulated strictly on the basis of race and color."[33]

This rigidity attempted to disguise and control the actual ambiguity of the situation. In the era of *Plessy v. Ferguson* (1896), millions of Americans may have visibly troubled the "stability" of racial categories on the sidewalk, on streetcars, and behind closed doors. While the 1890 census categorized roughly fifteen percent of African Americans as "mulatto," historian Michele Mitchell has drawn upon the statements of Charles Chesnutt, T. Thomas Fortune, Pauline Hopkins, and Du Bois to suggest that "estimates regarding the percentage of Afro-Americans who had either European or Native American ancestors—or both—were legion." At the turn of the century, Chesnutt stated, "More than half of the colored people of the United States are of mixed blood." In 1901, Fortune advocated for the use of "Afro-American" because terms such as "mulatto" and "Negro" were exclusive: "The Afro-American is already a mixed race; otherwise he would not be an Afro-American, but an African." Superintendent of the census Robert P. Porter, Fortune added, was "reported to have declared it as his belief, in accounting for the apparent decrease of the

Afro-American population as compared with the tenth census,—that quite half a million mixed-blooded Afro-Americans had been counted as white, because the census enumerators could not determine that they were black!" William S. Scarborough, professor (later president) at Wilberforce University, had estimated that twenty per cent of the "Afro-American" population was "of mixed blood." Fortune noted, "I think this estimate entirely too small. Thirty per cent would be nearer the truth." Du Bois and several others concurred with Fortune's figure of thirty percent. Du Bois added, "It is quite possible that the mulattoes form an even larger percentage than this, but I should be greatly surprised to find that they formed a smaller proportion." Hopkins, through her character of Mrs. Willis in *Contending Forces* (1900), suggested that there existed "no such thing as an unmixed black on the American continent." Of those designated "negro" or "mulatto" at the turn of the twentieth century, perhaps as many as one in three had a parent or a grandparent who was designated "white."[34] For these individuals, the transition from slavery to (racially circumscribed) freedom often required the active destruction of kin networks. Leaving behind a mother's grave, knowing return would be prohibited; giving up established, if informal, claims to a modest inheritance; being unable to visit an ailing aunt at the end of her life; abandoning books, maps, and other resources: this, too, was freedom.

Before and after emancipation, African Americans frequently lamented the racial and sexual hypocrisy of the South, which the aforementioned statistics bespoke. Women and men alike called attention, however subtly, to the sexual violence, including rape and concubinage, that underlay the numbers and spanned slavery and freedom. Sophia Cox Johnson, in an essay about "uplifting" freedwomen, "achingly notice[d] . . . differences in the color of families! . . . Brothers and sisters from the darkest shades of ebony to the fairest of the fair calling the same woman mother!" Living in the long shadow of *partus sequitur ventrem*—the legal intervention that guaranteed children's status (slave or free) would follow their mother's (typically enslaved) status beginning in the seventeenth century—and its postemancipation racialization as the "one drop rule," freedpeople lamented the fact that "immoral, hierarchical sexual relationships during slavery had managed to create color hierarchies within families."[35]

Black southerners had always lived with the daily consequences of this hypocrisy, those "walking indictments," but white southerners, increasingly, did not. The rapid racialization of southern class structure, the replacement of free-over-slave with white-over-black hierarchy, and the growing impulse toward segregation—of schools, churches, streetcars, and family histories— sealed the incorporation of "mulatto" southerners into black life. The poste-mancipation period was marked by the relative collapse of preexisting disparities among antebellum African Americans. Some "had just been freed from the darkest and most brutal slavery on the southwestern frontier," historian Joel Williamson notes, while "others had been slaveholders and planters themselves." With emancipation, however, "the mulatto elite joined missionaries from the North—white, mulatto, and black—in moving into the hinterland to raise up the freedman. . . . Close engagement in the economy as free individuals, in national patterns of education, family, and society, and in politics and civic affairs—along with a lingering engagement in white Christianity and with white denominational orders—plugged black people into a ready-made cultural system and gave them a valuable degree of unity." At the same time, expanding racial nationalism papered over long-standing class divisions among white southerners as well: "The line of division between the old elite and the white mass was still visible, but total fusion was inevitably coming. Even then lower-class whites were being rapidly integrated into Southern life—politically, economically, and socially."[36]

Among African Americans, the process of acquiring a "valuable degree of unity" was not altogether smooth. Some expressed discontent with the ubiquitous presence of "whyte mans children" across African-American communities, calling attention to the prevalence of sexual violence against African-American women and girls. In his letter to the American Colonization Society in 1891, would-be migrant James Dubose noted that many of these "whyte mans children" attended "collord" schools. He asked, "Can we Raise our Daughters hear with no law to pretec them[?]" In the late nineteenth century, what began as disgust with rape, sexual assault, and coercion by white men manifested in emerging ideas about racial purity, Africa, and black nationalism. During this same period, historian Michele Mitchell notes, pan-Africanist Edward Blyden "made no secret of his belief that antiemigrationists were likely to be 'mulatto' as he implored African Americans—especially darker-skinned members of the race—to view themselves as 'independent and distinct . . . [with] a mission to perform.'" In the early 1900s, a freedman in Clarksdale, Mississippi, wrote this letter to American Colonization Society secretary William Coppinger: "I am home bound. Where I can be free and act independent. . . . I go where my nation first come from. The yellow and the mixed negros don't belong to me as a people. I am one of the tribs of Hebrews and now I am asking for healp and aide carry my mother and my self back home . . . for the benefit of men and women of the Ethiopian or Hebrew's race." On the other hand, occasionally African Americans embraced emigrationism in the hopes of interracial escape. George Giles, for instance, wrote from Pittsburgh to the ACS that he "wanted to reside in a land where a black man and white woman could live, unharrassed, 'a[s] man and wife.'" While this appeal was unsuccessful with the ACS in the postemancipation years, Mitchell notes that there was some "precedent regarding emigration and interracial couples" in the antebellum era.[37]

Against this diverse backdrop, some "whyte mans children" willed to hold on to their white kinship connections longer than others. But for those children who remained near the homeplace, straddling two increasingly separate worlds, their lives grew more precarious with each passing day. Writer Ronne Hartfield recalled of her mother's upbringing on the other side of the state: "Our mother had grown to puberty in a multiracial context that, to an outsider, could seem crazily confusing." Her British father "was prohibited from being a full-time, fully present male figure in her life," while her mother, "the illegitimate daughter of a German Jewish merchant and a mulatto woman," had died when Day, Hartfield's mother, was a child. Thus the "important lessons of her life, along with her most consistent emotional nurturance," came from "her colored extended family." When her father died in an accident, however, Day was fifteen years old, and the death forced her into a choice common to this class of children at the time. Hartfield writes:

Deprived of his sure protection, our mother left all that she knew as home to follow the careful plan that he and Emmaline had made to ensure a more secure and more promising future for his daughter than life on the plantation would allow. Day was sent off to work as a live-in nursemaid for white friends of her father in New Orleans. There, our mother, in her blooming young womanhood, had her choice of paths. She could take her tenuous place in what was then called octoroon society, among other girls like herself whose bloodlines were mostly white (their one-eighth black blood was noted in the nomenclature). In this way she could "pass over the line" and live the remainder of her life in the white world, like many young women who shared her situation. Or she could find another way, looking white and living colored.[38]

Thus as the nineteenth century came to a close and Day's parents' generation faded away, such openly multiracial families began to disappear. The last vestiges of shared kinship were legislated and then threatened away, and family papers, oral histories, genealogies, and memory were increasingly segregated by race. "Folk stopped repeating all the details," Thulani Davis writes, "and in my own childhood . . . the white folks' papers were kept in a segregated library I could not visit if I wanted." African-American and "mulatto" freedpeople began to coalesce between the end of Reconstruction and the beginning of the Great Migration under the banner of "racial destiny." Freedpeople of diverse origins began strategizing a *collective* way out.[39]

In this way, the Carrollton Massacre in Ransom Edmondson's hometown sparked both black and "mulatto" Mississippians to consider another way. "The disfranchised citizens of Mississippi and other states where the minority rules by force and fraud should be helped to emigrate with their families to states where they will not be liable to massacre, where they will not be robbed of their political rights, nor defrauded of their wages." The *National Republican* went on to say that it was the "duty of patriotic citizens" of the North to organize the emigration society for this purpose of "transferring the oppressed from bondage to freedom, from darkness to light, from danger to safety." If the Republican Party were to lose the next election, this journalist warned, it would be due to its "cowardice and indifference" while freedom was "strangled to death" and government controlled by a party "satisfied with murder as its title deed to power." Later that summer, the *Chicago Observer* affirmed the "most important act" of the Colored Press Association's August 1886 convention was an adopted resolution "urging migration of colored people from the South to the West."⁴⁰

Building upon deep emigration roots in the lower South—from antebellum colonization efforts to the "exoduster" movement of the 1870s—the Carrollton Massacre motivated a new wave of emigration "fever" in the last decade of the century. Two hundred miles north of the Coleman homeplace, the infamous Memphis lynchings of Tom Moss, Calvin McDowell, and Will Stewart added fuel to the fire, while altering journalist Ida B. Wells's perspective on African-American prospects in the South. Moss, a respected postman, had founded in 1889 the Peoples' Grocery, a cooperative grocery store which he coowned with McDowell and eight other prominent black Memphians.

In 1892, William Barrett, a nearby white storeowner threatened by the competition and perhaps the visibility of this prideful black business, enlisted off-duty deputy sheriffs to destroy the building. When Moss, McDowell, and clerk Stewart resisted, gunshots rang out; they and one hundred African Americans were arrested. White vigilantes removed the three men from the jail to a railroad yard, and then murdered them. Wells spoke out against the Memphis police and their refusal to arrest the men who committed these murders. The murders stunned Wells, "opened my eyes," she said, "to what lynching really was": "an excuse to get rid of Negroes who were acquiring wealth and property and thus keep the race terrorized and 'keep the nigger down.'" This was the beginning of Wells's renowned investigation—"I then began an investigation of every lynching I read about"—and exposure of the true reason behind lynching: black economic progress.⁴¹

A lesser-known consequence of the Memphis lynchings, however, was emigration. After Moss pleaded for his life "for the sake of his wife, his little daughter and his unborn infant," his last words, according to the *Appeal-Avalanche*, were: "If you will kill us, turn our faces to the West." Wells wrote from her office at the *Free Speech*, "The City of Memphis has demonstrated that neither character nor standing avails the Negro. . . . There is nothing we can do about the lynching now, as we are outnumbered and without arms. The white mob could help itself to ammunition without pay, but the order was rigidly enforced against the selling of guns to Negroes. There is therefore only one thing left that we can do; save our money and leave a town which will neither protect our lives and property, nor give us a fair trial in the courts, but takes us out and murders us in cold blood when accused by white persons." Months later, in a speech delivered at Boston's Tremont Temple, Wells recalled this moment as "our first object lesson in the doctrine of white supremacy; and illustration of the South's cardinal principle that no matter what the attainments, character or standing of an Afro-American, the laws of the South will not protect him against a white man." In turn, "a great determination seized upon the people to follow the advice of the martyred Moss and 'turn our faces to the West,' whose laws protect all alike." Alongside the *Free Speech*, ministers and businessmen urged black Memphians to "leave a community whose laws did not protect them." Six years after the Colored Press Association began trumpeting westward migration as a collective response to southern violence, two years after the land runs, Oklahoma was the obvious destination. Within weeks, hundreds of black Memphians "left on foot to walk four hundred miles between Memphis and Oklahoma." One Baptist minister "went to the territory, built a church and took his entire congregation out in less than a month." Just like that, "the nation's first antilynching movement had begun."[42]

Freedom and Racial Destiny in Oklahoma

Oklahoma was an especially attractive destination for the children of southern white planters, whose space in the postemancipation South was rapidly, violently shrinking. Townsend D. Jackson had already left Memphis by the time of the Moss lynching. Jackson was said to have been seven years old when his father, and likely slaveowner, "hauled him into battle" near his home in Georgia. Jackson recalled that his wartime experience ended in Tennessee, at the Battle of Lookout Mountain. Townsend Jackson's father might have been John Jackson, a Confederate general from Georgia, whose brigade was stationed on Lookout Mountain during the battle. Years later, "Captain Jackson," as Townsend was then known, recalled that after the

Confederate regiment retreated at Lookout Mountain, he gained his freedom. One historian has speculated about the terms: "What passed then between slave and master could only be guessed at later. Was there genuine
affection between them, feeling that perhaps derived from parentage? Did
the white man offer the boy any advice, any money? Did they embrace as
they parted? Or did the young slave simply escape? All that could be known
for sure was that shortly after the Rebel defeat at Lookout Mountain,
Townsend Jackson was free."[43]

After reuniting with his African-American mother in Memphis, Jackson
worked as a waiter at the Gayosa Hotel; a fellow waiter taught him to
read, and at school he studied math, history, literature, and Latin. "He thus
fortified himself for the affluent, intoxicating swirl that was black Memphis,
a city whose population in the decades after the Civil War was nearly
half Negro, a place where every manner of black commerce sprouted
from the brown-brick buildings on Beale Street." Years later, Townsend's
daughter shared stories of her father, who "became sort of a Colored
man who energized other Colored men to arm themselves and take
measures as a group to protect themselves." Jackson helped organize an
African-American militia, and when a wave of yellow fever took off, Jackson
stayed in Memphis to support the relief effort. In the aftermath of this
Reconstruction-era epidemic, Jackson and fourteen fellow militiamen won
permanent positions on the Memphis police force. In so doing, they as-
serted their shared investment in the future of Memphis—their belief in
Reconstruction's unprecedented experiment in multiracial democracy—in
spite of what were surely frequent experiences of racial violence and
exclusion. But political recognition and prosperity for this group of freedpeople did not last. In the 1880s, just as Ransom Edmondson was settling
into life at Fisk University, on the other side of Tennessee, Townsend Jackson and his officers lost their jobs in the Memphis police force to several
Irish men.[44]

In 1889, Jackson faced mob violence that resulted in an "escape from
Memphis," which has lived on in his family history. "One day he went
to the local store to purchase a cigar. Some Whites there resented his
perceived elitist attitude, and his other militant activities, and they chided

and threatened him at the store. He decided that night, and told his wife
that he needs to leave town. That night he walked for days, along the railroad track, probably hopped on a freight train heading for the Indian Territory, which is now called Oklahoma." Thus, when "the KKK came looking
for him that night," they found no one there; the nightriders moved on and
"lynched three Negroes that night." In fact, Jackson's wife and children escaped too, though it is sometimes remembered as his solitary flight. His
wife, Sophronia — "native American with very long black hair" — and children had hidden at friends' homes and later boarded a car on the Rock Island Railroad. Jackson and Sophronia's granddaughter, Wilhelmina Guess
Howell, told the story this way: "My relatives [came] to Oklahoma to get
away from racism, violence, and death. In fact, my grandfather . . . just
barely made it out of Tennessee alive. The night before he left Memphis,
the mob came for him. But he had gotten word that the mob would be coming . . . [so he] fled to a neighbor's house where he was hidden until he
could get safely out of Tennessee. If it had not been for those kind, courageous neighbors, the mob would have lynched nine black men that night
and I wouldn't be here today." In Oklahoma, Jackson "became involved in
Tulsa with local law enforcement and civic activities," organizing the first
and only black militia. In the face of political violence, African Americans
and "mulatto" migrants "voted with their feet," heading west for Oklahoma
and Indian Territory.[45]

Long before he decided to leave Mantee, Mississippi, Monroe Coleman
had heard of Oklahoma as a possible site for black emigration. As early as
1881, on the heels of the Kansas exodus, black Missouri promoter James Milton Turner had said thousands of freedpeople were prepared to enter the
territory. The excitement was driven both by the historical specificity of Indian Territory and more broad-based rumors of "free land." In 1866, the U.S.
government had made treaties with the Creek, Cherokee, Choctaw, and
Chickasaw nations, requiring them to make certain provisions, including
land, for freedmen of the Indian Nations. Rumors of redistributed land for
freedpeople spread so widely that Secretary of the Interior Samuel Kirkwood queried the commissioner of the general land office, Curtis W. Holcomb, to review whether African-American freedpeople had rights to settle

18. Captain T. D. Jackson. *Tulsa Star*, 1914, courtesy
Oklahoma Historical Society

in the Oklahoma Territory in accordance with the 1866 treaties with the
Five Civilized Tribes. Holcomb replied, "The treaty stipulations, as uni-
formly understood and construed, have no application to any other freedmen than the persons freed from Indian bondage." Echoing this opinion in
1881, Judge Isaac C. Parker, presiding over the federal court in Fort Smith,
ruled: "Colored persons who were never held as slaves in the Indian country, but who may have been slaves elsewhere, are like other citizens of
the United States, and have no more rights in the Indian country than other
citizens of the United States."[46]

In fact, a whole host of active and hidden relationships entwined the two
groups. In Kansas, for instance, Eda (Ratlaft) Lowe had been separated from
her mother while enslaved, and sought, in the 1890s, a reunion with her
mother, presumably a Cherokee freedwoman. In July 1894, Lowe wrote to
the *Christian Recorder*:

INFORMATION WANTED of my mother. Her name is or
was Phoebe Ratlaft. She was in the South during the war. She

belonged to one Lewis Helterlirant, a Cherokee Indian, on or near Grand River, Indian Territory. I was an infant when she was run South, and am her first child. I heard from her once when she was in Topeka, Kansas and went from there to Oklahoma Territory. Any information concerning her whereabouts will be thankfully received by her daughter Eda Ratlaft, but now Eda Lowe of Parsons Kansas, in care of Rev. J. R. Ransom, Pastor of the A.M.E. Church.

Declarations that government land for freedpeople would not apply to stateside African Americans fell on deaf ears throughout the South, where dashed dreams of "forty acres and a mule" were not easily forgotten.[47]

By 1882 forty-five delegates said to represent sixty thousand African Americans convened to lobby Congress for the establishment of a black state. At the same time, Senator Henry Blair of New Hampshire introduced a bill in favor of creating such a state. As late as 1890, newspaper editor Murat Halstead entertained the possibility of an all-black state within Oklahoma: "It would afford the colored people a rallying point, a land of actual liberty and equality, a place where they could develop according to their capacity, where there would be none to molest and make them afraid; and there is no question of the importance of the popularity of the movement. . . . It is not only possible, but probable, that this is the beginning of a solution of the question of the races, the most important and dangerous question for the people of the United States. . . . With a black state, populous, prosperous, enlightened, and honored." William Eagleson organized a company at Topeka, Kansas, that actively recruited African Americans to Oklahoma, including Kansas "exodusters" from the 1870s movement. While the promotional activities of Eagleson and other black boosters resembled those of white promoters, they also reflected the specific plight of African Americans in the post-Reconstruction South.[48]

As he approached his twenty-first year, perhaps Coleman heard of Edward McCabe's 1890 meeting with President Benjamin Harrison to establish a "black state." Envisioning black freedom and economic opportunity in the Oklahoma land run of 1889, McCabe traveled to Washington in the spring of 1890, where he met with Harrison about the possibility of a "Black state" under his leadership. "We are here, first, as American citizens. We are here because, as such, we have the right to be here." When Harrison questioned why Oklahoma, McCabe replied, "We wish to remove from the disgraceful surroundings that so degraded my people, and in the new territory in Oklahoma show the people of the United States and of the world that we are not only loyal citizens, but that we are capable of advancement, and that we can be an honor to those who broke down barriers of our slavery; some of us have blood of those who owned us as chattels, but disavowed us as sons and daughters. We are willing to abide by that decision, but in a new country, on new lands." By 1890, those "disgraceful surroundings" included Coleman's home state's "Mississippi Plan," as well as passage of the 1890 state constitution, which laid the foundation for the disfranchisement of black voters across the South.[49]

Responding to this last straw in their political and economic paralysis, as well as the promise of a more free place, freedpeople departed in the 1880s on wagons, by foot, and now by railways. While individuals like Thomas Jefferson Brown had migrated earlier, the scale of this phase of westward migration was new. In the decades after the Civil War, white southerners often blamed freedpeople's migration across state lines on labor and emigration agents, unwilling to see or acknowledge black autonomy during this period. Notwithstanding the role agents sometimes played in the circulation of information and resources, freedpeople increasingly moved "on their own," including the migration of 100,000 African Americans to Oklahoma and Indian Territories between 1890 and 1910. "All-Black towns and settlements in the windswept Oklahoma plains," writes one local historian, "captured the collective imagination of an entire people." By the early twentieth century, Oklahoma claimed more than fifty black towns and settlements.[50]

Yet the notion of any group of settlers migrating "on their own" to Indian Territory is vastly incomplete. Practically, the movement was made possible by the dissolution of collectively held Indian lands and the federal expansion of railroads, a combination of corporate and settler incentives supported by the state. Although twentieth-century historiography kept the study of African-American lives largely separate from the history of American capitalism,

19. Original map of African-American towns and settlements of
Indian Territory/Oklahoma. I have identified sixty-four, including the
Coleman settlement of Mantee.

black towns were part of American westward expansion. Writing against the
grain of black town literature, one historian argues that "economic motives,
rather than racism, led to the inception of western black towns." Indeed, the
founders of these towns were speculators aiming to profit, as were founders of
surrounding white towns, "by fostering a migrant population's quest for social
equality and financial security." But "fostering" this movement was not a one-
way, top-down effort, and the "migrant population," while rooted in slavery,
was hardly homogenous. In the name of "racial destiny," black-led efforts
across Oklahoma to establish black towns and settlements and a black state
required not only the rhetoric of speculators and newspaper editors but the
knowledge, networks, hardship, and aspirations of a diverse population of
farmers, preachers, and schoolteachers.[51]

News of the movement traveled fast, facilitated by long-established
networks and a rapidly growing black press. The *New York Times* reported,
"Hundreds of letters were written to the negro preachers and school

teachers in the Southern States, and tens of thousands of printed circulars were sent to Arkansas, Mississippi, the Carolinas, and Georgia. The result was soon observable, as Arkansas and Mississippi negroes began to pour into Oklahoma, adding strength to the thousands who had already gone from Kansas. Negro settlements began to grow and new ones were started." Black and white boosters and sympathetic journalists took great pains to assuage white fears and elevate black and white understanding of the movement. The *Philadelphia Times* reported, "There is nothing at all alarming or disturbing over the prospect of a negro state. The negro has had no chance in the South." To bolster confidence, the Philadelphia editorialist added, "This movement to create a negro state is not undertaken in the haphazard way of most movements made either by the colored race or for its advancement. It is organized and directed by level-headed men both white and black." The paper noted that William Waldorf Astor had promised an endowment of $500,000 "for a colored university" in Oklahoma, with additional "liberal contributions" of $100,000. Typical of the movement, the paper also qualified the "class" of emigrants being "invited": only "able-bodied and energetic negroes" with "resources to sustain themselves for one year, are invited to emigrate to Oklahoma."[52]

White arrivals to Oklahoma were unpersuaded. "An official just returned from Oklahoma," wrote a *New York Times* reporter, reported "much bitterness over the candidacy of Edward P. McCabe, colored, for Governor of that Territory. He declares emphatically that if President Harrison appoints McCabe Governor, the latter will be assassinated within a week after he enters the Territory." White settlers quickly outnumbered black settlers in Oklahoma Territory. Ultimately, the rapid growth of white settlement and interest in Oklahoma diminished the likelihood of such an outcome. Throughout the 1870s and 1880s, white ranchers and farmers settled Oklahoma and Indian Territory in growing numbers, and publicity about the territory's lands led to lobbying for the opening of the lands for general settlement. At noon on April 22, 1889, fifty-thousand "sooners" entered Oklahoma territory. While some black soldiers helped to keep "intruders" and others out of the area before public lands were opened, the majority of "sooners" were white.[53]

African Americans continued, however, to stitch together a vision of a black Indian Territory. Some six thousand African Americans called Indian Territory home by 1870. Arriving in Guthrie in 1889, Townsend Jackson took a job as a jailer—in the first prison in Oklahoma Territory—and was elected justice of the peace. Following his appointment to the police force in Guthrie, Jackson helped organize the territory's first black militia. Monroe Coleman would have been listening closely for the backlash. Having lived through the violent backlash to black political power in Reconstruction, perhaps he eschewed formal politics in favor of land and economic opportunity. Surely he had heard the news of once-hopeful black settlers being pushed out of Indian and white communities in the 1890s and 1900s. In November 1891, the *Lexington Leader* reported, "The Choctaws are driving the negroes out of the Nation. Anyone employing a colored servant is subjected to a $50.00 fine." In the southern portion of Oklahoma Territory, the *Kingfisher Press* reported in 1896, "white Cappers are running the negroes out of the country. At Norman, not one negro remains." While a black-Native alliance might have challenged white domination, instead many Native Americans began to distance themselves from African Americans and black Indians.[54]

Thus by the time Monroe Coleman entered his thirties in Mississippi, perhaps he nodded knowingly when he heard the news that many African Americans originally invested in Oklahoma Territory and the fleeting promise of a "black state" had turned instead toward the establishment of black towns. McCabe himself began promoting the "all-black" towns in Oklahoma and, a decade later, Indian Territory. By the early 1900s, with allotment on the horizon, many African Americans set their sights on the newly opening lands of the Creek and Seminole nations (now eastern Oklahoma), where black Indians had a longer history of political participation and economic success. Indeed, at emancipation there were many more African-descended people living in Indian Territory than in Oklahoma Territory. Most were former slaves of the Indian nations. The black Indian towns of Arkansas Colored, Canadian Colored, and North Fork Colored were all established in the 1870s and 1880s, before the development of the "all-black" towns. Ultimately, at least twenty-four of the black towns emerged in Indian Territory, especially in the former Creek and Seminole nations. Facilitated by the 1866 federal treaty, freedpeople of these nations acquired land and experienced remarkable agricultural success in postemancipation years. While "patch farming" characterized much of this initial postwar activity, the building of railroads led to the production of some cash crops for sale in more distant markets. After the 1870s, "cotton production underwent tremendous expansion." But the railroads also led to further encroachment by American settlers. Soon McCabe's efforts in Oklahoma Territory began producing fruit in the older communities of Indian Territory.[55]

Perhaps Coleman heard about economic opportunities in the Creek nation, for instance the Abe Lincoln Trading Company, the officers of whom were "all Negro men of fair business ability . . . and new settlers in the Creek Nation." In 1904, the *Lincoln Tribune* declared, "Once to Every Man and Nation comes the moment to decide. . . . Follow the Procession WESTWARD to the land of NOW. . . . The better class of colored people are invited to come and dwell in a land of freedom." The *Christian Recorder* urged:

> OF THE vastness, bountifulness, and inviting capacity of our United States, the average Afro-American can have but the faintest conception. His non-acquaintance with the attributes mentioned has cost him untold sacrifices of life, liberty, and fortune. . . . The class of our people who should be encouraged to emigrate to more desirable sections if they wish to, is the thrifty, aspiring manhood loving set. Another class to whom the future under ordinary circumstances, seems none too inviting, either North or South, to the young colored man prepared for life through the schools and industrial shops. . . . Henceforth it shall be our aim through the RECORDER'S columns from time to time, to give emphasis to the long ago advice of Horace Greely [*sic*] and say to the unsettled but ambitious Afro-American youth, "Go West, young man."[56]

While Coleman, "unsettled but ambitious," responded to black newspaper reports, such as those in the *Lincoln Tribune*, the *Clearview Patriarch*, or the *Boley Progress*, ultimately he did not settle in Boley, Clearview, Bookertee, or other black towns. He settled in the towns' outskirts, on the border of Hughes and Okfuskee Counties, in the heart of Creek and African Creek country. There, in the wake of Indian allotment, salable land was plentiful for "stateside" African Americans. In contrast to participants in the emerging Great Migration, the vast majority of these settlers were farmers in search of land. "Real estate is the basis of all wealth," McCabe had declared in 1892.[57]

Especially in the wake of Indian allotment, Coleman would have heard Indian Territory was a place where one could easily get "a free home"—that is, land. Upon arrival, Coleman purchased a plot of land from Thomas Jefferson Brown's ten-year-old grandson, Creek Freedman Washington ("Wash") Bruner, an increasingly common practice following federal allotment of Indian lands. Coleman and his family named their settlement Mantee, after their home community in Mississippi, and applied to Washington for a post office. These are the well-trodden stories of the "all-black" towns and settlements and prideful black community formation. Upon closer examination, this moment was undergirded, in Indian Territory, by the Americanization of transnational space, the disconcerting confluence of racism and settler imperialism, and intensive masculine pride. As one settler had forecast in 1894, "The next move will then be upon the five civilized tribes, who own their lands in common. Then the whole of Indian Territory will have been swallowed by the white man. Many lots of black men help in the swallowing." In the name of racial uplift, the vast majority of the celebrated "all-black" towns of Oklahoma were in fact built upon Indian allotments— and publicized by motivated white railroad investors, who hired black town promoters to recruit black southerners.[58]

Monroe would have learned a great deal about life in Indian Territory from his neighbor and friend, Thomas Jefferson Brown, of adjacent Brownsville. Recall that perceptions of Brown when he first arrived in Indian Territory, in the 1870s, were less about his racial identification than his national (or *non*national) identification; indeed, Brown was initially categorized in Creek records as a "non-native" or "intruder." By the time Monroe arrived, however, migration to Indian Territory, and federal intervention, was so widespread that the future of a Creek nation was in question. In fact, the 1904 and 1908 changes in the law had made it possible for African Americans like Monroe Coleman to purchase land in the region for the first time,

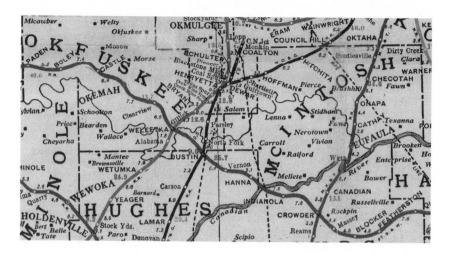

20. Railroad map, 1917, showing Mantee and Brownsville communities.
Courtesy Edmon Low Library, Oklahoma State University

exacerbating tensions between freedpeople of the Indian Nations and African-American newcomers. African-American immigrants were buying freedpeople's allotment lands, as were white migrants. "The market in allotment lands," David Chang notes, "gave rise to class divisions that ran across the boundaries of ethnicity dividing Freedmen from newcomers." Allotment sales and leases attracted "stateside" African Americans into historical African Creek districts, while yielding "at least some return" to allottees. "This return was paltry, however, compared with what land speculators could achieve." It was the sale of freedmen children's land that made it possible for many of the newcomers to purchase the farmland surrounding the "all-black" town of Boley.[59]

Certainly, the search for "free" land motivated many white and black migrants alike; in the case of black and "mulatto" migrants of some means, like Coleman, it was also the search for inalienable land, or land that would not be easily threatened by growing racial animus. "Beyond the natural yearning for freedom," one historian notes, many "held firm to a perceived economic truth: land ownership held the key to success." Moreover, many "thought land ownership would lead inexorably to full citizenship." Meanwhile,

Frederick Douglass, having been his whole life opposed to emigration—"full of mischief to the coloured people"—lamented the growing hold of colonization on public sentiment, all "owing to persecution," he argued. Responding to such persecution, Lewis Dolphin migrated to the black town of Boley, Oklahoma, in the former Creek nation. Lewis Dolphin, born in 1855 and the "son of the master," became free at eight years old. Lewis "chose the name 'dolphin' because he liked the word," and began raising his family in Alabama. "Because he had done well for himself, and his sons had horses, the Klan threatened his family, so he decided to move to Oklahoma." As a result of this move, his daughter Velma "has spent nearly all her life separate from the white world."[60]

Once in Indian Territory, "mulatto" settlers like Monroe Coleman sometimes played singular roles in the Territory, folding themselves into a long tradition of thriving "mixed-blood" entrepreneurs within the Indian Nations. Newspapers continually attest to the notable role that "mulatto," "creole," and "mixed-blood" individuals played in the settlement of Indian Territory, as well as rampant suspicion of African-American settlers allegedly "passing for Indian." White settlers, journalists, and politicians frequently commented on these supposed trends throughout the late nineteenth century. Commenting on the "leaders of this new movement," one journalist noted in racist parlance, "Being both black and mixed in blood, they bring to their enterprise the cunning and wisdom of both races." Their past included the prevalence of white parentage among "mulatto" settlers, as well as the abiding literal and symbolic presence of Africa and "Liberia fever."[61]

Participation in the settlement and cultivation of Indian land, witting or unwitting, would not have been entirely new to Coleman and his fellow African-American migrants. Indeed, Coleman learned and inherited his ambitions, ideals, and knowledge, not only as the son of an enslaved mother but as the son of a slaveowning father. Two generations before his birth, many of Monroe's white antecedents had expressed a kindred desire to escape settled American society for the "Old Southwest" of Alabama and Mississippi. As Alexis de Tocqueville wrote in 1835, "They have been told that fortune is to be found somewhere toward the west, and they hasten to seek it." To secure their fortune, they forcibly removed nearly one million enslaved men and women from the seaboard to the southern interior, including Monroe's mother; these men and women did the massive work of clearing the land and preparing it for cotton planting. From the start, the white planters who settled the region were, in one historian's words, "pioneers who owned other pioneers."[62]

Recall Townsend Jackson, who, dismissed by his white father in war, arrived from Tennessee to Oklahoma Territory in 1889, took a job as a jailer in the first prison there, and was elected justice of the peace. Jackson organized the Territory's first black militia, and after statehood, the white Oklahoma governor appointed him to a national conference on Negro education. Around this same time, Johnson C. Whittaker found his way from South Carolina to Oklahoma in 1908. In a speech delivered at Brown University in 1979, Ralph Ellison recalled his teacher in Oklahoma City:

> Professor Whittaker was a *white* black man. Which is to say that visually he was whiter than almost anyone here in Sayles Hall. But by birth and native background he was a South Carolina slave who had been born the property of the family of U.S. Senator James Chestnut, Jr. His mother was the personal servant of Mary Boykin Chestnut. . . . Johnson C. Whittaker was appointed to West Point, which is an example of the type of transformations that were made possible by Emancipation. But it was also an example of the reversal of expectations wrought by the betrayal of Reconstruction. Whittaker's career ended in a racial attack during which he was seized by other cadets, who tied him to his cot and notched his ear. My mother, who knew Professor Whittaker in South Carolina, told me that this was done so that he could not measure up to a West Point tradition which held that its graduates had to be physically perfect. This incident caused much indignation in the North, but Cadet Whittaker had to leave the Point, and thus the Army's loss was to become the Territory's gain. After taking a law degree and practicing in South Carolina, Professor Whittaker became the principal of Douglass High School, where he was to introduce elements of West Point

discipline and military style to young Oklahoma Negroes. Thus once again we have an example of the unnoticed logic of the democratic process.[63]

Ellison told this story to a largely white audience at Brown, in the midst of commemorating another black Oklahoman—and one of Brown's first African-American graduates, in 1877—Inman Page, in order "to suggest that our unknown history doesn't stop having consequences even though we ignore them," and to give an idea "of the scene and the political and social climate which led such people as Dr. Page" and Ellison's parents "from the southeastern part of the country to make a life out in the Old Territory. Geography is fate." With Oklahoma statehood, however, came Jim Crow legislation. A few years later, when the mayor of Guthrie demanded that Townsend Jackson police only black neighborhoods, Jackson resigned and moved on to Indian Territory.[64]

21. Johnson Chesnut Whittaker, c. 1900. Courtesy South Carolina State University Historical Collection and Archives

Such individuals were instrumental to the construction of "all-black" towns, a state, and a nation. Their complex relationship with the southern planter class before and after emancipation is an important part of the hidden history of the construction of "racial destiny," and the "golden age of black nationalism." The making of Oklahoma was every bit enmeshed in the rapid transformation of race that accompanied the immediate postemancipation era. If, as historian Wilson Jeremiah Moses has suggested, the development of nineteenth-century black nationalism can be seen as "the reaction of a formerly disunited group to a sense of mutual oppression," that is, slavery, then the emergence of "racial destiny" at the close of the century—the absorption of diverse (black, "mulatto," white, indigenous) kin networks under the umbrella of "the race"—can be understood further as a critical response to the violence and exclusion of southern "redemption." "The centrifugal energies of the late 1890s—pushing 'black' further and further away from 'white,'" Matthew Pratt Guterl writes, meant that "'Genteel' African Americans—no matter how light skinned or well mannered— increasingly found their only possible outlet in the leadership and uplift of 'the race.'"[65]

By 1904, when Monroe left for Indian Territory, a new term was in fashion within and beyond Atlanta University: "no-nation." Historian David Levering Lewis notes, "The children of white fathers, or of parents whose fathers or grandfathers were white, came to the university from all over the South. Complexions in early morning chapel ranged from Anglo-Saxon alabaster to African bronze. So many of [Atlanta University's] students straddled the South's vigilant categories of black and white that a curious term, no-nation, came into common use among them and many of the townspeople, denoting people who in time would face the wrenching choice of either falling back into consolidating blackness or exiting from it into troubled whiteness." The possibility of emigration and separation catalyzed this "racial revolution." By the 1920s, the lines of racial classification had been "redrawn with a heightened emphasis on race-as-color. . . . It was this new sense of race that obscured many of the ambiguities in turn-of-the-century racial classification and divided the world's peoples into the simple categories of white, brown, yellow, and black."[66]

The emergence of twentieth-century biracialism eclipsed the category of "mulatto" on the United States federal census after 1910; from this point on, "one could only choose between the calcifying borders of whiteness and blackness." Thus by 1920, David Levering Lewis notes, "almost half a million of the mulattoes counted in the 1910 census had 'passed' over into the white race during the intervening decade." Of course, the federal census alone cannot capture the complexities of daily experience. By the close of this momentous decade, W. E. B. Du Bois's old classmate Ransom Edmondson had moved from Galveston to Washington, D.C., where he worked as a government clerk. In 1920, he was living alone and classified as "White" on the federal census. In 1925, Charles Johnson, editor of the National Urban League's *Opportunity*, commented on the choice forced by the invention of American segregation in an article titled "The Vanishing Mulatto": "Men who, by and by, ask for the Negro, will be told—'there they go, clad in white man's skins.'" Whether or not Edmondson deliberately shaped the census taker's actions, "passing," especially for purposes of employment, became a more likely possibility for "mulatto" southerners like Edmondson following their migration to northern cities. Yet during the same period, Edmondson maintained regular contact with his alma mater, writing numerous letters to Fisk University President McKenzie throughout the 1910s and 1920s. This was not necessarily experienced as a contradiction. Memoirist Ronne Hartfield recalls that during the same decade, her mother, Day Shepherd, obtained a job at the Automatic Electric Company, following her move from Mississippi to Chicago: "She was good at her job and knew it. . . . But there was this: there were no visibly colored girls on the line. No one asked her any questions about race, and she didn't volunteer any information about herself." Hartfield concludes, "This was the kind of tacit passing that allowed my mother to gain a foothold in Chicago in 1918 and 1919." In addition to the foreclosure of the category of "mulatto," part of what made such acts of "tacit passing" more likely beginning in the 1910s was the emergence of mass migration and the relative anonymity of urban employment. At the same time, migration and urbanization expanded opportunities for the consolidation of kin networks, the growth of racialized kinship, "racial destiny," and the development of modern black nationalism. As the

Great Migration took off in the 1910s and 1920s, Du Bois himself began "to speak of race in a way that was decidedly 'new.'" Indeed, "the advent of bi-racialism" was "a revolution of sorts."[67]

Kinship was an essential ingredient in making freedom "real." As Day Shepherd later relayed to her children, "In slavery days, people got cut off from their families and everything they knew . . . but then there was nothing they could do about it. But these passing people who *choose* to do that? . . . I have my family and my true history. That means something." If slavery was defined, at least in part, by a lack of control over one's family life, so was the idea of freedom entwined with the pursuit and control of family and kinship. In the antebellum period, abolitionists believed that with emancipation, "the immorality of slave-breeding, and the cruelty of the separation of parent and children, will be extirpated together." For many African Americans, the vision of an emancipated future rested upon the sanctity of one's family life. Moreover, in numerous societies—including African and indigenous communities—slavery was defined "as an absence of kin." In West Africa, "slaves were viewed as kinless outsiders," historian Dylan Penningroth writes, "who were gradually assimilated into society by being absorbed into the family that owned them." Similarly, in the North American context, "If, in the Anglo world, whiteness was equated with freedom," historian Tiya Miles writes, "the corollary of freedom in the Cherokee world was clan membership." Thus "in the Native view, as in many African societies," Christina Snyder observes, "the opposite of slavery was not freedom; the opposite of slavery was kinship." In this sense "modern Western ideas about freedom" failed to resonate with indigenous Americans. Such individualized notions about freedom may have also failed to resonate with many African-descended men, women, and children.[68]

In the long postemancipation period, freedpeople and their children came to terms with lost kin. Some were kin lost to the domestic slave trade, "apprenticeship," and separation under slavery; others were loved ones—black, "mulatto," white, and Indian—lost to the Civil War and its violent aftermath; and still others were parents who exiled their children—and embraced others—in the name of racial "order." In short, a great number of freedpeople had experienced a rupture in their existing kin networks and set out to find, or create, kinship networks and peoplehood in order to make freedom "real." The growth of racial destiny after emancipation, and especially after Reconstruction—the "golden age of black nationalism"—was shaped, in part, by this simultaneous erasure and reconstruction of kinship. In fact, "sense of kinship" is at the heart of one scholar's definition of black nationalism: "Black nationalism . . . has not necessarily been concerned with the establishment of a geographical state but only with asserting a sense of kinship among the African peoples." Thus the "linchpin of race and empire in American history," George Hutchinson notes, is the "articulation of race with family, the recruitment of familial intimacy, psychic formation, and social as well as financial inheritance to the reproduction of race and its inevitable companion, racial hierarchy."[69] The making of the black West was every bit enmeshed in the construction of racial hierarchy and the rise of racial nationalism that expanded after emancipation. African-descended children of antebellum privilege, including the children of white planters, played critical roles in the establishment of the black West. In this sense, the "golden age of black nationalism" did not emerge in a vacuum, but was in fact rooted in the violent destruction of kinship and the coterminous creation of black peoplehood.

THREE

"He Dreamed of Africa"

Kinship, Class, and Peoplehood

Before heading to Indian Territory, Monroe Coleman stopped first in the Mississippi delta, following the path of his older cousin and friend Alexander "Elic" Davis. Raised by the Colemans, Davis had moved his family to a farm near the "all-black" town of Mound Bayou, before moving on, with Coleman, to the newly founded state of Oklahoma. Elic Davis's early life experiences, however, were hardly identical to those of Coleman. Without the benefit of a white planter father—a critical factor in Monroe Coleman's early life—Davis was "sold" (probably "apprenticed") after general emancipation. While Monroe and the Coleman boys were educated, Davis—boarding in the same home—worked; come nightfall, he would study his cousins' schoolbooks. While Coleman honed his skills as a landowner and "never worked for anyone," descendants recall, Elic Davis worked as a "huckster" and "country preacher." Among descendants, while the narrative of Coleman's migration to Indian Territory was celebratory, Davis's story centered on fear and persecution. Elic Davis's daughter remembered two families—the Colemans and the Griffiths—as wealthy, compared to the Davises. About the Griffins, she recalled, "Some of my relatives . . . in Mississippi . . . Oh they were very wealthy. They didn't pay attention to the rest of us. I don't know how they got that way, but they was . . ." Then she described the Colemans: "They seem to have gotten up in the world."[1]

And yet it was Elic Davis who would eventually "pick up" first, leading his kinfolk from the family homeplace in northeast Mississippi to Mound

Bayou, and from there to the "all-black" towns of Oklahoma. Following the passage of Oklahoma's "grandfather clause" in 1910—which exempted from literacy requirements the lineal descendants of citizens who could vote on or before January 1, 1866, effectively limiting the vote to anyone whose father or grandfather was white—Elic Davis abandoned his efforts "in getting blacks to go vote" and instead "turned more seriously to a new way," ultimately choosing to leave the United States entirely. Nurtured by the zenith of black emigration, Davis was about twenty when Bishop Henry McNeal Turner began speaking about Africa as the next great "exodus"—emancipation was the first—and he died in his sixties in the Gold Coast at the height of Garveyism. Raised in what Wilson Moses called "the golden age of black nationalism," Elic Davis "dreamed of Africa," and his actions throughout most of his life were increasingly driven by the vision of a "potential *black space*."[2]

The years between Reconstruction and the Great Migration were marked by a steady wave of emigration movements within and beyond the South composed, in the main, of poor, rural black laborers like Elic Davis. Between 1886 and 1892, this included thirty-four people from Davis's home village of Sturgis, Mississippi, who took off for Liberia; surely thirty-year-old Elic noted their departure. Indeed, the movement also included millions of freedpeople "left behind," who were nonetheless shaped by emigration "fever" and kept alive the idea of a more free place. Historian Steven Hahn notes that it is "difficult, if not impossible, to determine how wide the embrace of African emigrationism" was in the closing years of the century. In the summer of 1892, one emigrationist in Conway County, Arkansas, wrote "that there are no less than two million negroes in the South who would leave America, for Africa this Fall, were they able."[3]

Unlike thousands of planter sons and professionals, Elic Davis was not run out of the delta for being "too prosperous," for owning his own carriage, holding on to his land, or looking "too white." He could not "pass" for white while selling his produce, as Coleman did, nor for Indian, as Brown may have. He had no land to sell to finance his trip to West Africa, nor was he compensated as a town "booster" like Edward McCabe; he traveled "on his own" and on behalf of his family group. In short, Davis's experiences in the delta and his decision to emigrate to Indian Territory reveal the ways that rural emigration to black settlements across Kansas, Indian Territory, Oklahoma, and West Africa functioned for many freedpeople, as a response to political and economic exclusion, poverty, and violence at the nadir. In this sense, Davis's migration was part and parcel of what scholars have called "the great age of global mobility," and "the most intensive period of migration in human history," the years between 1850 and 1930. During this period, "economic liberalism fostered remarkable freedom of movement, while the advent of steam ships and railways made travel cheaper and faster. . . . Adventurous and ambitious, cowed or courageous, people travelled in pursuit of work, to make a new life, to provide fresh opportunities to their families or simply to satisfy their curiosity about foreign lands." These included "colonised and coloured people . . . everywhere in revolt." So when freedpeople took to steamships and railways in search of "real freedom," they participated ecumenically in this "great age of global mobility."[4]

Yet by the close of the century, amid the rise of Jim Crow, itself a response to such resistance, "real freedom" for Americans of African descent had become increasingly dependent upon—if not inseparable from—the development of racialized kinship and "black space." "Neither the fact of blackness nor shared experiences under racism nor the historical process of their dispersal," Robin Kelley and Tiffany Patterson write, "makes for community or even a common identity." Instead, the invention of racialized kinship was "the reaction of a formerly disunited group to a sense of mutual oppression," especially slavery. In the postemancipation era, the violent backlash to Reconstruction added fuel to the rise of racial destiny and pan-Africanism. The fact that Reconstruction quelled such sentiment—and southern "redemption" dramatically amplified it—illustrates the argument that diaspora is not merely a condition but a process. "As a process it is constantly being remade through movement, migration, and travel," Kelley and Patterson write, "as well as imagined through thought, cultural production, and political struggle."[5]

During the Civil War and Reconstruction era, a key component of the "mutual oppression" that shaped the development of black nationalism was the rupture of family and kinship networks that accompanied political and economic exclusion from the postemancipation United States. Against this backdrop, many freedpeople ascribed to increasingly racialized and nationalistic ideas of peoplehood and destiny. Over the course of Elic Davis's migratory life, "real freedom" began to look like nascent black nationalism, or what Henry McNeal Turner spoke about as "negro nationality." At the turn of the twentieth century, borrowing and broadening the elite emigrationism of the antebellum era, rural farmers like Davis participated in the construction of black nationalism and modern pan-Africanism. So it was that the "great age of global mobility" (1850–1930) coincided with the "golden age of black nationalism" (1850–1920) in the shape of Elic Davis and his peers.[6]

Davis's life illuminates the devastating poverty and disfranchisement that shaped the lives of freedpeople after Reconstruction, precipitated the nadir of African-American history, and instilled in millions of rural black southerners the desire to "pick up" in the name of "real freedom," self-determination, and "black space."

Freedom's Kin

During the first few days of December 1882, Elic Davis and Della Watkins probably rode into West Point, Mississippi, and paid the three-dollar fee in order to be "authorized to celebrate the Rites of Matrimony." Perhaps the twenty-two-year-old Elic and Della enjoyed a small gathering on their church grounds in Maben. Notwithstanding the complexities of legalized marriage in the postemancipation era, weddings were a momentous occasion for many freedpeople in the 1870s and 1880s. For some—possessing, for the first time, the right to legally formalize an existing bond, or to choose one's spouse—weddings, and the ornate license to marry, symbolized the very essence of freedom.[7]

For many freedpeople, carrying recent memories of the domestic slave trade and the separation of parent and child, husband and wife, the vision of an emancipated future rested gravely on the sanctity of one's family life. This began quite literally with the search for loved ones. For the largely rural people that composed freedom's first generation, family and kinship networks—with their attendant economic value—were necessary to make

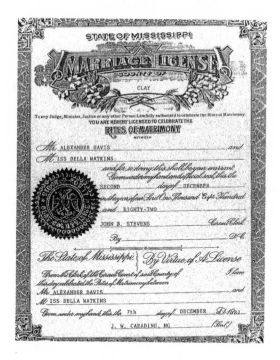

22. Marriage certificate of Alexander Davis and Della Watkins, 1882.
West Point Courthouse, Clay County, Mississippi

freedom "real." Recall that in many African and indigenous societies, "the opposite of slavery" was not freedom but kinship. Following emancipation, for many, the very meaning of freedom lay in the freedom to "move about" and, ultimately, the possibility of reuniting with family.[8]

In the aftermath of the Civil War, perhaps Della Watkins's mother yearned to return to South Carolina in search of her own mother. Only eight years earlier, Rebecca Watkins had begun her thousand-mile journey from South Carolina to Mississippi. Born enslaved in South Carolina in 1848, at the age of nine she was separated by sale from her parents and siblings in South Carolina and sold as a nursemaid to a white planter family preparing to move to Mississippi. She was, according to her granddaughter, "old enough to recognize 'being sold.'" Rebecca did not make the migration with a long-standing owner or with her own kin network, but was sold shortly before the journey, like hundreds of thousands of children who endured this Second Middle Passage. While she did not travel with a slave trader, and was not purchased at auction in Natchez, Rebecca was nonetheless "sold south." Barely ten years old, she probably knew she might never again see her homeplace or loved ones.[9]

Watkins's recollection of her experience fording a river somewhere along the journey has lived on for nearly two centuries within family lore; Della shared the story with her daughter Lomie in the late 1890s, and nearly a century later Lomie shared it with her great-nephew in the 1980s: "Rebecca was holding the baby of a white woman while they were crossing the river on a ferry. Both Rebecca and the baby fell off the ferry into the river. Rebecca was rescued, but the baby drowned." Significantly, the same story was passed down to a white descendant of the Coleman planters. Both descendants reveal that this story was memorable for a reason—perhaps because the white child was *not* saved in an antebellum world of "slave" and "free." While this outcome may have seemed paradoxical to descendants, in fact southern migrants would have perceived Rebecca's survival—and that of thousands of freedwoman of childbearing age—as central to their pursuit of material wealth on the southern "frontier." Rebecca Watkins's forced migration from South Carolina took place at the bitter, speculative end of southern expansion, on the eve of the Civil War and emancipation. In the late 1850s, in the midst of exponentially rising prices—what contemporaries called the "negro fever"—Rebecca's imminent reproductive labor offered tremendous wealth to the Watkins planters who owned her. Indeed, six years after leaving her homeplace, fifteen-year-old Rebecca gave birth to a daughter she named Della. The baby's father was recalled by Lomie as a "mixed-Indian" named David Blackwell. "They didn't always marry," Lomie said. "In slavery times, those white men would get children by the black women. . . . They just had to do whatever they told them to do. They had no control over their own bodies." Lomie's narration of her maternal ancestors' lack of control "over their own bodies" captures the reality not only of antebellum forced reproduction but of forced migration. These twin modes of exploitation formed the foundation of southern expansion and the origins of Della Watkins's family tree, while necessitating the erasure of the exploitation itself.[10]

While the Civil War put an end to the Davises' and Watkinses' financial investment in Elic and Della, both the history and continuing presence of their "white people" loomed powerfully over their childhood and adolescent memories after emancipation. That eighteen-year-old Rebecca Watkins felt three-year-old Della clinging to her leg as she boiled the Watkins family's laundry perhaps made a return to Carolina seem a distant dream. Meanwhile, Alexander "Elic" Davis entered the world in Colfax County, Mississippi, in the spring of 1859. He might have been owned by the sixty-five-year-old Thomas Davis and his wife, Nancy Ann (Lampkins). Thomas and Nancy Davis had settled in Alabama on the eve of statehood. They purchased Cherokee land from the U.S. office before the birth of their first son in 1818. Thomas Davis set to the task of clearing and preparing it for cotton, for which he depended almost exclusively upon enslaved labor. By 1830, following his stint as sheriff of Pickens County, Thomas and Nancy Davis owned sixteen slaves, including one adult man, one adult woman, five young adults, four little girls, and five little boys, one of whom could have been Elic's father, Alexander Davis, and one of whom could have been his mother, Sarah. Over the next two decades, they moved into northeastern Mississippi, bringing with them Alabama-born laborers who may have included Elic's mother and father. Perhaps owing to the reproductive labor of Elic's grandmother and countless other enslaved women, the Davises' slaveholdings nearly quadrupled. On the eve of the Civil War, the sixty men, women, and children the family owned constituted a major portion of the Davis's massive estate—which would amount to $6 million in 2017 dollars. These enslaved people may have included Alexander Davis and Sarah Davis, Elic, and his several siblings Sarah bore in Sturgis, Mississippi, beginning in 1853. It also included others who had been "sold south," women and men who knew no mother, father, uncle, sister, child, or loved one when they landed in this newly established settlement on the southern "frontier."[11]

After the Civil War, freedom, too, was constrained by the denial and destruction of family bonds. Although legally free, Elic Davis and Della Watkins, Lomie recollected, had been "sold to someone" and "given," respectively, to families of ex-slaveholders. This was some time after the legal end of slavery and the passage of the Thirteenth Amendment. They may have been formally "apprenticed," or informally coerced, or "given," into the homes of former slaveowners, yet Lomie invoked the language of purchase and sale in the telling. Indeed, the term "apprentice" had multiple meanings during this period. "It could refer to a state of legal paternal guardianship or to a period of craft training," one historian notes, "or it could be shorthand for 'former slave,' as uttered by former 'masters'—an expression, therefore, of the hope that one could" reduce freedpeople "to some poor measure of their previous existence." Under apprenticeship laws, parents had little to no recourse or parental claim. By this time, abandoned and reclaimed lands had been returned to former slaveowners, and most former slaves were required to sign annual labor contracts, with little to no wage and growing debt. Elic's "sale" occurred only after the entire Davis planter family died in the final year of the Civil War. A few years later, he was returned to his mother.[12]

Thereafter, Elic Davis continued to experience the vulnerability of his family and kinship networks. Whereas Monroe Coleman grew up working on the Coleman plantation in close proximity to his mother and her family, when Elic was ten or twelve years old, his mother died. His daughter recalled Davis saying that "at his mother's funeral, they put her casket on a wagon, and set her children on her box for the ride to the cemetery." After her death, two of his mother's relatives—William and Kaziah Coleman—took Elic and his siblings—Andrew, Moses, Henry, and Dinah—into their own homes in the Mantee area. (His father appears to have died or moved away by this time, either in Alabama or Mississippi.)[13]

Elic Davis's marginal position within the household of William Coleman was highlighted in his daughter's memory of his struggle for education. Like many newly free children coming of age during Reconstruction, Elic wanted to attend school. As a young child, he witnessed the cultivation of informal schools throughout the Mississippi countryside: "Not only are individuals seen at study, and under the most untoward circumstances," John Alvord noted in 1866, "but in very many places I have found what I will call 'native schools,' often rude and very imperfect, but *there they are*, a group, perhaps, of all ages, *trying to learn*. Some young man, some woman, or old preacher, in cellar, or shed, or corner of a negro meeting-house, with the alphabet in hand, or a torn spelling-book, is their teacher." But Elic Davis struggled mightily to get the education some of his Coleman cousins received while living in his uncle William Coleman's household. Lomie recalled, "He (William Coleman) sent *his* children to school. But he didn't send my father. My dad had to work. And they would go to bed at night. He said he would get up, light the lamp, and study their books. He would hear them, and he'd get enough from what they would be saying to be *able* to study." Growing up among the Colemans who had "gotten up in the world," Elic Davis had not had the same opportunities.[14]

Unlike his cousin Monroe Coleman, Elic Davis did not have the advantage of a planter father or a living mother to secure his education. While Monroe and the Coleman boys were educated, Davis worked; come nightfall, he would study his cousins' schoolbooks. By the close of the century, Coleman was a landowner, while Elic Davis worked alongside his wife, Della Watkins. In the early 1900s, Davis moved his family to a farm near Mound Bayou, before moving on, with Coleman, to the newly founded state of Oklahoma. While the Davises, too, sought land, like most freedpeople, they worked as sharecroppers.[15]

Constant naysaying about Elic's prospects both within and beyond his family may have shaped additionally his willingness to "just pick up." Perhaps Elic Davis had a bit less to lose in the gamble that was emigration. As he approached his twentieth birthday, perhaps he read circulars about "The Liberian Exodus" and the 1878 voyage of the *Azor* from the port of Charleston to Monrovia, Liberia. A year later, he may have considered joining the "Exodus" for Kansas. Had it not been for his growing connection to neighbor Della Watkins and her extended kin network, he might have left with the thousands of Mississippi exodusters. Certainly he shared their disgust with economic and political conditions for African Americans after Reconstruction, and their growing commitment to self-determination and "black space."[16]

Instead of leaving Mississippi, however, Elic Davis married Della Watkins. In the preceding year, he had begun boarding with Monroe Coleman's mother, his aunt Kaziah. At night, after leaving the cotton fields, Elic would walk several miles to the local night school. Meanwhile, Della cooked and washed for Jane Blackwell Little, whom she called "Miss Jane." While daughter Lomie emphasized goodwill "between Della and Miss Jane," Della's older siblings expressed deep resentment toward Della's "white people."[17]

Throughout the 1880s, after their marriage, Della and Elic Davis chipped away at their dream of owning their "little place." Perhaps they kept track of their peers who had risen into landownership. Indeed, "The petty

23. Alexander Davis, Della Watkins Davis, and children, c. 1900. Courtesy Mississippi Department of Archives and History

accumulations of land and personal property that African Americans had struggled mightily to attain," Steven Hahn writes, created a diversity of conditions. "Even in 'forlorn and forsaken' Dougherty Country . . . where the rack-renting remnants of an older plantation regime seemed to be squeezing everything . . . W. E. B. Du Bois found that most had lifted themselves out of the 'submerged tenth' of sharecroppers and that somewhat more than an 'upper tenth' had become cash renters and freeholders." So in the decade after their wedding, Della and Elic worked mightily to secure a farm of their own, which they finally did outside the town of Maben in 1895. There Elic ran the farm and a sugar mill, while serving as a "country preacher" throughout the area. As they raised their family, acquired some modest property, and a steady church following, it may have been difficult for Della and Elic to grasp that the political backlash to Reconstruction by then under way was in fact the new normal. Memories of Reconstruction were vivid. Barely ten years before, black soldiers had been stationed throughout the countryside, a visceral symbol of African Americans' myriad contributions to the nation. As Elic and Della entered their second decade of marriage, they bet on the promise of freedom at home.[18]

"Some Quiet Haven"

If, on a Sunday afternoon, one saw them walking from one of Elic's revivals in West Point to their cabin in Maben, children trailing behind, staving off the next day's work with their slowing steps, one might imagine a "turning inward" to matters of family, education, and worship. "We ask but an equal chance before the law, no more, no less," the *Huntsville Gazette* editor wrote the year of Della and Elic's marriage. "We do not seek your society, we only ask you as Christians, as servants of the Master," the editor wrote, "to help us safely anchor our little boat in some quiet haven." "This was the world," Steven Hahn writes, "in which Booker T. Washington began his tenure" at Alabama's Tuskegee Normal and Industrial Institute.[19]

What they talked about as they walked, however, skirting the edge of the Natchez Trace, was probably the fact that Elic Davis could no longer vote. Indeed, for Davis, as for most freedpeople, starting a family in the post-Reconstruction South eventually raised the specter of peoplehood. By the time Elic and Della welcomed daughter Lomie at the close of the century, Mississippi had become the first state to formally disfranchise African-American citizens. Meanwhile, the federal government turned a blind eye time after time to white southern violence, exploitation, and disfranchisement. As Della and Elic labored to provide for their growing brood of seven (two additional children died during this period, and two more would be born in the twentieth century), the Supreme Court was busily "reversing the action of the Government, defeating the manifest purpose of the Constitution, nullifying the Fourteenth Amendment, and placing itself on the side of prejudice, proscription, and persecution."[20]

In the 1890s, Elic and Della probably worried more and more about their family's lack of protection from violence and exploitation. They found themselves in a nation that could, in the words of Frederick Douglass, "claim service and allegiance, loyalty and life, of them," and yet "cannot protect them against the most palpable violation of the rights of human nature." The government "can tax their bread and tax their blood," Douglass wrote, while having "no protecting power for their persons." While Douglass continued to speak out against southern political exclusion and violence from the North, so, too, did black southern newspaper editors closer to home, albeit in "more muted tones." The "enormous explosion" of African-American newspapers and religious papers between 1890 and 1910 was entirely unprecedented. We can probably assume that Elic and Della received a portion of their news from the papers; for while most came from larger cities, Hahn asserts, "a growing number" were published in smaller towns "for the benefit of a largely rural readership." In fact, Elic and Della Davis's "poor and overwhelmingly rural state of Mississippi" boasted 150 African-American newspapers and religious journals during this period — more than any other state. All but forty of them were in largely rural areas, and Chickasaw County alone — the county where Elic and Della Davis were tending their children, fields, and small congregation — had four; the county they soon moved to had twelve.[21]

As a "country preacher" in Mississippi, Elic Davis would have paid close attention to the bulletins circulated by the African Methodist Episcopal

Church, as well as the American Colonization Society, especially when they featured the voice of Bishop Henry McNeal Turner, who had served in the late 1870s as vice president of the ACS and, by the 1890s, was the leading proponent of emigrationism. In the 1880s and 1890s, Elic probably shared copies of Turner's *Voice of Missions,* of which he was editor, as well as the ACS's *African Repository,* eagerly promoting emigrationism. As Steven Hahn has shown, the *Repository* reached especially remote areas of the countryside, including Coleman's northeast Mississippi, and collective reading and discussion were critical to this circulation. A single letter was often composed on behalf of multiple family groups or whole communities of freedpeople. For instance, in the next county over from Coleman, freedman Eli Morrow wrote on behalf of "a but 300 pepel in the foth and fifth be[a]t of Munro and Chickasaw Countey," Mississippi: "I am re cuseted to rit with a most hastey . . . to no Sumpting" and to be sent copies of the *African Repository.*[22] Perhaps Elic began a letter to Coppinger himself, or contributed to one or more of the many collectively written letters sent from Mississippi to the ACS in the three decades after Reconstruction. Turner's ideas about African emigration had begun to take root among black southerners in the 1870s, preceding the rise of Booker T. Washington and Tuskegee.

While African emigration has often been framed as a reaction to more conservative Washingtonian solutions, in fact Washington's famed "Atlanta Compromise" speech of 1895—his stated domestic vision—was itself a response to the growing wave of African-American emigration activity, including "fever" for Africa, Mexico, and the Caribbean. In light of the widespread appeal of emigrationism, Washington called on black southerners to embrace agriculture, commerce, and domestic service. Yet it was the combined threat of widespread black exodus from the South as well as recruitment of immigrant labor by southern planters that formed the backdrop, the raison d'être, of Washington's speech: "To those of my race who depend on bettering their condition in a foreign land . . . I would say: 'Cast down your bucket where you are.'" Similarly, "To those of the white race who look to the incoming of those of foreign birth and strange tongue and habits for the prosperity of the South, were I permitted I would repeat what

I say to my own race, 'Cast down your bucket where you are.' Cast it down among the eight millions of Negroes whose habits you know." He assured white southerners that African Americans would eschew politics and "questions of social equality" and instead content themselves with living "by the production of our hands." He celebrated the American South and the opportunities it represented for "business, pure and simple." While they did not necessarily accept or accommodate the new order, in the wake of Reconstruction many African Americans nevertheless "saw their survival and growth as families, as communities, and as a people best served by turning inward, by pursuing self-reliance."[23]

At the same time, while still eschewing a "foreign land," Washington began supporting an emerging third way. As freedpeople entered their thirty-fifth year of freedom amid growing racial violence and debt peonage, Washington began to actively publicize those black rural settlements already begun in the American South and Southwest as the pinnacle achievements of "the race." Some years later, in 1912, Washington would recall that the "Negro rural communities" which have "grown up" since emancipation were the result of black farmers' attempts to become landowners. Freedpeople had discovered that "in communities where there was very little encouragement for a Negro to vote," Washington wrote, "there was nothing which prevented him from owning property." At the turn of the twentieth century, "the masses of the people were learning to save their money and buy land." He pointed to "Negro rural communities," with their black landowners, schools, and businesses, as an example of "what can and is being made of farming life by Negroes under favorable conditions; that is to say, where they have had a chance."[24]

The "Negro rural community" that Washington touted more than all others was the town of Mound Bayou, Mississippi. Throughout the late 1880s and 1890s, word of the fertile land and "cheap land prices" had begun to draw freedpeople from across the state to the Mississippi delta. There, new habits of life and cotton production had been under way since the early nineteenth century, as many of the region's tobacco and indigo planters led the transition to a cotton economy. In the 1880s, five hundred freedpeople had left Oktibbeha County for a single delta plantation. In the previous decade, Isaiah Montgomery had begun an experiment in black landowner-ship, founding the black town of Mound Bayou. As violence escalated across the state, the population surged. By 1904, Mound Bayou's population was 400, "with an additional 2500 farmers scattered over the township." The lat-ter number probably included Elic and Della Davis.[25]

Elic's brother Henry had moved to the delta around 1900, settling in Bolivar County. Around 1902, Elic and Della "picked up" with at least eight young children and headed west to join him, followed by his siblings and cousin Monroe. Their motivations appear to have been largely economic, including recent crop failure and opportunities to farm fertile delta land, in-cluding, by their daughter's recollection, "cheap land prices of seven or eight dollars an acre." Elic and Della Davis settled on an eighty-acre farm near Mound Bayou. Lomie recalled that the farm was "situated a mile from the Sunflower River, six miles from Mound Bayou and seven miles from Meri-gold." The town of Mound Bayou was a newly founded "all-black" settle-ment, and the town of Merigold, just a mile or two down the road, was a bit older.[26] The Sunflower River formed the foundation of these communities.

The sudden hush that overcame formal political participation—and the words of town boosters and professionals—has encouraged historians to read the establishment of such towns—and the families, churches, land-ownership, agriculture, and community formation therein—as reflecting the "domestic" politics of racial uplift. The movement that produced "Ne-gro rural communities," however, was not simply about town-building and domestic landownership. This was an emigration movement, and it was fundamentally about moving to a different kind of place, beyond the bounds of racial or national constraints. Beneath the surface and in the hinterlands of these celebrated American towns lay a different impulse that conflicted with Washington's domestic (as in home-centered) vision as well as with the conventional domestic (as in nation-bound) interpretation of this period as a "turning inward." Indeed, as Steven Hahn has noted, African-American responses to the demise of Reconstruction "were not necessarily Washingto-nian" in the late nineteenth century; and emigrationism was the alternative path.[27] As Elic Davis's story reveals, African emigrationism was less a re-sponse to than an inspiration for Washington's plan. Moreover, a closer look at the rural black southerners like Elic Davis who formed the engine of such movements reveals the diverse cultural and political meaning of "domestic" black colonization. For men like Elic Davis, "turning inward" was often about African Americans engaged in diasporic thought, action, and dreams, and many of the same freedpeople in different moments engaged in both "domestic" and "foreign" emigration activity.

As white violence rose and formal segregation hardened, African Americans struggled mightily to adjust. Some preached accommodation, others took a bolder stance, and many more quietly searched for a way out. Some of these freedpeople initially on the move were refugees—men and women uprooted by the Civil War who spent the better part of the 1870s and 1880s moving across county and then state lines. By the close of the century, political exclusion, economic uncertainty, and widespread racial violence encouraged even those with deep roots and kinship networks—people like Elic and Della Davis, who had barely left their homeplace and, in Della's case, who continued to work for their former slaveowners—to consider another way. While streetcars and public protest were far afield from Maben at the close of the century, the symbolism of the *Plessy* decision was not lost on Elic and Della Davis. How many arguments they witnessed throughout the 1890s over the perennial question, for African Americans, of whether to stay or go. So as they entered their forties and surveyed the changing times, Elic and Della Davis reconsidered their earlier decision to remain home in Maben.[28]

Even as they returned from a visit to Elic's mother's grave, perhaps Elic and Della began to rethink the very meaning of home. In spite of "cheap land prices," Elic and Della Davis ultimately worked as sharecroppers for most, if not all, of their time in the delta. There by the riverbed, according to Lomie, the farm where they lived for the next several years was owned by "either a Bowman or a Mansfield"—white men who lived on adjoining farms just on the other side of the river. Having farmed their own plot for five years back home, this loss of land and related autonomy did not go unnoticed by Della and Elic's children. Since the Civil War, "news that land was not to accompany their emancipation" was "almost invariably interpreted . . . as an unfaithful characterization of the freedom offered to them." In part due to this circumstance, "no single strategy guided rural societies"; instead, enslaved peoples "sought someplace secure enough, time long enough, or wages high enough to ground claims born with the dawning of freedom."[29]

Long after entering their sharecropping relationship in the delta, Elic and Della actively maintained connections with their old community and land in northeastern Mississippi—Maben and West Point. Della's mother, Rebecca Watkins, continued to visit them during their time in the delta. When she passed away in the first years of the twentieth century, perhaps Della and Elic made the hundred-mile trek back home together. Indeed, throughout the postemancipation years, freedpeople took many measures to maintain links with particular lands. They did this by walking or riding home to see loved ones. They did this by visiting family gravesites. They did this by planting on the old homeplace after they took up residence elsewhere. By such measures, the rhetorical shorthand of "forty acres and a mule" barely captures the breadth and depth of freedpeople's land claims, revealing the cost of leaving one's homeplace and the complicated social and emotional burden of "making freedom real."

As one generation gave way to the next, freedpeople made meaning of these passages of time and space. By the close of the century, historian Heather Williams has shown, while African Americans were still placing ads in newspapers for lost loved ones, "many of them now included a phrase that had appeared only sporadically before: 'my people.'" Williams writes, "The term said, 'My people who help to give me a sense of history and identity, a sense of having come from somewhere and someone.'" At the close of the nineteenth century, the search for "real freedom" broadened from the literal recovery of loved ones to increasingly symbolic, nonetheless strategic, constructions of racialized kinship.[30]

"Escape from Mississippi"

While Elic Davis farmed to make good on the economic promise of the delta, his daughter recalled he was "more of a preacher than a farmer" and continued to serve their home community in this capacity. Decades later, Lomie recalled that her father's ministry grew during these years, and he eventually picked up a nickname, "The Singing Preacher," because of his beautiful voice. Moving back and forth to Maben and West Point to run revivals, Elic Davis was frequently away for a week at a time; often Della would join him Sundays, for just the last day and night of service. When Lomie's brother Brad was just a baby, Della would rise early in the morning to get "all the little things together" for him, as well as the things "that my dad would be wearing," and her own clothes. Subtly reflecting their family's economic shortcomings as well as their sense of propriety, Lomie recalled her mother "didn't have a white dress . . . she had a little dress with green stripes." Indeed, Lomie's memory of her mother's detailed attention to the family's clothing as she returned to her homeplace and kin reminds us of freedwomen's careful self-presentation against the backdrop of childhood slavery and the economic and political fragility of the post-Reconstruction moment.[31]

Come Monday mornings, they were back farming in the delta. Like most freedpeople there, primarily "we raised cotton," Lomie recalled with little emotion; her father had a "horse or two" he used to plow. This was shared with the landowners. In addition, however, "maybe we'd have a patch of black-eyed peas." Perhaps best of all, in Lomie's memory, the family "raised cane, sugarcane." Her father had a mill he would use to "make syrup for peoples for miles around. They'd come and bring their cane, and my father would make syrup for them." Lomie helped him "to skim off" and process the syrup.[32]

Around twelve years old, Lomie began working alongside her father, helping to relieve her mother and her older sisters from the burden of field labor, so closely associated with experiences of enslavement. Nearly eighty years later, Lomie recalled: "I liked to work. And lots of times, we'd have work to do in the field. And the two girls, they'd be ashamed. And they didn't want anybody to come to the field and see them working. So they'd be at the house. And my mother and I—She started working. So I went on down there and I said, 'Mama, you go on back to the house.' . . . I guess I was about twelve years old. Well then—I worked. I said, 'Mama, you go on back to the house and let *me* work.'" Like many freedpeople, the Davis family marked the distance between their present and their past, in part, by attempting to limit women's field work. In the postemancipation era, the opportunity to delineate labor and gender roles in various ways emerged as one of many emblems of freedom. Yet as Lomie's replacement of her mother in the fields reveals, the supposed "withdrawal" of black women's plantation labor during Reconstruction, a subject of significant historical debate, was ambiguous at best. Lomie recalled that her mother was "a very smart person," her intelligence marked especially by her role in managing the household economy. Freedwomen leveraged economic opportunities, including the household economy and the southern credit system, to turn emancipation into substantive freedom. Indeed, part of the promise of legal freedom lay in "the possibility of reconstituting families and remaking households, family economies and familial relationships" on freedpeople's own terms.[33] Freedwomen's work and leadership were central to this project.

In the last years of the nineteenth century, as the household economy became increasingly central to survival, so too did women's work. In a political and economic world increasingly hostile to black landownership, black businesses, and black prosperity, the fruits of household labor were often one of the few things freedpeople could claim and protect as their own, as household property. Indeed, the Davises' particular sharecropper arrangement left Elic, according to one descendant, "little prospect for prosperity" based in cotton. Instead, survival often depended upon household production. Lomie recalled: "You know, back in those days, if you had a milk cow and had pigs, you could, you could feed your family . . . you could feed your children very reasonable . . . that was the way they lived. Because if you made anything, sometimes they would take it all away from you if it was on the farm." For this reason, she recalled, "My father never liked being on a plantation. He liked his little place." W. E. B. Du Bois acknowledged in the early twentieth century that the question of land was central to the fate of Reconstruction, and possession of one's own "little place" was precisely what most planters were unwilling to allow. Indeed, in the early 1900s, Elic and Della were living on a plantation, and the fruits of their labor went to the nearby Mansfield or Bowman planter family. This family lived on the other side of the Sunflower River, though their land stretched out on either side of it. "They had a big white house," Lomie recalled, "and had peafowls. I remember those peafowls calling every evening: 'Calldall. Calldall.' I'll never forget it." On this farm, the Davis family worked planting and harvesting cotton.[34]

The kinds of exploitation associated with sharecropping in the postemancipation period began with the federal government's failure to implement land redistribution and economic transformation during Reconstruction. Once the system was in place, planters systematically exploited sharecroppers in increasingly brutal ways, through manipulative contracts and pricing, as well as theft. It was increasingly difficult for freedpeople to escape this system in favor of their own land. "There is, to be sure, no law forbidding the selling of land to the colored people," Frederick Douglass wrote a decade earlier, "but there is an understanding which has the full effect of law. That understanding is that the land must be kept in the hands of the old master class." As a result, Douglass wrote, "The colored people can rent land, it is true, and many of them do rent many acres, and find themselves poorer at the end of the year than at the beginning, because they are charged more a year for rent per acre than the land would bring at auction sale." The sharecropping system was thus well established by 1880, dominating much of the cotton South.[35]

Lomie recalled in painstaking detail how exploitative sharecropping was for her family: "One time my father was on a farm. We made fourteen bales of cotton. . . . And so my father said, 'I guess we'll go sell the cotton.' And so this man says, 'No. I sells the cotton.' And he took *all* the cotton and sold it. And he was living on his place." Indeed, what distinguished this labor system was that workers lacked the political power needed to protect them from brutal exploitation. Moreover, the terms and constraints of emancipation did not necessarily match freedpeople's aspirations. Planters employed violence and coercion to impose contracts, and these contracts communicated to freedpeople that "self-employment was not a condition of their emancipation." Instead, emancipation was accompanied by new obligations and forms of coercion.[36]

These new forms of coercion included the abandonment of land and customary property, including "fowl, stock, and farm tools, as well as access to small gardens . . . and the time in which to work them." In the minds of many freedpeople, these were the very first "casualties of free labor." As sharecroppers, not even Della and Elic's household economy was safe. When they had first moved "down in the delta" onto the Mansfield (or

Bowman) land, Lomie recalled, they brought with them "the finest cows," as well as horses and mules, that her mother had been given by the Watkins planters. By Lomie's recollection, "My mother got those cows from, from her white people." Lomie then rephrased thus: "Those horses and cows were given to my mother from the people that owned her." She recalled most poignantly the loss of this property: "Well . . . they took *everything*. . . . And we lived in this little house. They took all the cows, horses. I think they let them have the hogs. And either fourteen or twenty bales of cotton. I don't know. And all of the cotton. They took *ev-ry-thing*." Whether the planter family took the Davis belongings and migrated elsewhere, or whether they stayed put, the point remains that the appropriation of the Davis household property represented, for Lomie, the ultimate violation. Property played a central role in the making of African-American communities before and after emancipation. In this respect, as one historian notes, emancipation was a great rupture in property relationships. It was about more than the moving of four million enslaved people "out of the category of property"; it was also about the history of enslaved people and the experiences of freedpeople as property owners. Freedpeople entered into Reconstruction with their "eyes wide open," fully aware of the importance of property. Under slavery, property might well have been more important to enslaved families, as the primary entity, in the absence of a wage, enslaved people had to show for their labor. For many years, planters had required slaves to make their own clothing and food, shifting the burden of slavery on to the slaves themselves; later, when the institution itself was threatened, planters attempted to deprive slaves of these functions and to prevent others from trading with slaves. As one witness wrote, "The tendency was . . . to take away the capacity of the negroes to take care of themselves."[37]

In the postemancipation era, the Davis family experienced this familiar vulnerability when the Bowman (or Mansfield) planters seized their cows (for dairy) and their horses (for plowing). Immediately afterward, Lomie heard her father say, " 'I believe I'll see if I can get this house.' He went over and got that house, and we moved in." Indeed, it seems Elic was able to secure a small house of his own at this point, at least for a short time. But supporting one's family without the "fine cattle," horses, and everything that had been taken from them was nearly impossible. Lomie recalled their daily life after this loss:

> Left us high and dry. You see, we didn't have anything else. I remember my mama, she took the children and went off to work. And sometime my father, he would maybe come home and he'd make us some mush out of cornmeal. . . . And that's all we could have to eat until . . . at night, maybe, mama would take the older ones and they'd go work and bring in something. At night, maybe, when she come in, she would have a little something else for us. But I remember *well* we had nothing but (cornmeal) . . . he would use cornmeal for cereal. . . . And that's what we had.

Harkening back again to all that they had just lost, she added: "They kept everything . . . done raised fourteen bales of cotton, and those fine cattle. Mama had some fine cows . . . took them, and the horses. Took everything but the hogs. . . . I say, I say, they took everything. We had a dog named Bulgia. They took everything but the children and Bulgia."[38]

Looking back on her childhood in the Mississippi delta, Lomie Davis recalled most vividly the bond between her parents. After it rained, Elic and Della would walk outside together: "It seems like I can see it now. My mother and father. . . . After this shower . . . they would go down there and walk around. . . . And then they'd . . . just come back to the house. It would be a little too wet to work." Her nephew replied, "They must have been a fairly close couple." Lomie responded, "Very close. Very close. O, I mean very close. There's nothing between them."[39]

Today this land where Della and Elic once walked lies on the border of Sunflower and Bolivar Counties, just a few miles from Mound Bayou, Mississippi. A cursory view of this distant place and time suggests a proud community of black women, men, and children intent on owning their own homes and institutions, and controlling their familial and communal lives. Moreover, Elic and Della's story—their 1880s marriage certificate, memories of their "closeness," and the only extant family photograph—fits easily within a collective narrative of racial destiny and abiding ambitions about the future of "the race."[40]

A closer look reveals homeplace after homeplace abandoned amid the backlash to Reconstruction. To the east, the land they once called home abuts Parchman Penitentiary. Beginning in 1900, the state of Mississippi began purchasing land parcels, accumulating approximately sixteen thousand acres, including the large landholdings of the Parchman family; these lands were soon refashioned into the infamous southern penal plantation. Under the emerging "Mississippi plan," law enforcement came to mean controlling African-American labor and mobility, including convict labor and penal plantations. Mississippi Governor James Vardaman, in particular, represented a new era of reactionary politics, racial subordination, and prison development. He openly endorsed mob rule and defended lynching; his 1904 campaign slogan was "a vote for Vardaman is a vote for White Supremacy, the safety of the Home and the protection of our women and children." After his election, Vardaman stated that had he lost, "we would have had to kill more negroes in the next twelve months in Mississippi than we had to kill in the last twenty years." In his first days in office, Vardaman urged law enforcement to launch "a most vigorous campaign" in response to "criminal negroes" who had become a "menace to the safety of the white man's home."[41] Walking along the banks of the Sunflower River, Elic and Della witnessed firsthand, in their backyard, the emergence of Parchman, one of Mississippi's leading contributions to state-sanctioned racial violence.

By the turn of the century, these once-prospective landowners were sharecroppers on the brink of starvation. "In the Southern States to-day," Frederick Douglass wrote several years earlier, "a landlord system is in operation which keeps the Negroes of that section in rags and wretchedness, almost to the point of starvation. . . . Their hands are tied, and they are asked to work. They are forced to be poor, and laughed at for their destitution." In Lomie Davis's recollection, it was "time to move on." By 1903, Elic's brother Mose Davis had already moved to Indian Territory, and so had Della's sister Mahalie Watkins. Subsequently, Elic's brother Henry made a monthlong trip to see for himself what it was like: "First, he left Mississippi and went to Oklahoma . . . and looked around to see if it was any better than where we were living. He was going to find out before he made the move." Henry Davis returned from Indian Territory with the news that "everything was different." Months later the Davises left the delta.[42]

Leaving the delta was no easy feat. Planters attempted to contain and control the local labor force, including many who had been coerced into unjust contracts and conditions. Lomie explained that their family's departure was no simple move, but instead a well-orchestrated "flight from Mississippi." In her words, "Well you see, if you lived there, they wouldn't want you to leave, you know—especially the black people. They had to slip away." She told the story of how one man they knew left town: "One man, they put him in a box like he was a dead man. Made holes. And they shipped him away." At the same time, Lomie implied that it mattered little whether you were sharecropping or not. "See, if you was a good farmer, and a, if you had, if it was your land or you was working their land," she recalled, "they didn't want you to leave. At all." Lomie's slight hesitation over the language of land ownership here: "if you had, if it was your land . . ." speaks volumes about the fragility of black ownership in this setting.[43]

When contemplating migration, there was little to be salvaged from any value the family may have built up during their time in the delta. Lomie's interviewers at one point asked her to explain how her "dad was trying to buy a farm, but you couldn't." She promptly corrected them, saying that Elic did in fact buy the farm, but he did not have the right to sell it. In her recollection, "Well, he bought this farm. And we could stay there. It would be ours *as long as we stayed there.* But when he got ready to leave, he couldn't sell it. Uh-uh. In other words, he couldn't just go and catch the train in broad open daytime." Like many freedpeople, they had to abandon all of their property and make their way westward in the night: "You couldn't buy anything. Stayed on it till you leaved. This place. And my brother, they sold everything they could. And I remember, they sold their furniture, what-ever they couldn't carry—which we didn't have a lot of that." Having said unspoken farewells to their belongings, their house, and "this place," family members left under the cover of darkness with barely a murmur: "I remem-ber they made a pallet *on the floor.* And we all went to bed. . . . We left way in the middle of the night. To keep anyone from seeing us. And we went to Mound Bayou . . . and we got a train out from there. It must have been midnight, or just before day. But I think it was midnight. And we went to Oklahoma." Monroe Coleman soon followed.[44]

One of Elic's sons, Thad, stayed behind. Thad was "a logman," and Lomie recalled he stayed behind because of his lumber work. "He worked . . . way out in the place where there were a lot of long, you know, tall trees that you could make good lumber out of," Lomie said. "Well he worked there . . . They would cut these trees. And then they would haul them in to whatever town they wanted to. So, that was all he knew. And he *liked* it." According to Lomie, when Elic announced the move to Oklahoma, Thad replied, "Well, I'm not going. I'm going to stay here." And while Elic left, "and brought all the children and my mama to Oklahoma," Thad stayed. Upon marrying, however, Thad was forced to leave, under even more violent circumstances. Some of the white landowners in the area threatened violence if he stayed. Finally, as he prepared to leave for the safety of his family, "those mean people . . . they watched him" and then attempted to kill him: "Late at night one of the neighbors say they heard . . . my brother had guns, and all kinds of ammunition. And he couldn't carry it with him because they would see it. He carried *some* of it. So, this man said they went and set the house afire. They was going to burn him up. And they called him 'That's a smart nigger,' you know. That's the way they talked about you. He said he heard just guns shooting." Afterward, Lomie said, they were "so sure that my brother had been killed." But "they went the next morning and saw he wasn't dead. He wasn't even there." Like many black farmers facing hunger, debt, and violence in the "redeemed" South, without the slightest state protection, Lomie's family left their home in Mississippi for the West on the promise of kin that "everything was different."[45]

Jim Crow Statehood

Just as Oklahoma became a state in November 1907, ten members of the Davis family arrived in Wetumka. Since Wetumka was an "all-white" town, Davis settled just outside of town, soon moving on to Weleetka. With little property to their name, the family rented a one-room house, with a kitchen in an attached tent. Wetumka, like other towns in Oklahoma, had only recently emerged as an "all-white" setting. For many years, this part of Indian Territory had been populated almost exclusively by members of the Creek nation, including African-descended Creeks, and, starting in the 1870s, occasional "intruders," including Coleman's soon-to-be-neighbor, Thomas Jefferson Brown. By the time Davis and Coleman migrated, the racial map of Indian Territory was much changed by widespread settlement, but the idea of a white town in Indian Territory was yet a new one.

As they incorporated Indian Territory into the expanding United States, settlers, speculators, reformers, and politicians employed the rhetoric of manifest destiny, and the tools of capitalism and statehood, working quickly to flatten the complexities of this long-standing middle ground. Government officials and humanitarian reformers alike pushed policies that would ensure the assimilation of Native peoples (and land) into Anglo-American society while seeking at the same time to define and segregate African Americans within a rigid racial dichotomy. When Native American representatives to the constitutional convention objected to sharing schools and other facilities with African Americans as a result of constitutional segregation, delegate Robert Lee Williams offered an amendment; regarding the constitution, "the word or words 'colored' or 'colored race,' 'negro' or 'negro race,' . . . shall be construed to apply to all persons of African descent. The term 'white race' shall include all other persons." In other words, "the provision defined Indians as legally white," historian David Chang writes, and this became part of the 1907 constitution.[46]

Within months of Oklahoma statehood, the legislature effectively segregated all facilities within the state. As the New York Times reported, "The Democrats carried Oklahoma on the race issue. They planned Jim Crow cars and all the other means of segregating the races which are in vogue in the Southern States." In turn, they "were expected by the people to lose no time in making good the issue on which they were elected." One after another, Jim Crow laws were passed to restrict African Americans from assembling and to impose segregation in housing, schools, railroad cars, and beyond; in subsequent years, while Thomas Jefferson Brown's sons and Monroe Coleman could reportedly "pass" for Indian or "creole"—Coleman, perhaps when selling his farming produce in town, and Thomas Jefferson Brown's sons at the movie theater—Elic Davis could not.[47]

Moreover, African Americans were effectively prohibited, through policy and racial violence, from participating in state and local politics.

On Christmas Eve following statehood, African-American James Garden became the victim of Oklahoma's first lynching; over the next eight years, nearly forty people were lynched in the new state, and the victims were almost exclusively black. Echoing the Mississippi State Black Codes, which prohibited African Americans from renting land outside of cities, required written labor contracts, and criminalized black autonomy, white Oklahomans began to limit African-American access to land in the early 1900s. Recall that in 1911, white farmers of Okfuskee County (which would soon form the base of the Sam movement) signed oaths pledging to "never rent, lease, or sell any land in Okfuskee County to any person or persons of Negro blood, or agent of theirs; unless the land be located more than one mile from a white or Indian resident."[48]

That same year, a mob of white Oklahomans had lynched a thirty-three-year-old woman, Laura Nelson, and her fourteen-year-old son, L.D. Mother and son were hanged together over a bridge, while a large crowd of men, women, and children watched. Her "suckling babe" was left lying on the bridge, until a neighbor picked her up. Perhaps not surprisingly, this bridge was just a few miles from the land that would soon become known as South Gold Coast. This was a far cry from the dream of Oklahoma as an "all-black state" for freedpeople that had circulated—and received momentary consideration by President Harrison—just two decades earlier.[49]

Moreover, hundreds of African Americans who had been slaves of the Indian Nations (and thus granted land allotments), or who had married into their families after emancipation, lost their landholdings, many of them oil-rich, in the years after statehood. As one Oklahoman commented to the *Professional World*, "Practically all the rich oil fields in this State were originally the property of Negroes. When the restrictions preventing the sale of freedmen's lands were removed by Congress in 1908, it was the signal for wholesale robbery of these freedmen's lands." The loss of land and economic opportunities was accompanied by political exclusion; in 1910 the grandfather clause disfranchised the majority of African Americans in Oklahoma. In Oklahoma, resistance to disfranchisement was aided by a robust socialist movement, including numerous northern leaders, who argued against the clause. This resistance, however, was largely driven by concern for the

24. Circulated as a postcard, this photo shows the aftermath of the lynching of Laura and L. D. Nelson, May 25, 1911, on a bridge over the Canadian River. James Allen and Jon Lewis, *Without Sanctuary: Lynching Photography in America* (Santa Fe, NM: Twin Palms, 2000).

suffrage rights of poor white citizens. Although several black Oklahomans endorsed socialist candidates in the 1914 elections, the success of socialism in Oklahoma was linked to its role as a "vehicle for white agrarian politics."[50]

While he was not a landowner in Oklahoma, Lomie Davis's father was a political man. Leading up to the gubernatorial election in 1911, Davis was prohibited from attending local political meetings. Lomie recalled that her father "went to the meetingplace and stooped beneath a window to listen. He heard someone say: 'We'll have to keep them Negroes down'"—something that was occurring throughout the state. Racial violence expanded throughout the 1910s, including lynchings and widespread terrorization of African-American communities. As his nephew later reflected, "if Elic had expected everything to be different in Oklahoma, he was surely soon disappointed." According to Lomie, his efforts "in getting blacks to go vote" had been undermined, and he "turned more seriously to a new way."[51]

In the years that followed, Elic Davis was said to have visited bustling Chicago and, possibly, Jamaica in search of somewhere to move his family. Displaced and disillusioned, the family groups and whole communities that migrated to Indian Territory between the 1880s and 1910 were soon searching again for a new destination. Several hundred black Oklahomans migrated in family groups to the Canadian plains of Alberta and Saskatchewan in the few years immediately following statehood; others headed southward for Mexico. Some doubled down on the "all-black" towns and settlements, and others, like Elic and Della Davis, revived older dreams of Africa. As Mary Evans once wrote to the ACS, "we have no home in Mississippi and we aint got no home in Indian T[erritory]."[52]

As Elic Davis scrambled to locate the family's next place of settlement, Lomie recalled, her father became a "full-time preacher," though it is difficult to know exactly what this meant: whether he ministered to a single church or served as an itinerant preacher, and whether he was compensated for this labor. It is almost certain that Della continued working and supporting the family, most likely doing laundry for white families, perhaps in Wetumka. Della also cooked "dinner on the ground" for the church crowd in Zion Hill, Oklahoma, and beyond. Lomie referred to the Zion Hill church and community on several occasions; her family and those of her uncles Mose and Henry occasionally met there "to attend services and visit."[53] Against a hostile backdrop, the church became an increasingly important part of Della and Elic Davis's lives.

A few short years in the delta, followed by sudden disillusionment in the newly founded state of Oklahoma, soon marked indelibly Elic Davis's drive to emigrate and, ultimately, to escape the United States altogether. As an adult, Lomie recalled, Davis "dreamed of Africa." Davis participated in several emigration movements, and served as "lieutenant" in the 1913–15 back-to-Africa movement—the subject of the following chapter. When he entered his fifties, Elic Davis finally made it there "on his own."[54]

The very idea of a "potential black space" depended upon increasingly expansive understandings of black peoplehood or "racial destiny." Together "racial destiny" and emigration "fever" papered over divides that had historically separated freedpeople like Elic Davis from their own African-descended kin, such as Monroe Coleman. Recall Wilson Moses's declaration that beyond "the establishment of a geographical state," the critical dimension of black nationalism was concerned with "asserting a sense of kinship among the

African peoples." If there is "one *essential* quality," he writes, "it is the feeling on the part of black individuals that they are responsible for the welfare of other black individuals, or of black people as a collective entity, simply because of a shared racial heritage and destiny." This spirit emboldened freedpeople like Davis, while also welcoming "mulatto" men like Coleman into the expanding nationalist fold. Ultimately, circumstances of the late nineteenth century urged both Davis and Coleman toward emigrationism.[55]

Still, the Davis family remembered the lingering distinction. Throughout his life, Elic was ridiculed by his mother's family with the phrase "he didn't get around much"— that is, for not being "as ambitious as [they] thought he should be." If Elic overheard talk of his lack of "ambition," he would have easily deduced that Rebecca and others were comparing him to his cousin Monroe. As former slaves "reestablished and expanded social ties," including the control of labor and property, "community and family ties may have become more important than ever before and thus more contested."[56] Certainly, talk of Elic's lack of "ambition" was linked to communal conflict over material resources, land, and property—to "freedom" as much as "character."

Elic Davis's life choices illuminate both the historical diversity of freedpeople's experiences and the remarkably consistent solution—emigration—at which so many arrived. As southern class structure grew increasingly racialized, and long-distance travel became more accessible, emigration emerged as a leading response to the economic and political challenges of being black in the post-Reconstruction era. In the wake of economic warfare and political disfranchisement, while many African Americans "turned inward" toward reconstructing families, communities, and spiritual lives in the name of "racial uplift," others of myriad racial and class backgrounds organized emigration clubs, went "prospecting," and established politically and culturally independent communities. In fact, many who "turned inward" at the same time "turned outward," migrating to black "colonies" on the margins and beyond the bounds of the American nation-state in the hopes of becoming an independent "people."

The lessons of southern "redemption" were painful to black farmers in the 1880s and 1890s, as the heart of African-American emigrationism shifted across the southern interior to freedpeople in the Mississippi Valley. It shifted, too, from African Americans of some means to poorer, rural African Americans who were especially vulnerable to the tragic exploitation of the sharecropping system, debt peonage, and to the constant threat of racial and sexual violence. The majority of these would-be emigrants were black farmers in the rural South. Many joined emigration clubs, allowing the stories and sentiments of hundreds to survive through the letters of a fellow farmer or preacher who could write to the American Colonization Society, Bishop Henry McNeal Turner, and other hopeful outlets. Most were not steadfast disciples of Booker T. Washington or W. E. B. Du Bois, but instead built their politics from the ground up and in direct response to the circumstances of their daily lives as laborers in the rural South.

African-American emigrationism resists monolithic accounts, revealing instead how diverse threads of nationalism were put to practical, powerful, and complex purposes, especially visible during the nadir in the literal and symbolic building of new homes and communities in places like Nicodemus, Kansas; Boley, Oklahoma; and Canada, Mexico, and West Africa. At the same time, the Davis family saga illustrates the ways in which African-American emigration carried within it the ritually deferred question of black citizenship. Long after the Civil War and Reconstruction, the question of African-American citizenship was yet unresolved; at the same time, emigrationist sentiment remained an actively contested constant in black political discourse, such that the possibilities for citizenship and emigrationism were inextricably tied. "Emigration," Robin D. G. Kelley writes, "remained at the heart of a very long debate within black communities about their sense of national belonging." "As paradoxical as it may sound," James Campbell notes, "Africa has served historically as one of the chief terrains on which African Americans have negotiated their relationship to American society. To put the matter more poetically, when an African American asks 'What is Africa to me?' he or she is also asking 'What is America to me?'" In his decision to ally with thousands of African Americans and depart the United States altogether, as the subsequent chapter reveals, Elic Davis answered this question decisively.[57]

FOUR

"No Such Thing as Stand Still"

The Chief Sam Movement and the "African Pioneers"

Fifteen years following his family's trek to Oklahoma, Elic Davis would compose one concerned letter to his daughter from the Gold Coast, telling her that he was sick and asking for her help in order to return to America. Lomie Davis recalled, "That's when I got the letter. . . . He wrote to me to come and help him." Back in Texas, Lomie tried her best to obtain a loan to reach him. "Well I, I had sixty dollars. And I went to the bank. And I tried to get the money to go. And they told me they couldn't." She added, "That was all I knew to do." No one heard from Elic again. Lomie believed he passed away in the Gold Coast shortly thereafter.[1]

The previous chapters have revealed that the years leading up to Lomie's loss of her father, between Reconstruction and the rise of Jim Crow, were marked by constant movement. In his lifetime, Lomie's father migrated from northeast Mississippi to the delta hinterlands of the "all-black" town of Mound Bayou, from the delta to Indian Territory, and from Oklahoma to West Africa. Along the way, he also ventured to New York, Chicago, and, possibly, Jamaica. And as we have seen, Elic Davis was not exceptional in this respect. Like thousands of former slaves and their children, Davis and his peers were men of meager means, rural black southerners who time after time "voted with their feet," creating a constant flurry of movement that spanned both "domestic" and "foreign" destinations across the American South and West, Mexico, Canada, and West Africa, long before the first steps of the Great Migration.

In this final chapter, I recover and tease out the intricacies of the little-known 1913–15 Chief Sam back-to-Africa movement and the lifelong migrants who created it. One hundred years ago, Sam and his followers set sail on the S.S. *Liberia* for the Gold Coast (present-day Ghana). The movement began in Oklahoma and ended on the Gold Coast during the First World War. Yet its roots extended across the American South. Here I use the continuing stories of Elic Davis and Monroe Coleman—in Oklahoma and Texas, New York and West Africa—to show that this movement was no mere prelude to Garveyism and the Great Migration, but the culmination of what Carter Woodson once called "a century of negro migration" within and beyond North America.[2]

More specifically, my analysis illuminates the link between the western and Liberia movements, and the common ground beneath the two. That so many westward migrants attempted to move decisively beyond the borders of the United States following Oklahoma statehood underscores my claim that part of what attracted African Americans to Indian Territory in the first place was its momentary status as a political and economic space on the margins, if not beyond the bounds, of U.S. oversight. Thus this story reveals Indian Territory and early Oklahoma as one of the first sites of African American transnational movement in the postemancipation period, decentering the United States in North American history even at the turn of the "American century." At the same time, it further illuminates the long transition from slavery to freedom and the gradual emergence of American biracialism.[3]

In the century since the S.S. *Liberia* set sail, the Sam movement has received sporadic scholarly attention, focused either on crediting Sam as a forgotten precursor to Garvey's Black Star Line or illustrating the tragedy of Sam's "utterly desperate group of people." My research—the first to move beyond the charismatic leader and his nameless, faceless followers to detail the individual lives of participants—reveals that this movement was anything but an "ephemeral flash." While their actions were "early rumblings" of twentieth-century emigration—including the Great Migration and modern repatriation—most of Sam's participants had migrated two and three times into the southwest American borderlands before joining this back-to-Africa movement. Throughout, they retraced enslaved people's antebellum paths, echoing the lore of national and transnational journeys lit by the North Star.[4]

Marking both endings and beginnings within this family history and the long arc of black emigrationism, the Chief Sam movement links stories too often classed separately. This little-known movement joins "domestic" and "foreign" migrations, encompassing a continuum of flight from the late nineteenth-century United States. In short order, the Sam movement encapsulates this book's reimagining of the postemancipation period as a series of unbound migrations, deepening the roots of the Great Migration, while highlighting the centrality of migration and geopolitics in African-American history.[5]

"South Gold Coast" and the Transnational Nadir

Lomie Davis was about seventeen when her father moved the family from Salt Creek to a nearby "tent city" in Weleetka, Oklahoma, in November of 1913. After only a few years in Oklahoma, they joined hundreds of African Americans who had hastily "disposed of their property," Lomie Davis's descendants recalled, readying themselves to set sail for the Gold Coast with a native of the country known as Chief Alfred Sam. By the first week of December, the *Wewoka and Lima Courier* reported "not less than 50,000 vacant farms and houses throughout our eastern section," as a result of "the people selling out getting ready to go to Africa on the 15th of Dec." Fifty thousand was an exaggeration, but certainly "hundreds" were residing "in tents near Weleetka and in other parts in order to be ready to pack up on short notices." The vast majority of these were "born farmers," said a correspondent for the *African Mail*; accustomed to raising cotton, corn, and rice, many were "good ranchmen" and had managed "horses, mules, and the plough from their early years." Repeated postponements meant that by January 1914, food was becoming scarce and the migrants were ill-prepared for freezing temperatures; nevertheless, most "shivered through the cold winds of the Oklahoma winter," J. P. Owens, the son of one participant, recalled. Although the ship was still delayed in New York at the end of the month, the *Courier* reported, "There are hundreds who have not despaired of the ship sailing nor languished in the hope of seeing the promised land." These hopeful migrants named their temporary camp "South Gold Coast."[6]

Several months before setting up camp at "South Gold Coast," on a Thursday night in October, more than one thousand men and women had gathered outside the First Baptist Church in Weleetka. As the opening prayer service began, the *Courier* reported, "one could hear all over the assemblage, yes, let us get ready for the exodus." When Chief Sam rose to speak, the crowds pushed toward him, trying to touch his clothing. He spoke of "the conditions of the negroes in America," the grim details of which were well known by listeners; according to an American correspondent for the *African Mail*, these included "lynchings, disfranchisements, peonage, segregation in church, school, and public careers," all of which had "embittered the lives of Negroes." Sam then spoke of "the golden opportunities that awaited them at Gold Coast Africa," saying that there was "plenty of room in Africa for the American Negro" and that they would "go home and build up a powerful kingdom."[7]

This was new: information about Africa from an African, let alone a man with claims to a chieftaincy. Especially since the demise of Reconstruction, African-American men and women across the South had begun to express a renewed interest in Africa, and many were ready to go, if only they could access reliable information about the place and the resources to get there. Would-be migrants formed hundreds of local emigration clubs, writing time and again to the American Colonization Society (ACS) in the 1880s, 1890s, and 1900s, enclosing stamps or money orders for "25 cts," requesting copies of the Society's *African Repository* (later the *Liberia Bulletin*), "printed matter," or simply "information" about Liberia and occasionally other parts of Africa; in so doing, they remade this antebellum organization in their image as freedpeople. In the early 1890s, the ACS reported that "a careful estimate . . . shows that one million or more of the people of color are seriously considering the matter of an early change of residence from the United States to Africa." In particular, the letters coming from Oklahoma skyrocketed after statehood, and the state soon became the new heart of "Liberia fever." In the ninety years since the founding of the ACS, surviving records suggest that the epicenter had moved westward in two waves, first from the antebellum Carolinas to the post-Reconstruction delta (especially Arkansas, Mississippi, and Louisiana), and on to Indian

Territory and Oklahoma during the first decade of the twentieth century. In the three years immediately following Oklahoma statehood, the number of letters written to the then-obsolete ACS that originated in Oklahoma (fifty), while a far cry from nineteenth-century numbers, nearly equaled the number coming from all the other U.S. states combined (sixty-two); meanwhile, thousands of letters circulated throughout the emerging black press, and more were written directly to shipbuilding companies. Those written to the ACS asked for "the terms upon which the society will furnish transportation."[8]

In fact, the ACS no longer had the capacity to "furnish transportation" to any of the tens of thousands interested in migrating; following the crises of 1892—in which hundreds of impoverished African Americans from Oklahoma and Arkansas arrived in New York City mistakenly expecting passage to Liberia—the ACS had lost much of what remained of its credibility and funding. What it did have, however, was "printed matter," especially the *African Repository* and subsequent *Liberia Bulletin*. Also circulating throughout the South was the *African League*, published in Liberia by a former Mississippi editor who had migrated with his printing press at the request of AME bishop and emigrationist Henry McNeal Turner, by now a familiar face to black Oklahomans. So it was that in the tiny black farming settlement of Mantee, Oklahoma, sometime in 1912, Peter J. Dorman, a young black doctor from South Carolina and president of the local emigration club, could be found reading a recent issue of the *African League* when he came across an Akim Trading Company advertisement for "Agricultural Lands in Africa and How to Obtain Them." Dorman composed a letter to the company's founder, "Chief Sam," asking for "information concerning conditions in the Chief's country."[9]

Alfred Sam was born in 1879 or 1880 in Akim Swedru, Gold Coast. He was born at the dawn of a new phase of European imperialism in Africa, the infamous "Scramble for Africa"; between the year of Sam's birth and the launch of the movement he founded, European control of the African continent increased from ten to nearly ninety percent. In the wake of four centuries of European settlement and slave trading, the British Gold Coast had been formed in 1867; for several decades before, the British had been

25. Chief Alfred Sam, c. 1910. Courtesy James Anquandah

busily expanding the colony, usurping local kingdoms, resulting in four Anglo-Ashanti wars between the 1820s and the close of the century. In the 1880s, Alfred Sam was educated at the Basel Evangelical Mission day school at Kyebi. By the time he reached adulthood, the Gold Coast was controlled entirely by Britain, facilitating the replacement of traditional mining practices with capitalized mining companies and the extraction and exportation of vast natural resources, including gold, diamonds, and cocoa. Amid an economic boom driven especially by cocoa and a minor gold rush, Sam shifted away from his career as a missionary to become a produce trader of cocoa and crude rubber. At the same time, however, Sam grew increasingly enmeshed in a growing transnational network of African, African-American, and white American missionaries that eventually included the African Methodist Episcopal church in Liberia, as well as the Holy Ghost and Us Bible School in Shiloh, Maine. These friends may have shaped and assisted his first visit to the United States in 1910 and the establishment of the trading company in 1911 in New York. At least one of the African AME missionaries in Liberia was on the company's board. When he returned to the Gold Coast, Sam acquired African shareholders and a plot of land, and he made plans to trade West African resources including cocoa, mahogany, and rubber.[10]

While Sam's original interest lay in trade, however, he mentioned land in his 1912 newspaper advertisement, which caught the eye of black Oklahomans who were quickly being dispossessed of their landholdings in the new state. The migrants sought the Gold Coast for "protection under the laws of the country," said the *African Mail*, and the "vast opportunities" available "for the development of the natives and themselves." Dr. Peter J. Dorman's letter expanded Sam's pan-African interest. According to an American correspondent for the *African Mail*, Sam brought the letter to "several chiefs," who recalled "the history of the Negroes' expatriation" and "their blood relationship" and invited "those who wished to accept their hospitality." "The movement for a migration back to Africa, whence they had been taken by force years ago and brought here without their consent," Sam later told a reporter for the New York *World*, "has been inherent to the negro race in America for generations." When Dorman received Sam's affirmative reply—at last, "reliable information"—he and his neighbors "lost no time to scatter the news among the people." In May 1913, Sam stepped off the train in Wetumka, Oklahoma, and headed to the small community, "nine miles through the country," known as Mantee. Dorman and his neighbors welcomed Sam, and there the "African movement" began in earnest with a four-hour meeting, in which sixty-four black Oklahomans joined the cause.[11]

Among these were Elic Davis, his brother Moses, who, movement theologian Orishatukeh Faduma reported, paid "the first 50 dollars in it," and his cousin Monroe Coleman. Although Coleman had founded the small farming community of Mantee just a few years earlier, he was about to become a "well-known financier" of an international emigration movement. In a parallel transformation, by the time Davis walked through the doorway of Weleetka's First Baptist Church several months later, the life of this country preacher had been changed forever. As he stood listening, Davis heard Sam describe himself as "the Moses that has come to deliver them." If people chose not to come, Sam said, they could "stay here and die in the wilderness." Bridging various religious denominations, those who stood to speak would have emphasized a common dream, as did one *Courier* reporter, "to plant manhood and justice into the unborn" or "to rise up and call us blessed." Before the close of the Weleetka meeting, the *Courier* reported, Elic Davis walked toward the pulpit where Sam had stood. There, he sang "a good old song" which "brought tears and great hallelujah by the delegates." Perhaps it was at that moment, as he looked out across the glistening faces of one thousand devotees (who could scarcely fit in the room), that Davis decided to sell his belongings and move his family into a tent at South Gold Coast. The "tent city," where they would live for much of the year, may have resembled those that were constructed two decades before, in the land runs that facilitated African-American migration to the state. It may have also prefigured the camp several years later in which hundreds of black Oklahomans would be forced to live through the winter of 1921, after the burning of their homes and property in the Tulsa riot.[12]

As the participants gathered at South Gold Coast, Coleman prepared to travel with Sam to New York to locate and purchase a ship. Within a day of the October church service, they had taken up a collection of six thousand dollars, largely in twenty-five-dollar shares. Following a series of rallies throughout Okfuskee County (home to many communities with black majorities), the company was "capitalized at $1,000,000"; "6,300 men and women, mostly Southern negroes, have bought shares and are ready to go." Chief Sam urged them "to unite in a union of confidence and Christian love," and to "start to Africa free upon their own ship." "They have sold their

26. Tent following Tulsa riot and burning of Black Wall Street, 1921.
Courtesy Oklahoma Historical Society

farms in Oklahoma, packed their goods and are ready to go to Africa for the rest of their lives," wrote one reporter for the *New York Sun*. They planned to "build model cities, have large farms, and establish a form of government of their own."[13]

In the spirit of racial uplift, reporters noted that "the stockholders are all negroes," highlighting the movement's independence from white capital. Chief Sam was "looked upon by the hundreds who have bought shares as a leader who will deliver them from all 'Jim Crow' regulations." Delegates would later be found by reporters "having a religious meeting in the dining saloon of the ship" and "singing negro camp meeting hymns." Sam's political and religious vision stood alongside a commercial one. "After we land our immigrants," the company's business agent A. E. Smith told a reporter for the *Sun*, "we will then tear out the partitions and load the ship with African products such as goat skins, mahogany, cocoa beans, rubber, coffee, and ostrich feathers. These products will be brought to this country where I have already found markets." Throughout the fall, black Oklahomans carefully considered the righteousness of the movement, debating in the *Courier* pages the legality of the path—"What we want is a definite understanding of the contract"—and the providential spirit of the movement:

were there "substantial grounds to argue a negro inheritance or secular sovereign" in "the land of Africa"? By Thanksgiving 1913, "men of noble rank"—dozens of lawyers, schoolteachers, and representatives of "every profession"—who had previously "had their heels against" Chief Sam had been "converted to the project." By January 1914, an old German ship had been purchased for sixty-nine thousand dollars and was undergoing thousands of dollars in repairs, including the installation of wireless communication believed essential in the wake of the *Titanic* sinking two years before.[14]

The movement's "delegates" included, according to the *Gold Coast Leader*, "distinguished Afro-Americans," such as Dr. Peter J. "P.J." Dorman, "who was in full practice in the States" and volunteered as "ship's doctor." Another, "the aged Mr. Garret," was described as "a highly respected man in his State" and a veteran of "the Emancipation war." Mr. M. A. Sorrell was a "successful lawyer" and justice of the peace in the "all-black" town of Boley. While he initially tried Chief Sam for disturbing the peace in Boley, Judge Sorrell later emerged as the "ship's purser" or treasurer, while Mr. W. H. Lewis, a graduate of Fisk University, "volunteered as second mate." Rounding out the list of Oklahoma delegates were "a goodly number of sound business men," including "Messrs. Coleman, Langhorn and Parker, the well-known financiers." Responding to rampant attacks on the movement and claims of fraudulence, the *Gold Coast Leader* emphasized that such judges and doctors "can hardly be regarded as adventurers in quest of fortune." By the spring of 1914, the movement's newspaper, the *African Pioneer*, was up and running, and both Davis and Coleman, with hundreds of other black Oklahomans, had moved their families directly to Galveston Island—some living in makeshift tents, others boarding with locals—to await their ship.[15]

The presence of South Gold Coast, Oklahoma, reveals an unsung relationship between continental and overseas movement, expanding views of black emigrationism and nationalism. It highlights the misguided tendency among U.S. historians of this period to treat the "western" and "Liberia" movements separately, as historian Steven Hahn has noted. Present-day categories of "foreign" and "domestic" belie the history of the long-standing middle ground that was the American Southwest at the turn of the twentieth

27. Coleman homestead near Weleetka, Oklahoma, c. 1910, before
departure for the Gold Coast. Monroe Coleman and Ida Coleman
(seated), and children. Author's collection

century—those parts of early Oklahoma that were in some ways as "foreign"
as West Africa. For most of the period, just as ownership was restricted in the
Gold Coast, white and black settlers could not own land in Indian Territory;
many married Indian and black Indian women squatted on collectively held
Indian lands or worked for Indian landlords until the early twentieth century. The presence of this middle ground supports Hahn's suggestion that
the western and Liberia movements were probably "manifestations of a
more general and remarkably widespread impulse," or what historian
Michele Mitchell calls "incipient forms of black nationalist thought." Even
rural African Americans who may have had less exposure to antebellum
(elite) pan-Africanism engaged "the notion of becoming a 'race,' a 'people,'
a 'race of people,' or a 'nation.'" More specifically, Mitchell has noted, "African American people associated freedom with territory"; this was of a piece
with larger global patterns of migrating laborers at the turn of the twentieth
century, but also "a relatively unique phenomenon, if not a delayed reverse
migration of a people rented by the Atlantic slave trade generations earlier."
Increasingly on the margins of American cities, towns, and states, these men
and women sought a place apart.[16]

As we have seen, between 1890 and the arrival of Oklahoma statehood in 1907, African Americans entered Indian Territory by the tens of thousands, and the African-American population nearly quadrupled; their presence quickly overwhelmed that of African-descended Creeks and the Indian population as a whole. Recall that just a few years before, however, white and black settlers alike were considered "intruders" on these lands. Again, Monroe Coleman's neighbor, Thomas Jefferson Brown—born in 1850s Arkansas to an African-American man and an Irish woman—had entered "I.T." and married twice to African-American descendants of the Creek and Seminole nations, securing more than a thousand acres of land, a school, church, and post office, and shaping a distinct black and Creek settlement in Indian Territory known as "Brownsville." Indeed, by 1900, there were more than three times as many non-Indians as Indians in Indian Territory. Indian Territory's African-American population had grown to more than eighty thousand before Oklahoma statehood. Letters to the ACS suggest that many African Americans had come to see Indian Territory as "a potential *black space*" that might function as "a substitute for the longed-for African homeland."[17]

In other words, twentieth-century African emigration can instead be rooted in the longer durée of Indian country as "open and even marginal space, a psychic territory where black subjects find safety solace, autonomy, and family." African Americans "searched outside the United States for political allies," Robin Kelley writes, "and often sought connections with North America's colonized people—the Native Americans." Of course, words like "family" and "community" often "conjure a romance of past and present" that is defied by reality. Indeed, promoters envisioned "a place where Indians were necessary but peripheral." In the name of racial uplift, the vast majority of the celebrated "all-black" towns of Oklahoma were in fact built upon Indian allotments—and publicized by motivated white railroad investors, who hired African-American men as town promoters to recruit black southerners; at least twenty-four black towns, and many more settlements, emerged within Indian Territory.[18]

The first issue of the *Boley Progress*, in 1905, stated the paper's mission as serving "homeseekers and colored capitalists . . . who desire cheap homes, unrestricted privileges, and paying investments, [with] information pertaining to the advantages possessed by Boley." Soon the *Progress* equated moving to this black town in the Creek nation with the Pilgrims' search for freedom. In 1908, Booker T. Washington wrote that "Boley . . . represents a dawning of racial consciousness, a wholesome desire to do something to make the race respected; something which shall demonstrate the right of the negro, not merely as an individual, but as a race to have a worthy and permanent place in the civilization that the American people are building." And yet, he added, "Boley, although built on the railway is still on the edge of civilization. You can still hear on summer nights, I am told, the wild notes of the Indian drums and the shrill cries of the Indian dancers among the hills beyond the settlement." In this sense, the concept of a black Indian Territory "transformed Indians into a vehicle for black identity formation and racial uplift." Though for much of the twentieth century, "the black flight to Oklahoma, like the movement toward Africa at the same time," was framed as simply a "response to white racism," recent scholarship reveals that black migrants were in fact engaged in modern nation-building, including vibrant debates over where the nation might be "at home."[19]

If African Americans in West African colonies sometimes "gained their liberty through forfeiting the freedom, property, and lives of others," so they did in Indian Territory. Indian Territory was thus a place for African Americans to "demonstrate their fitness" for national inclusion, even as it functioned as a space to some degree outside of the nation. Having chosen for a debate the question of whether African Americans should "celebrate George Washington's birthday," Boley's Union Literary Society "decided in the negative." Black towns were emblematic of this pervasive tension between national fitness and expatriation, proximity and distance. But even as black southerners gravitated to this "pretty country" that "the Negroes own"—as Boley town poet "Uncle Jesse" added, "with not a single white man here to tell us what to do"—others were forming "Africa Societies" and preparing to emigrate there. As A. G. Belton wrote in 1890 from Mississippi to the ACS, "We as a people believe that Affrica is the place but to get from under bondage are thinking of Oklahoma as this is our nearest place of safety." Following Oklahoma statehood, when such migrants "picked up" yet again, this time for the Gold Coast, they were, in the words of Faduma,

"African Pioneers": "They know what the life of pioneers means in a new country. They have counted the cost, and have been prepared by years of suffering and injustice, and by years of endurance, to attempt what others have attempted to do in the history of the struggles of the human race for self development and freedom of the soul." The haunting coalescence of freedom and settler imperialism in "pioneering" is thus part of the common ground shared by black continental and overseas emigration in the postemancipation period.[20]

As much as the Sam movement is a story about the transnational dimensions of the nadir, so it is one about its multiracial dimensions. Encompassing the lives of freedom's first generation, this story illuminates the gradual emergence of twentieth-century American biracialism. The construction and maintenance of the division between black and white required a great deal of ideological labor, especially the papering over of historical fractures

28. Orishatukeh Faduma, c. 1900. Courtesy Special Collections and Archives, Drew University Library

within each of these emerging communities; these included fractures between enslaved and free African Americans, and others between white slaveowners, traders, and yeoman farmers. The emergence of white and black racial nationalism obscured a more complex past. "The relentless search for the purity of origins" is indeed "a voyage not of discovery but of erasure."[21]

I have documented the continental journeys of Monroe Coleman and Alexander Davis, first cousins of disparate backgrounds who together joined the Sam movement. Together their migratory pasts reveal the rapid rise of racial nationalism among turn-of-the-century African Americans. Born in 1869 to a freedwoman and, perhaps, her former slaveowner, and identified by census-takers as "mulatto," Monroe Coleman had migrated to Indian Territory at the turn of the twentieth century, drawn by the recent growth of black towns and settlements. Recall that participation in American expansionist policies and the settlement and cultivation of Indian land would not have been entirely foreign to Coleman. While most enslaved men and women were considered property for the duration of their lives, they nonetheless inherited a complex relationship to American national expansion. When they first arrived in Indian Territory in the late nineteenth century — as categories of black and white replaced slave and free — "mulatto" settlers like Brown and Coleman may have initially, or sporadically, folded themselves into a longer tradition of thriving "mixed-blood" entrepreneurs within the Indian nations, sometimes passing for Indian or white (as Coleman did when selling his vegetables in town). Ultimately, however, the (African) Americanization of transnational space obscured critical fractures within African-American communities, including those that had historically separated Monroe Coleman from his own cousin, Elic Davis.

Recall that Monroe Coleman had stopped first in the delta before moving on, with his older cousin Elic Davis, to the newly founded state of Oklahoma, More than 100,000 African Americans — most from the newly "redeemed" southern states — had migrated to Indian Territory and Oklahoma between 1890 and 1910, only to witness the rapid construction of a racial regime proudly modeled after the Jim Crow South. In the aftermath of Oklahoma statehood, while several hundred African Americans (including Coleman's brother) headed north to the Canadian Plains, and others southward for Mexico, thousands formed emigration clubs and sought passage to Africa. Emigrationist Bishop Henry McNeal Turner indeed found a "ripe audience" in Oklahoma. Some soon sold their land for a lump sum, camped near railroad stations and "began a vigil" for the trains to New York City and "the ships for Africa."[22]

Thus when Chief Alfred Sam arrived in Oklahoma in the summer of 1913, inviting black farmers across the countryside to "become pioneers" and "cross the Atlantic," Elic Davis and thousands of others heeded the call. As he listened to Sam speak at Weleetka First Baptist a few months later, Davis may have noted that Sam spoke "in plain language" and "without any modifiers"; a reporter for the movement called him "Christlike . . . plainly dressed, kind and humble." Perhaps Davis thought back to that first summer meeting, and the fact that Sam did not go directly to the black doctors, teachers, and financiers of Tulsa (of famed Black Wall Street), or to the professionals of Boley and other towns, but instead walked those "nine miles through the country" to their little farming settlement.[23]

Reporting on the influx of local refugees to the "tent city" and their devotion to the new movement, a *Courier* reporter wrote that Sam "has a power of collecting more colored people *into one unit* than we have ever witnessed of any flock leader." Another (perhaps the same) reporter encouraged followers to "lay aside factions":

> No need for us to carry church divisions, social strifes into the land of Africa in the hope of God blessing us for he will not. . . . *We as a race may often feel as individuals among our race*, friendless, down trodden, an object of scorn and hate. But the only remedy to this is to stand pat for what you know is right regardless who it affects so long as you are under the guidance of God.[24]

Color—ambiguously linked to questions of parentage, class, and proximity to slavery—was central to these divisions in Oklahoma. Bind together "every hue and color," the *Courier* specifically urged, allowing "only principle" to be the basis "upon which one is received or rejected." By contrast, numerous back-to-Africa movements of the late nineteenth and early twentieth century had been shaped, if not divided, by color and class. Recall Anderson

Palmer's words to the ACS two years prior: "I am home bound. . . . The yellow and the mixed negros don't belong to me as a people." Part of what collected Sam's followers "into one unit" was, in fact, the construction of a new racial hierarchy in Oklahoma. In the end, an emigration movement that began, in part, in the spirit of national expansion ended as a powerful experience of racialized land loss and disfranchisement—for black, "mulatto," and black Indian residents alike. The turn-of-the-century emergence of a global color line—experienced, for instance, in a vast wave of racialized land loss and disfranchisement, and consolidated, for instance, by the elimination of the category of "mulatto" from the federal census after 1920—encouraged both Coleman and Davis to become "fastened in the colored group."[25]

"There Is No Steamship . . . Owned by Negroes": Unthinkable Movement at the Nadir

As the migrants in tents at South Gold Coast persevered in the winter of 1914 through several months of freezing temperatures and an outbreak of small-pox, Booker T. Washington received a letter from a man named Tom Johnson. Writing from the town of Margaret, Alabama, about a hundred miles from Tuskegee, Johnson told Washington that he had heard in the paper that "yo and Mr chief-Sam" were "caring the colord Peoples to Aferica, to ther own homes." Johnson noted, "if it is true I wants to go my Self an four other familys. we or wating for an ancer from you an then we or ready to go as soon as we get a ancer from yo." Upon closing, Johnson added, "Please ancer at once. we will meet yo at any Place that yo say for us to meet yo."[26]

At the time that he received this letter, the fifty-seven-year-old Booker T. Washington kept a busy schedule of speaking, fund-raising, and various activities at Tuskegee Institute. Still the reigning African-American voice at the turn of the twentieth century, Washington kept close watch over a variety of African-American movements taking root across the United States—including the Chief Sam movement that Johnson referenced in his letter. But Johnson was sorely mistaken about Washington's involvement in Sam's back-to-Africa movement. Instead, Washington had "employed an agent to spy upon and try to frustrate Chief Sam." Not surprisingly, when Washington responded to Tom a few weeks later, he wrote, "I write to say that I have no connection, whatever, with the scheme of 'Chief Sam' to carry a colony of Negroes from the South to Africa. Personally, I am not in favor of such a movement, for the reason that there are better opportunities offered to Negroes in this country than in any other country in the world; and my advice has always been that they remain in this country, and, as far as possible, in the South."[27]

During the same month, W. E. B. Du Bois spoke out publicly against the movement. In the February 1914 issue of the *Crisis*, the esteemed editor wrote, "The Oklahoma movement for migration to Africa is a poorly conceived idea and we warn our readers against it. Migration to-day is a serious matter and should be planned and financed on a large scale. It is foolish for individuals with small sums of money and no knowledge of the country to go to Africa. . . . Let the migration idea stop at present. Fight out the battle in Oklahoma and protect the masses against the charlatan who is stealing their money." In closing, Du Bois added, "There is no steamship in New York building for the African trade and owned by Negroes, and the alleged African chief traveling in Oklahoma is nothing but a common cheat who belongs in jail."[28]

Certainly Du Bois had reason to doubt. At first glance, the migrants living at South Gold Coast in the winter of 1914 would have resembled those hundreds of African Americans who had left Indian Territory and nearby Arkansas throughout the 1890s with dreams of an African return, only to find themselves stranded in rail cars and on the streets of New York City. Throughout the decade, according to historian James Campbell, numerous "charlatans and confidence men" busily exploited the "frustration, despair, and desperate need" in the South under the auspices of African emigration. One man claiming to be Doctor Edward W. Blyden, the renowned pan-Africanist, was in Arkansas collecting a dollar from each would-be emigrant during the summer of 1890. At the time, "the real Blyden was in Africa," and this man was exposed as an imposter.[29]

But Sam was not, as it turns out, one more "swindler" in this succession of emigration leaders. In spite of rampant claims of fraudulence—including a steady stream from ministers, officials, and professionals of Boley, who had a vested interest in people staying put—the U.S. and British governments were ultimately unable to find fault in his handling of the movement. Sam could frequently be heard discouraging followers from selling their homes or rushing to the camps until a second Atlantic passage was secured. Notwithstanding their refusal to wait, Sam's followers shared with him a genuine vision for the future; they lived together—on and off the ship—for more than a year, weathering the attacks of the press alongside a harsh winter and dwindling resources. As the movement's agent commented in the New York Sun, "If a 318 foot steamship, formerly the Curityba of the Munson Line, can be regarded as an earnest of Chief Sam's intent to take American negroes to the gold coast of Africa, give them lots of land to farm and win huge profits for them by shipping their produce to the markets of the world, it may be said that the project is well under way." Two leaders had "a personal interview" with the governor of Oklahoma, explaining the movement's "raison d'être." As the Okfuskee County attorney wrote to Oklahoma's Governor Cruce, "If this is a swindle, it is open and above board, and there is nothing secret about it."[30]

This is not to say that the Sam movement was without liabilities. In addition to the material constraints of a grassroots movement of rural southerners—many of them former slaves—at the height of Jim Crow, the movement faced a series of governmental challenges, including intervention by U.S. and British officials, the imposition of a British head tax, and the outbreak of the First World War. So while some of the delegates who made it to the Gold Coast later blamed Sam for the government persecution, mounting debts, dwindling supplies, hunger, and illness they faced, there is little evidence that most felt themselves duped by the individual. "Among the forty now quartered on the Curityba in Erie Basin are old mammies, who have sold their all out in the West that they may buy stock in Sam's enterprise. There are negroes above the average in intelligence, who tell you they are engineers, 'professors' or editors of negro publications, who also have sunk their savings in the scheme. And for many weeks their faith in Sam remained unshaken." After a conversation with migrant W. H. Lewis about the availability of land, the Sun reported, "The Oklahoma negroes . . . have been led to believe that the difficulty of getting land for colonization was overcome because Sam was a tribal chief . . . and that his tribe of Akim would adopt them as brothers and give them wide areas of land to build on and till as their own." Another migrant urged caution, "Remember, some of us who shall embark for Gold Coast, will never put foot on American soil any more; then how careful ought we to be in this final step which may be marked its last time by death's signal."[31]

The movement appears to have been largely "unified" across religious denominations, as well as color and class; it included "well-known financiers" like Monroe Coleman, as well as country preachers like Elic Davis. It included former slaves and the children of slaveowners. The rhetoric of "racial destiny" helped to paper over a more complex past. Recall that the category of "mulatto" had been eliminated from the United States census after 1910. Over the next decade, while nearly half a million "'passed' over into the white race," others left the country altogether, as in the case of Monroe Coleman, who mobilized his material and cultural relationship to whiteness and American expansion in the name of African-American freedom.[32]

So it was that in February 1914, instead of stumbling onto hordes of "desperate" migrants stranded in railway cars in Jersey City, New Jersey, or wandering a pier on the East River, reporters came upon a group of forty delegates, many of them professional men, on a steamship "owned by Negroes" and headed for Africa, at the height of Jim Crow. Both Coleman and "Rev. A. Davis" were on board the ship in Red Hook, Brooklyn, while it underwent repairs. When they returned to their families in the Galveston camp, perhaps Davis and Coleman tried to explain to their children what was happening: where they were going, and how far they had come. Five months later, on a rainy Thursday afternoon in July days before departure, hundreds had paid the twenty-five-cent admission fee just to board and witness the *Curityba*, now rechristened the *Liberia*, the steamship "owned by Negroes." Having waited for months, the *Galveston Daily News* reported, men and women "lined the dock and crowded aboard, all in their Sunday best." They "shook hands with each other and laughed and shouted and cried . . . sat in the deck chairs and touched the ship's brasses lovingly. 'Our ship,' they called the Liberia." On this day, Elic Davis spoke once more to the movement. As he looked out over the faces of Sam's followers—and

29. Piers at the foot of Wall Street in Manhattan, with the steamship
Curityba (renamed the *Liberia*), left, and the sidewheeler *Nantasket*.
Library of Congress

hundreds of others who had taken the train from Houston and beyond to get
a glimpse of the famed ship—Davis "spoke of the beginning of the movement." Throughout the speech, "at short intervals," Davis "paused and sang
a snatch of song, the audience joining in the chorus." For nine months,
Davis had lived, eaten, slept, and worked alongside these men, women, and
children, organizing Sam's "disciples" in Galveston. In May 1914, Davis was
recorded as the "General Vice President of Emigration Club," in a letter
Davis, Dorman, and Sorrell wrote to the British vice consul, in which they
vouched for Sam and the movement. But when the *Liberia* finally set sail
for the Gold Coast, Davis was not among the delegates. The scouting party

included his cousin Monroe, but Elic Davis and his wife Della were made to stay behind, with promises of a "next trip."[33]

Elic and Della were still waiting in Galveston in July 1915, by which time headlines of "Sam's Bunch Starving" were pouring in through the *Boley Progress* and other black and white newspapers, with news that many had "passed into the Great Beyond" and that all "are broke." While such stories confirmed outside skepticism of the movement, in fact, upon their arrival in Saltpond, the migrants had been welcomed by town leadership. Their resettlement plans were repeatedly delayed by colonial bureaucracy and land disputes, which drained their dwindling resources. Sam had pleaded to the British ambassador in Washington, D.C., in a May 1914 telegram: "Submit most respectfully that I have agreed and complied with every condition conveyed to me. . . . Steamer is ready for sea. The Delay in sailing is now entailing heavy financial loss." When the steamer finally reached the Gold Coast, British authorities initially prohibited the migrants from disembarking. When interviewed in the 1970s, Nana Kurantsi III, chief of Saltpond at the time of the migrants' arrival, cited food distribution, governmental taxes, and lodging among the challenges they faced. She recalled, "I was chief of Saltpond at the time of the visit of the Afro-Americans. . . . The ship was here for about 8–9 months. The ship was huge & the people many. . . . They had lots of food in it [but] they soon ran out of food. There was starvation. Some went home. The influenza killed many of them so it was not possible to keep track of them. Some walked to Winneba, Cape Coast." When this deadly wave of influenza swept through the Gold Coast, a great number died, while others scattered to cities along the coast, including Anomabo, Accra, and Sekondi, as well as Cape Coast, later engaging in the production of tobacco, gunpowder, gin, and cocoa. In spite of the movement's unraveling, sixty years later, Nana Kurantsi III could recall:

> I still remember some of the events as if they happened only yesterday. We organized a welcoming durbar for them. Many people came forward to present them with gifts of fruits—coconuts, bananas, oranges. . . . I had a gong beaten throughout Saltpond announcing that every man should make a contribution of two

shillings and every woman one shilling towards a hospitality fund for the Afro-American visitors. We collected a total of 160 (one hundred and sixty British pounds). This was presented to the Afro-Americans. Rev. James Reynolds was minister of the Methodist church at the time and he received the Afro-Americans. . . . They told us that many of them were members of the American Methodist Episcopal Zion Church. They attended the Methodist Church while here and some of the women evangelists who were in their party preached with power.[34]

On or about August 24, 1915, Alfred Charles Sam testified before B. M. Taplin, acting commissioner of the Central Province of the Gold Coast. Taplin, it seems, wanted an explanation for the dire straits and rising mortality among movement participants in the Gold Coast. When they landed in January of 1915, Sam reported, only twenty passengers had funds available to pay the hefty taxes imposed by British customs officials. Eventually, about forty people "went up to Akim Soadro" to see the land that Sam had acquired for the movement. "Whilst in the bush," the story unfolded, "three of these people died and one depositor." Meanwhile, "A member of the crew was drowned in the surf at Saltpond . . . and a passenger died at Anamabo of fever," bringing the death toll to six by April 1915. By the end of summer, according to Sam, it had risen to nine, and there were twenty-one people "living in tents at a place called Asuboi, on the banks of the Birrim river, where they intend to erect a town with the help of the natives."[35]

Sam swore that he had paid Nana Kurantsi III sixty-six pounds for "10 days supply of food to the American immigrants," and an additional portion to the Omanhene or ruler of the town of Anomabu, who "is still feeding them by my directions." Indeed, the Omanhene had promised "to feed the Delegates and Crew till I receive money from America." As his narrative stretched back to Oklahoma, Sam emphasized that he had initially been "sent for" by J. P. Dorman and J. P. Liddell, who had "organised a Club," having some who "wanted to go to Africa." "I told them I had land to give," Sam testified, "and I undertook to bring them here. Many of them sold their land to proceed to Africa." Under the guise of the Akim Trading Corporation, their goals were

HEAD OF BACK-TO-AFRICA MOVEMENT,
WITH SHIP AND SOME OF HIS FOLLOWERS.

LEFT to RIGHT.... MRS. OPHELIA STEWART,
MRS. W. H. LEWIS, MRS. C. C. HALL
and LUCILLE GARRETT.

ALFRED C. SAM

The CURITYBA...

30. Chief Alfred C. Sam, Mrs. Ophelia Stewart, Mrs. W. H. Lewis,
Mrs. C. C. Hall, and Miss Lucille Garrett, pictured in *The World*,
March 8, 1914. Courtesy Princeton University Library

to engage in commerce and agriculture, and establish schools and businesses; they brought cotton seeds with them. Sam insisted that the corporate
shares "entitled them to a free passage only." In other words, "they had to
subsist themselves on board the ship and on the Gold Coast," and "the share
did not entitle the people to a grant of land."[36]

As to the future of the movement, Sam said, "I offered to give the people
land at Asuboi near Auaba, River Birrim," but "the immigrants did not want
to stay on account of the weather." The desire to return was made more urgent by widespread illness. "I know some people at Anamabu are sick," Sam

testified, and "I understand that I must pay the Hospital fees." Sam noted one intriguing exception to this widespread desire to return: "*Mr. Coleman and his wife and two children, and Mrs. Garret and her child wish to remain. The others want to return to America.*" Having received word that the S.S. *Liberia* was "unseaworthy," Sam agreed to "arrange to send the immigrants back to America by another line." Some who were forced to return to the United States nevertheless continued to believe in the idea of the "African movement." Three months later, in October 1915, despite their commitment to the movement, Monroe Coleman, Ida Coleman, and their two sons returned to the United States. The following spring, Moses Davis—the man who had given "the first fifty dollars" to the movement—reentered the United States via Havana and New Orleans.[37]

In August 1915, while Sam was providing this testimony in the Gold Coast and arranging passage, a powerful hurricane hit Galveston. Winds of 120 miles per hour and a storm surge up to sixteen feet led to severe flooding, resulting in the death of several hundred people, including Della Davis. Several days later, her body was discovered, and she was buried in the

31. Destruction in the wake of the 1915 Galveston hurricane. Courtesy Galveston and Texas History Center, Rosenberg Library

potter's field in Galveston. For Elic, the summer of 1915 was full of tragedy. News of the "failed African venture" had arrived, and his companion of thirty-two years was found dead in the storm's wreckage.

In the years following Della's death and the end of the movement, Elic "continued to dream of Africa," and in 1916, remarkably, he left for the Gold Coast. On December 2, 1916, while residing on P Street in Galveston, he applied for a passport. The authority handling his application described Alexander Davis as fifty-seven years old, five feet, ten inches, "eyes: black," "nose: broad," "mouth: medium," "chin: round," "hair: black and gray mixture," "face: round," and "complexion: dark." The purpose of his trip was recorded as "visiting friends and prospecting," in "Freetown, Seirrialeon, West Africa." Assuming his plan held, several weeks later, "on or about December 19th," Davis headed for the port of Key West, Florida, and from there to Sierra Leone. Then, aside from the letter he wrote to his daughter pleading for help, none of his children heard from Elic again.[38]

A year and a half later, in the last week of 1916, a "barnacle crusted vessel" was towed into Erie Basin at the end of an eight hundred–foot line. "Pitted with rust" and "sticky with tropical mildew," the *Brooklyn Eagle* reported, the *Liberia* returned to the same Brooklyn port, within three hundred feet of the place where it had first departed for Galveston nearly three years before. After "tossing many months at anchor off the African Gold Coast, the last chapter of the romance of an African negro's dream of a black empire in Africa was closed." This time around, "curious seafarers from all the ships at the Basin wandered over the Liberia's deck tracing from what they saw the story of 'King Sam' and his voyage back to the land of black men, and they found the ship a veritable historical museum of the undertaking." These visitors observed seats with "scraps of hymnals" and "inscribed with names of the colonists and the home towns in Oklahoma and Kansas which they had left behind." Surely the name "Mantee" was carved on one of them. In the steward's office they found "a moldy rubbed stamp, moldy stationery and twenty-three keys, the whole outfit lettered imposingly, 'Ethiopian Steamship Line.' "[39]

Indeed, the "rusty 'ark' " made quite a spectacle in December 1916. But this was nothing new. From Erie Basin in the winter of 1914 to Galveston

32. Alexander Davis's passport application, December 1916.
National Archives and Records Administration, Washington, D.C.

Island in July, and on to West Africa, the *Liberia* had been a sight to behold. As early as January 1914, when the delegates first left Oklahoma to "take charge of the vessel that is said to be bought by the African pioneers," journalists had anticipated the symbolic value of the ship, especially in the American South, and in the eyes of former slaves and their descendants. In the words of the *Courier* reporter, "When it leaves New York City, it will touch the landing points of Norfolk and Charleston on its way down. It is said thousands will be at these points to get a glimpse of the ship that was bought by the black man; and the ship that shall traffic with the other nations of the world. . . . When the ship does land in the harbor of Galveston there will be thousands to gaze thereon." In the fall of 1913, as African Americans proverbially "turned inward" in the Jim Crow South, this unthinkable movement was under way. One year later, in spite of the movement's collapse at the outbreak of the First World War, the ship "owned by Negroes" had nevertheless made it "back home." Years later, Du Bois himself revised his opinion of the movement, from a narrative of individual fraud to one of material constraints: "I beg to say just before the outbreak of the World War one of the minor chiefs of the English Gold Coast came to America. . . . His scheme was feasible and he was personally honest but he did not take into account the attitude of the British Government. . . . His boat was kept outside the harbor on various pretenses and not allowed to land. Finally, the World War broke out before it had landed its cargo and the whole scheme naturally fell through."[40]

The spectacle of such a movement at the nadir was perhaps matched only by the appearance of the "all-black" towns of the same period. In the 1910s, in the last years of his life, Booker T. Washington was enthralled by these towns. In 1912, Washington wrote to Isaiah Montgomery, founder of Mound Bayou, that outside of Tuskegee there was "no community in the world" in which he was "so deeply interested" as Mound Bayou, Mississippi, the "all-black" town in the delta where the Davis and Coleman families had first migrated—and he expressed similar sentiments about Boley. In 1954, historian August Meier noted that as the infrastructure of Jim Crow emerged and African Americans turned toward ideologies of economic advancement, self-help, and racial solidarity, it was in the "all-Negro communities founded during the late nineteenth and early twentieth centuries (most extensively in Oklahoma) that we find this latter cluster of ideas institutionalized in its most radical form." Ironically, it was Oklahoma's "most radical form" of Washingtonian thought that readied the new state to become, at the turn of the twentieth century, the primary locus of the African emigration movement that Washington himself decried. Moreover, Washington called attention to the common ground beneath westward and Liberia emigration movements when in 1912 he wrote, "Liberia . . . merely represented a widespread movement among Negroes, who had escaped slavery, to establish homes and communities of their own, not only in Africa but wherever freedom was assured them." Not surprisingly, then, although he investigated the Sam movement, Washington could do little to stop it from moving beyond U.S. national borders. Among those shareholders on board the *Liberia* in the weeks leading up to its Galveston departure was "one colored woman, who said she was a graduate of Booker T. Washington's school at Tuskegee." Faduma, who joined expecting to become the movement's "Principal of the College of Ethiopia in the Gold Coast," modeled on Tuskegee, had written a letter to Washington in December 1913, hoping to visit his institute "for five days' thoro[ugh] examination of your methods." In the end, perhaps Tom Johnson's misguided assumption about "yo and Mr chief-Sam" was not so misguided after all. Indeed, the separatist impulse took many forms following the demise of Reconstruction, including both "domestic" town movement and "foreign" emigration; the two explicitly converged in turn-of-the-century Indian Territory and Oklahoma, almost predictably on the literal edge of the U.S. nation-state.[41]

African-descended peoples led bold political lives in Indian Territory, and when faced with Jim Crow statehood, many chose to emigrate once again. Their experiences in Indian Territory—exemplified by the Chief Sam movement—thus portend the emergence of Garveyism, the "New Negro" movement, and the Great Migration. As I have shown, this moment informs not only the "firsts" of African-American political life in the postemancipation era but the "lasts" of African-American experiences in Indian country. Moreover, at the turn of the twentieth century, African Americans were immersed in the expansion of U.S. domestic and overseas imperialism. As the African-American teacher and orator Alfred M. Green had prophesied four decades earlier, in the midst of the Civil War: "There is no such thing as stand still in this nineteenth century; you must progress backward or forward; the world is rushing on; he or they who will not move with her, must be crushed by her onward march."[42]

Epilogue

"Grandpa went back to Africa with Garvey," my grandmother recalled. I carried this precious refrain into the archives with me. In Garvey's place, I found Chief Sam, in the black and Indian borderlands of Oklahoma. While the Great Migration had largely displaced the preceding history of black rural emigration at the nadir, so had Garveyism displaced descendants' memories of the Chief Sam movement. Meanwhile, scholars portrayed the movement as the product of a single charismatic charlatan and his nameless, faceless followers. Relying almost exclusively on U.S. sources and the memories of those "left behind" in an economically depressed and politically repressed Jim Crow Oklahoma, the only book-length study of the movement, written in the 1950s, argued that the Chief Sam movement illustrated "the desperate hopes of an utterly desperate group of people." The image fit easily with twentieth-century American tropes of black victimhood and criminality.[1]

This image stood largely at odds, however, with the fragments of stories I had heard while excavating our family history. Notwithstanding their displacement of Sam with Garvey, my father's mother and aunts had spoken with great pride about Coleman's participation in the movement. When the ship steamed into the Gulf of Mexico, the fraction of the movement on board included my great-great-grandfather, Monroe Coleman, his wife, Ida, and two of their sons, Willie and Raymond. When I asked what happened next— why Coleman returned to the United States the year following, after successfully migrating to the continent—I was told the land was inhospitable, that life in the Gold Coast was not as they had expected. This seemingly rational explanation again stood at odds with the more dramatic stories of fraud and dispossession circulated among those "left behind." I had examined hundreds

33. Ellis Island, New York, c. 1920. Library of Congress

of articles from black newspapers and white newspapers, from the *Boley Progress* to the *New York Times*, with headlines such as "Sam's Bunch Starving! Appeal for Aid in America. Let them stand the pressure of their folly." I felt the vigor and visceral certainty with which many of Coleman's peers blamed the movement's collapse on Sam's fraudulence. I could not resolve this disjuncture for some time. I considered the possibility that Coleman was part of the scheme; in a family history that intermingles stories of gambling and marital infidelity alongside schooling, worship, and uplift, this was hardly taboo. But upon closer inspection, the Colemans had left several of their young children, and most of their extended family, in Galveston for a year while they inspected their future home. From a written interview conducted in the 1980s and numerous family stories, I knew about my great aunts and uncles left behind in Galveston, all anxiously awaiting the "next trip."

By the spring of 1915, famine and an outbreak of influenza resulted in numerous deaths among the migrants. The black press in Oklahoma reported based on letters received from migrants requesting support to return. While the majority of those who survived returned to the United States, some dispersed throughout the Gold Coast and Liberia, their existence and fate disappearing from most American records of the movement. These interviews indicate some engaged in the production of tobacco, gunpowder, gin, and cocoa. At least two brothers set up shop in Cape Coast, while another migrant ran a tobacco plantation close to Chief Sam's family home; others were remembered for building a motorized boat and operating a ferry service along the coast; a young woman who had married Chief Sam during the movement later migrated to England; and several appear to have moved on to Liberia with Sam. Such alternate endings had not appeared in any detail in the fledgling literature, or in the public history—urban and rural legends that had declared the movement an unmitigated failure.

In the summer of 2013, I shared these alternate endings and related evidence with a group of residents in Clearview, Oklahoma. Founded in 1903 along the tracks of the Fort Smith and Western Railroad, Clearview was one of the first black towns in Indian Territory, a bustling black metropolis of newly arrived southern migrants on the eve of Oklahoma statehood. In the decade that followed, the political and economic repression that accompanied statehood urged many to look again beyond the United States. By December 1913, Clearview had emerged as the heart of the "African

34. Main Street, Clearview, Oklahoma, 2013. Photo by author, author's collection

movement." Today, Clearview's population is about forty-nine, but along its historic main street, the old boarded storefronts, remnants of Dr. Alford's pharmacy, and numerous churches still offer an evocative picture of this rich history.

The residents I met included men and women in their seventies. Many had heard of Chief Sam from their parents and grandparents—men and women who bought shares in the Akim Trading Company and waited in vain for the S.S. *Liberia* to return for them; in the story they knew, Sam was a fraud. Some had heard it directly from Dr. Alford, who had tended to sick children in the camps of would-be migrants that emerged in the fall of 1913, and was still practicing in town decades later. I spoke with his daughter-in-law at the local nursing home. J. P. Owens, nine years old at the time of the movement, recalled a doctor traveling to the camps, where he found "many children with no shoes and people in rags." Amid repeated postponements,

35. Part of movement camp gravesite at "South Gold Coast," Weleetka, Oklahoma, 2013. Photo by author, author's collection

food was becoming scarce and the migrants were ill-prepared for freezing temperatures. Still, the local paper reported, "There are hundreds who have not . . . languished in the hope of seeing the promised land."[2]

In the public history of the movement, the mournful recollection of children dying in the camps—and subsequent illness and death in West Africa—have formed the core of the fraudulence claim. To be sure, the migrants living at South Gold Coast in the winter of 1913–14—and those in Gold Coast the following year—would have resembled the thousands of African Americans who escaped the American South and Southwest with dreams of an "African return," only to be taken in by "swindling schemes," stranded in rail cars, standing on docks, or huddled on the streets of New York City. As we have seen, however, Sam was not simply one more "swindler" in this succession.

Still, as I spoke with the men and women of Clearview whose parents and grandparents had been "left behind" by Sam, I began to understand how seamlessly the popular story of a charismatic charlatan had papered over the near-perfect storm of structural constraints that the movement faced at every step. On the eve of the First World War, these included a series of governmental roadblocks extending from the Boley courthouse and the Oklahoma state house to the U.S. State Department and numerous British officials in London and the Gold Coast. Mobilizing a long history of "Liberia fever" in the South and Southwest, Sam and his followers envisioned a practical future together; living in the camps and on the ship for more than a year, they weathered the attacks of the press, a harsh winter, and dwindling resources. Some who were forced by circumstance to return nevertheless continued to believe in the idea of the "African movement."

When the ship failed to return to Galveston in 1915 for the supposed "next trip"—when those "left behind" returned to Oklahoma penniless, when their children soon faced the depths of the Great Depression, the Dust Bowl, and the near-disappearance of whole towns and livelihoods— the now-familiar narrative of total failure and individualized fraud set in. To this day, descendants still living carry with them haunting memories of their parents' lost fortunes and of what might have been. I began to see this narrative, like many, as a yearning attempt to explain not necessarily the movement itself but the hard times that followed, to make peace with what happened next.

Before leaving Clearview, I witnessed two somewhat quiet reflections that did not fit the movement's popular narrative in Oklahoma. The first came from a middle-aged man who helped tend to an African-American gravesite in town, where many of the migrants had been buried. After showing me the headstones and sharing what he knew about the location of an unmarked "mass grave" behind these stones, he offered one opinion. He said that one thing that had never quite made sense to him was how Sam could have been a fraud when, in the end, he "bought that ship" and made the trip with the others. The second came from J. P. Owens's daughter, who had saved in her home an original stock certificate from Sam's Akim Trading Company. At the time of the movement, her father was nine years old. He had held onto his parents' certificate ever since; before he passed, he recorded his memories of the prideful movement.[3]

A year later, several of my aunts, uncles, cousins, and I organized a reunion around the centennial (1914–2014) of the Chief Sam movement, inviting by word of mouth and social media known and unknown descendants who had stories, memories, or any familial knowledge at all about the Sam movement. We located five large, discrete family groups and attracted more than 150 movement descendants who traveled from Illinois, Michigan, New York, Virginia, Missouri, Georgia, New Mexico, Colorado, Texas, and California to Oklahoma to commemorate the movement, and our forebears' participation in it. Descendants scattered by the Great Depression and the Great Migration met with present-day residents of Clearview and neighboring black towns, and together we trekked to the movement gravesite for a moment of silence.

Where Garvey's movement had stopped short, Sam's had succeeded, at least momentarily, in pulling off the African "return." In hindsight, however, the displacement of Sam by Garvey in the scattered public history of this movement is hardly surprising. In 1913 and 1914, the Sam movement engaged several thousand African Americans in one corner of the American Southwest; five years later, Garvey mobilized millions across the United

36. Monroe and Ida Carrell Coleman. Author's collection

States and the Western Hemisphere. By 1926, ten years after the dissolution of the Chief Sam movement, black Oklahomans had produced twenty-eight UNIA chapters—the eleventh-most of all states. In the wake of Garvey and the UNIA, impressions of Sam grew hazy and sometimes disappeared.[4]

In October 1915, Monroe Coleman, Ida Coleman, and their two sons stepped off the S.S. *Adriatic* and walked onto Ellis Island. They returned from the Gold Coast following the collapse of the "African movement," dreams of a more free life deferred. Listed as "U.S. Born Citizens," they walked the pier alongside thousands of European immigrants entering the United States with dreams not unlike those that motivated the Colemans to exit the country.[5]

Monroe Coleman died at the Okmulgee City Colored Hospital in the 1940s. Constructed at the corner of 3rd and Wood Streets around 1922, the hospital quickly emerged as a pillar of the African-American community within the then-bustling city of Okmulgee, especially following the 1921 Tulsa race riot and the burning of Black Wall Street. The Okmulgee City

37. Returning ship manifest for the S.S. *Adriatic*, including Coleman family members, via Liverpool. Library of Congress

Colored Hospital is one of the few segregated hospitals in the United States that is today still standing.

The same decade that Monroe died in the hospital, my father was born just a few blocks away, in the back room of "713" North Choctaw, as they called the twentieth-century Brown homeplace. While my grandmother carried with her memories of Brownsville, her life was largely shaped by twentieth-century biracialism and the world of black towns, hospitals, schools, libraries, and churches. My father eventually moved east and, following his kidney transplant, became a physician. The visible presence at the Okmulgee City Colored Hospital of highly respected African-American doctors and nurses played a powerful role in his life, and in the circumstances of my own.

Monroe Coleman was born to a former slave and died in a "colored hospital" at the height of Jim Crow. A narrative framed by such starkly defined beginnings and endings, however, fails to reflect the vast mobility that defined Coleman's life. Such a narrative belies the rich inheritance—the

38. Historic Okmulgee City Colored Hospital, c. 2000. Photo by
Michael Cassity

"family architecture"—in which we share. It also fails to encompass our collective inheritance as children of freedom's first generation. In this sense, I echo Thulani Davis's claim that one of the greatest gifts of this work has been "to come closer to the first generation out of bondage. . . . Never has one group of people acted on such a large scale in so many regions of the country to push this society to honor its foundational principles. They taught the rest of us how to do it and yet there is no cultural memory of those millions. They are freedom's 'Greatest Generation.' "[6] In this sense, the historical erasure of the Chief Sam movement was not only a function of scale but a failure of imagination.

In 1790, a French colonist named La Barre wrote to his wife from Saint-Domingue, "There is no movement among our Negroes. . . . They don't even think of it. They are very tranquil and obedient. A revolt among them is impossible. . . . Freedom for Negroes is a chimera." Several months later, the world's "most important slave insurrection in recorded history" began, creating an independent Haiti. In *Silencing the Past*, Michel-Rolph Trouillot used La Barre's words on the eve of insurrection to illustrate that the Haitian Revolution was an event "unthinkable even as it happened." Trouillot added that not even the "most radical writers of the Enlightenment" or "the extreme political left"—those presumably in favor of "freedom for Negroes"—had a "conceptual frame of reference" for the events that unfolded in Saint-Domingue at the turn of the nineteenth century.[7]

A century later, the question of "freedom for Negroes" had been decidedly put to rest for the children of enslaved Americans living in the period Rayford Logan termed "the nadir" of African-American experience in the United States. W. E. B. Du Bois wrote of the tragic consequences of the demise of Reconstruction, "The slave went free; stood a brief moment in the sun; then moved back again toward slavery." Historians have located in the nadir a stark reminder of a racial order that outlived the institution of racial slavery and a sober caution against privileging the "event" of emancipation. Yet even at this low point, as African Americans proverbially "turned inward" in the Jim Crow South, another "unthinkable" movement was underfoot in the Atlantic world.[8]

This was, after all, a group of ex-slaves who pooled nearly $100,000, purchased a German steamship, and journeyed to West Africa at the height of Jim Crow. The denial and distortion of the Chief Sam movement as another "failed African venture" by contemporaries and historians reveals much about the "deeply held beliefs" that dominated American lives and history in the years not only before the civil rights movement, but before the New Negro Movement, the Harlem Renaissance, the world wars, and the Great Migration.[9] One of the quieter legacies of the Jim Crow era has been the narrowing of historical imagination for what black lives and actions could and did look like.

NOTES

Preface

1. "mother's stories": Ronne Hartfield, *Another Way Home: The Tangled Roots of Race in One Chicago Family* (Chicago: University of Chicago Press, 2004), xvii. "so wonderful . . . the world for me": E. Frances White, *Dark Continent of Our Bodies: Black Feminism and the Politics of Respectability* (Philadelphia: Temple University Press, 2001), 3–4.

2. "intergenerational self": Robyn Fivush, Jennifer G. Bohanek, and Marshall Duke, "The Intergenerational Self: Subject Perspective and Family History," in *Self-Continuity: Individual and Collective Perspective*, ed. F. Sani (New York: Psychology Press, 2008) 131–41. "belong to something bigger . . . self-esteem": Bruce Feiler, "The Stories That Bind Us," *New York Times*, March 17, 2013.

3. On the separation of families, see Heather Andrea Williams, *Help Me to Find My People: The African American Search for Family Lost in Slavery* (Chapel Hill: University of North Carolina Press, 2012). "The reader": Frederick Douglass, *The Life and Times of Frederick Douglass, Written by Himself* (Boston: De Wolfe and Fiske, 1892). "haunted by the need to know . . . history of a people": Williams, *Help Me to Find My People*, 192. "some people are still stunned . . . reclaim that history": ibid., 198.

4. "I began as a woman alone": Dorothy Spruill Redford with Michael D'Orso, *Somerset Homecoming: Recovering a Lost Heritage* (New York: Doubleday, 1988; rpt. Chapel Hill: University of North Carolina Press, 2000), 158. "All the slaves on the plantation": Williams, *Help Me to Find My People*, 198. "worked hard . . . Black Jacobins": White, *Dark Continent*, 2.

5. Virginia Adams, "Organ Transplant Controversy: A Gift of Life or Lifetime I.O.U.?" *New York Times*, July 9, 1977. Odevia Field, quoted ibid.

6. "family architecture . . . children must live": Suzannah Lessard, *The Architect of Desire: Beauty and Danger in the Stanford White Family* (New York: Delta, 1997), 5.

7. John Henrik Clarke recalled Arthur Schomburg's first words to him in 1934: "Son, what you're calling Negro history and African history are the missing pages of world history"; John Henrik Clarke, *My Life in Search of Africa* (Ithaca, NY: Cornell University Press, 1994), 13–14.

Introduction

Epigraph: Ralph Ellison, "Going to the Territory," in *Collected Essays of Ralph Ellison*, ed. John F. Callahan (New York: Modern Library, 2003), 602.

1. *"real* freedom": Nell Irvin Painter, *Exodusters: Black Migration to Kansas after Reconstruction* (1977; New York: Norton, 1992), 4 (emphasis added). On Reconstruction and its aftermath, see W. E. B. Du Bois, *Black Reconstruction in America, 1860–1880* (1935; New York: Free Press, 1998); Steven Hahn, *A Nation under Our Feet: Black Political Struggles in the Rural South, from Slavery to the Great Migration* (Cambridge: Belknap Press of Harvard University Press, 2005); Gregory Downs and Kate Masur, ed., *The World the Civil War Made* (Chapel Hill: University of North Carolina Press, 2015); Leon Litwack, *Trouble in Mind: Black Southerners in the Age of Jim Crow* (New York: Knopf, 1998); Painter, *Exodusters*; Edward L. Ayers, *The Promise of the New South Life after Reconstruction* (New York: Oxford University Press, 2007); Michele Mitchell, *Righteous Propagation: African Americans and the Politics of Racial Destiny after Reconstruction* (Chapel Hill: University of North Carolina Press, 2004); Kevin Gaines, *Uplifting the Race: Black Leadership, Politics, and Culture in the Twentieth Century* (Chapel Hill: University of North Carolina Press, 1996); C. Vann Woodward, *Origins of the New South, 1877–1913* (Baton Rouge: Louisiana State University Press, 1971); Eric Foner, *Reconstruction: America's Unfinished Revolution, 1863–1877* (1988; New York: Perennial Classics, 2002); David Blight, *Race and Reunion: The Civil War in American Memory* (Cambridge: Belknap Press of Harvard University Press, 2001). Much of the Davis family history survives thanks to Elic and Della's seventh child, Lomie (Davis) Reed. Her great nephew Cecil Cade and his partner, Mark A. Phillips, interviewed Lomie extensively on her ninety-third birthday in 1988. Lomie (Davis) Reed, conversation with Cecil Cade and Mark A. Phillips, March 22, 1988 (Houston, Texas), transcript (in possession of the author), 13, A-5, 15; audiocassette, Alexander Davis Family Papers, Box 1, Manuscript Collections, Mississippi Department of Archives and History.

2. John Hope Franklin stated in 1961 at the Sidney Hillman Lectures at Howard University that "The Long Dark Night" continued until 1923; Leon Litwack dated the nadir as 1890 through the Great Migration. Rayford Whittingham Logan, *The Negro in American Life and Thought: The Nadir, 1877–1901* (New York: Dial, 1954), 52; John Hope Franklin, Sidney Hillman Lectures, 1961; Leon Litwack, *Been in the Storm so Long: The Aftermath of Slavery* (New York: Knopf, 1979). Studies of

specific emigration movements during this period include Painter, *Exodusters;* Leslie A. Schwalm, *Emancipation's Diaspora: Race and Reconstruction in the Upper Midwest* (Chapel Hill: University of North Carolina Press, 2009); Kenneth Marvin Hamilton, *Black Towns and Profit: Promotion and Development in the Trans-Appalachian West, 1877–1915* (Urbana: University of Illinois Press, 1991). Several important studies span multiple movements, and the long history of black emigrationism: James Campbell, *Middle Passages: African American Journeys to Africa, 1787–2005* (New York: Penguin, 2006); Hahn, *A Nation under Our Feet;* Edwin S. Redkey, *Black Exodus: Black Nationalist and Back-to-Africa Movements, 1890–1910* (New Haven: Yale University Press, 1969); Carter Godwin Woodson, *A Century of Negro Migration* (Washington, DC: Association for the Study of Negro Life and History, 1918); and Eddie S. Glaude, *Exodus! Religion, Race, and Nation in Early Nineteenth-Century Black America* (Chicago: University of Chicago Press, 2000). For generational studies of the era, see, for instance, Robert F. Engs, *Freedom's First Generation: Black Hampton, Virginia, 1861–1890* (Philadelphia: University of Pennsylvania Press, 1979); Ira Berlin, *Generations of Captivity: A History of African-American Slaves* (Cambridge: Belknap Press of Harvard University Press, 2003). Hahn, *A Nation under Our Feet*, 453–54; Redkey, *Black Exodus*, 73–149; Ellison, *Going to the Territory*, 602.

3. On the emergence of biracialism, see Matthew Pratt Guterl, *The Color of Race in America, 1900–1940* (Cambridge: Harvard University Press, 2001); Mitchell, *Righteous Propagation;* Gaines, *Uplifting the Race;* and Martha Hodes, "Fractions and Fictions in the United States Census of 1890," in *Haunted by Empire: Geographies of Intimacy in North American History*, ed. Ann Laura Stoler (Durham: Duke University Press, 2006), 240–70. George Hutchinson, "An End to the Family Romance: Nella Larsen, Black Transnationalism, and American Racial Ideology," in *Race, Nation, and Empire in American History*, ed. James T. Campbell, Matthew Pratt Guterl, and Robert G. Lee (Chapel Hill: University of North Carolina Press, 2007), 55–74, 55.

4. On the construction of race and racial categories in the United States, see Barbara J. Fields, "Ideology and Race in American History," in *Region, Race, and Reconstruction: Essays in Honor of C. Vann Woodward*, ed. J. Morgan Kousser and James M. McPherson (New York: Oxford University Press, 1982), 143–77; Thomas C. Holt, "Marking: Race, Race-Making, and the Writing of History," *American Historical Review* 100 (1995): 1–20; Hodes, "Fractions and Fictions"; and Ariela J. Gross, *What Blood Won't Tell: A History of Race on Trial in America* (Cambridge: Harvard University Press, 2008), 140–77.

5. "White men's countries": Marilyn Lake and Henry Reynolds, *Drawing the Global Colour Line: White Men's Countries and the International Challenge of Racial Equality* (New York: Cambridge University Press, 2008), 6. "global in its power": ibid., 3. W. E. B. Du Bois, "The Souls of White Folk," *Independent*, August 18, 1910, 339.

6. Historians Steven Hahn and Michele Mitchell have highlighted the common ground between western migration and "Liberia fever." See Hahn, *A Nation under Our Feet*, 331, chapters 7 and 9; and Mitchell, *Righteous Propagation*, chapter 1. On the UNIA in Oklahoma, see Epilogue, note 4.

7. Hahn, *A Nation under Our Feet*, especially chapters 7 and 9 and epilogue; Mitchell, *Righteous Propagation*, especially chapter 1. On "geopolitical nationhood," see Wilson Moses, *Afrotopia: The Roots of African American Popular History* (New York: Cambridge University Press, 1998), 26. On "geopolitical literacy," see Phillip Troutman, "Grapevine in the Slave Market: African American Geopolitical Literacy and the 1841 *Creole* Revolt," in *The Chattel Principle: Internal Slave Trades in the Americas*, ed. Walter Johnson (New Haven: Yale University Press, 2008), 203–33. J. W. Turner to American Colonization Society, June 20, 1892, Incoming Correspondence, roll 141, Records of the American Colonization Society, Library of Congress, Manuscripts Division.

8. Alfred M. Green, Letters and Discussion of the Formation of Colored Regiments, and the Duty of the Colored People in Regards to the Great Slaveholders' Rebellion, in the United States of America (Philadelphia: Ringwalt and Brown, 1862).

9. "lost to history": Campbell, *Middle Passages*, xxiii.

10. Richard White, *Remembering Ahanagran: Storytelling in a Family's Past* (New York: Hill and Wang, 1998), 4.

11. On gender, race, and respectability, see Evelyn Brooks Higginbotham, *Righteous Discontent: The Women's Movement in the Black Baptist Church, 1880–1920* (Cambridge: Harvard University Press, 1994); Darlene Clark Hine, "Rape and the Inner Lives of Black Women: Thoughts on the Culture of Dissemblance," in *Hine Site: Black Women and the Re-Construction of American History* (Bloomington: Indiana University Press, 1994), 37–48; Martha S. Jones, *The Woman Question in African American Public Culture, 1830–1900* (Chapel Hill: University of North Carolina Press, 2007); Brittney C. Cooper, *Beyond Respectability: The Intellectual Thought of Race Women* (Champaign: University of Illinois Press, 2017). On the erasure of sexual violence, see, for instance, Hazel V. Carby, *Reconstructing Womanhood: The Emergence of the Afro-American Woman Novelist* (New York: Oxford University Press, 1989), 39; and Gregory D. Smithers, *Slave Breeding: Sex, Violence, and Memory in African American History* (Gainesville: University Press of Florida, 2012). Hine, "Rape and the Inner Lives," in *Hine Sight*, 37–48, 43. See "Brown Family," Okmulgee Historical Society and the Society of America, comps. and eds., *History of Okmulgee County, Oklahoma* (Tulsa, OK: Historical Enterprises, 1985), 1: 587; Darlene Clark Hine, "Rape and the Inner Lives of Black Women: Thoughts on the Culture of Dissemblance," in *Hine Sight: Black Women and the Re-Construction of American History* (Bloomington: Indiana University Press, 1994), 37–48, 43.

12. On the relationship between migration and family history, see François Weil, *Family Trees: A History of Genealogy in America* (Cambridge: Harvard University

Press, 2013). "hidden transcripts": James C. Scott, *Domination and the Arts of Resistance: Hidden Transcripts* (New Haven: Yale University Press, 1990).

13. Clifford Fields and Terry Smith, family history presentations, Brown/Coleman Family Reunion, video recording, July 2007, author's collection.

14. "family architecture": Suzannah Lessard, *The Architect of Desire: Beauty and Danger in the Stanford White Family* (New York: Delta, 1997), 5; "Our unknown history": Ellison, "Going to the Territory," 602.

15. "Three-fourths of the testimony": Du Bois, *Black Reconstruction*, 725; "prompted Black historians": Painter, *Exodusters*, 265.

16. On "objectivity," see Peter Novick, *That Noble Dream: The "Objectivity Question" and the American Historical Profession* (Cambridge: Cambridge University Press, 1988).

17. On "agency," see Walter Johnson, "On Agency," *Journal of Social History* 37 (2003): 113–24. "all human subjects have agency": Mae Ngai, "Western History and the Pacific World," *Western Historical Quarterly* 43 (2012): 282–88, 288. "emptied . . . meaning": Johnson, "On Agency," 114. "trope": ibid., 113. "binary of free and unfree labor": Ngai, "Western History," 288. Du Bois, *Black Reconstruction*. "all-but-unsinkable . . . to counter present-day racism": Jim Downs, "The Future of Civil War Era Studies: Race," *Journal of the Civil War Era*, journalofthecivilwarera.org, accessed Jan. 2015, 1–2. "tangled in this mess . . . sainthood": ibid., 3–4.

18. "sweeping accounts": Nicole Etcheson, "Microhistory and Movement: African American Mobility in the Nineteenth Century," *Journal of the Civil War Era* 3 (2013): 392–404, 392. "details that often find . . . as heroes": Downs, "The Future of Civil War Era Studies," 6. "What is the object . . . future may be built": Du Bois, *Black Reconstruction*, 725.

19. Here I am interested in African-American migrants' origins in the southern states as well as the complex, multiracial, multinational terrain onto which they stepped—including the freedpeople (formerly enslaved peoples) of the Indian Nations whose communities they joined and, in some cases, with whom they built new communities. On the history of African-descended peoples within the Southeast Indian nations, see Tiya Miles, *Ties That Bind: An Afro-Cherokee Family in Slavery and Freedom* (Berkeley: University of California Press, 2005); Tiya Miles and Sharon Holland, eds., *Crossing Waters, Crossing Worlds: The African Diaspora in Indian Country* (Durham: Duke University Press, 2006); Celia Naylor, *African Cherokees in Indian Territory: From Chattel to Citizens* (Chapel Hill: University of North Carolina Press, 2008); Theda Perdue, *Mixed Blood Indians: Racial Construction in the Early South* (Athens: University of Georgia Press, 2003); Claudio Saunt, *Black, White, and Indian: Race and the Unmaking of an American Family* (New York: Oxford University Press, 2005); Gary Zellar, *African Creeks: Estelvste and the Creek Nation* (Norman: University of Oklahoma Press, 2007); David A. Chang, *The Color of the Land: Race, Nation, and the Politics of Landownership in Oklahoma, 1832–1929* (Chapel Hill: University of North Carolina Press, 2010); Barbara Krauthamer,

Black Slaves, Indian Masters: Slavery, Emancipation, and Citizenship in the Native American South (Chapel Hill: University of North Carolina Press, 2013); Kevin Mulroy, *The Seminole Freedmen: A History* (Norman: University of Oklahoma Press, 2007); Fay A. Yarbrough, *Race and the Cherokee Nation: Sovereignty in the Nineteenth Century* (Philadelphia: University of Pennsylvania Press, 2007); Circe Sturm, *Blood Politics: Race, Culture, and Identity in the Cherokee Nation of Oklahoma* (Los Angeles: University of California Press, 2002); Daniel Littlefield, *Africans and Creeks: From the Colonial Period to the Civil War* (Westport, CT: Greenwood, 1979). Sarah Deutsch, "Being American in Boley, Oklahoma," in *Beyond Black and White: Race, Ethnicity, and Gender in the U.S. South and Southwest,* ed. Stephanie Cole and Alison M. Parker (College Station: Texas A & M University Press, 2004), 97–122; Christina Snyder, *Slavery in Indian Country: The Changing Face of Captivity in Early America* (Cambridge: Harvard University Press, 2010), 182–212; and Gross, *What Blood Won't Tell,* 140–77.

20. "white men's countries": Lake and Reynolds, *Drawing the Global Colour Line,* 6. "cramped for land": Charles Pearson, "On the Land Question in the United States," *Contemporary Review,* November 1868, quoted *ibid,* 37. "But what on earth is whiteness? . . . Amen!": Du Bois, "Souls of White Folk," 339 (emphasis added).

21. On the scholarly emergence of African-American and diasporic family histories and microhistories, largely since the turn of the twenty-first century, see Adele Logan Alexander, *Ambiguous Lives: Free Women of Color in Rural Georgia, 1789–1879* (Fayetteville: University of Arkansas Press, 1991); Adele Logan Alexander, *Homelands and Waterways: The American Journey of the Bond Family, 1846–1926* (New York: Vintage, 2000); Adele Logan Alexander, *Parallel Worlds: The Remarkable Gibbs-Hunts and the Enduring (In)significance of Melanin* (Charlottesville: University of Virginia Press, 2010); Mary Frances Berry, *We Are Who We Say We Are: A Black Family's Search for Home across the Atlantic World* (New York: Oxford University Press, 2014); Erica Armstrong Dunbar, *Never Caught: The Washingtons' Relentless Pursuit of Their Runaway Slave, Ona Judge* (New York: Atria, 2017); Mamie Garvin Fields with Karen Fields, *Lemon Swamp and Other Places: A Carolina Memoir* (New York: Free Press, 1983); John Hope Franklin and Loren Schweninger, *In Search of the Promised Land: A Slave Family in the Old South* (New York: Oxford University Press, 2006); Annette Gordon-Reed, *The Hemingses of Monticello: An American Family* (New York: Norton, 2009); Angela Pulley Hudson, *Real Native Genius: How an Ex-Slave and a White Mormon Became Famous Indians* (Chapel Hill: University of North Carolina Press, 2015); Lawrence P. Jackson, *My Father's Name: A Black Virginia Family after the Civil War* (Chicago: University of Chicago Press, 2012); Karl Jacoby, *The Strange Career of William Ellis: The Texas Slave Who Became a Mexican Millionaire* (New York: Norton, 2016); Malinda Maynor Lowery, *Lumbee Indians in the Jim Crow South: Race, Identity, and the Making of a Nation* (Chapel Hill: University of North Carolina Press, 2010); Miles, *Ties That Bind;*

Sydney Nathans, *To Free a Family: The Journey of Mary Walker* (Cambridge: Harvard University Press, 2013); Sydney Nathans, *A Mind to Stay: White Plantation, Black Homeland* (Cambridge: Harvard University Press, 2017); Nell Irvin Painter, *Southern History across the Color Line* (Chapel Hill: University of North Carolina Press, 2002); Adam Rothman, *Beyond Freedom's Reach: A Kidnapping in the Twilight of Slavery* (Cambridge: Harvard University Press, 2015); Carla Peterson, *Black Gotham: A Family History of African Americans in Nineteenth-Century New York City* (New Haven: Yale University Press, 2012); Martha Sandweiss, *Passing Strange: A Gilded Age Tale of Love and Deception across the Color Line* (New York: Penguin, 2010); Claudio Saunt, *Black, White, and Indian: Race and the Unmaking of an American Family* (New York: Oxford University Press, 2005); Rebecca Scott, *Freedom Papers: An Atlantic Odyssey in the Age of Emancipation* (Cambridge: Harvard University Press, 2014). "proudly small": Etcheson, "Microhistory and Movement," 392. "ordinary . . . change up close": ibid., 393. "one of the last fields . . . sweeping accounts . . . difficult to achieve": ibid., 392. John Blassingame, *The Slave Community: Plantation Life in the Antebellum South* (New York: Oxford University Press, 1979); Ira Berlin, *Many Thousands Gone: The First Two Centuries of Slavery in North America* (Cambridge: Belknap Press of Harvard University Press, 1998); Laurel Thatcher Ulrich, *A Midwife's Tale: The Life of Martha Ballad, Based on Her Diary, 1785–1832* (New York: Vintage, 1990); John Demos, *The Unredeemed Captive: A Family Story from Early America* (New York: Vintage, 1994); Martha Hodes, *The Sea Captain's Wife: A True Story of Love, Race, and War in the Nineteenth Century* (New York: Norton, 2006); Miles, *Ties That Bind*; Alexander, *Parallel Worlds*.

22. "belief in American exceptionalism": Clement Price, "On Anchoring a Generation of Scholars: P. Sterling Stuckey and the Nationalist Persuasion in African American History," *Journal of African American History* 91 (2006), 385–88, 386. "essential humanity": Du Bois, *Black Reconstruction*, 725. "long dead": Downs, "Future of Civil War Era Studies," 1.

23. "eclipse of institutions": Thomas Bender, "Historians in Public," *Transformations of the Public Sphere*, Social Science Research Council, July 2010, http://publicsphere .ssrc.org/bender-historians-in-public/. "scraps of evidence . . . and the arc": Downs, "Future of Civil War Era Studies," 7.

24. Letter from Annie Davis to Abraham Lincoln, August 25, 1864; Letters Received, 1863–1888; Records of the Adjutant General's Office, 1762–1984, Record Group 94; National Archives (National Archives Identifier 4662543).

25. On kinship and the binary of slavery and freedom, see Snyder, *Slavery in Indian Country*, 5; Miles, *Ties That Bind*, 51; and Dylan Penningroth, *The Claims of Kinfolk: African American Property and Community in the Nineteenth-Century South* (Chapel Hill: University of North Carolina Press, 2003), 13; "wrote letters": William H. Robinson, *From Log Cabin to the Pulpit, or, Fifteen Years in Slavery* (Eau Claire, WI, 1913), http://docsouth.unc.edu/fpn/robinson/robinson.html,

quoted in Heather Williams, *Help Me to Find My People: The African American Search for Family Lost in Slavery* (Chapel Hill: University of North Carolina Press, 2012), 143. "opposite of slavery": Snyder, *Slavery in Indian Country*, 5. "haunted by the need to know . . . negligence of history . . . a people": Williams, *Help Me to Find My People*, 192.

26. On queer genealogies, see Laura Doan, "Genealogy Inside and Out," in *Disturbing Practices: History, Sexuality, and Women's Experience of Modern War* (Chicago: University of Chicago Press, 2013), 58–97. Dylan Penningroth notes that not only did families make property, but property helped to "make" families. Penningroth, *Claims of Kinfolk*, 86, 88. On the construction of family and race, George Hutchinson writes, "The subordination of 'family' to 'race,' the attempt to ensure that families would always serve to reproduce race, is one of the greatest constants in the legal, social, cultural, and spiritual history of the United States." George Hutchinson, "An End to the Family Romance," 70.

27. Painter, *Southern History across the Color Line*, 5.

28. "stories that we refuse to tell": E. Frances White, *Dark Continent of Our Bodies: Black Feminism and the Politics of Respectability* (Philadelphia: Temple University Press, 2001), 24. "American history": James Baldwin, "A Talk to Teachers," delivered October 16, 1963, as "The Negro Child—His Self-Image"; originally published in *Saturday Review*, December 21, 1963, rpt. in James Baldwin, *The Price of the Ticket: Collected Nonfiction, 1948–1985* (New York: St. Martin's, 1985), 325–32, 332.

29. "bi-racialism" and "revolution": Guterl, *Color of Race*, 156.

30. "The slave went free": Du Bois, *Black Reconstruction*, 30. Greeley's advice: *New York Tribune*, July 13, 1865. See also Elliott West, *Growing Up with the Country: Childhood on the Far Western Frontier* (Albuquerque: University of New Mexico Press, 1989). "place near the border": George Coleman, "Interview with George M. Coleman," interview 10449, April 13, 1938, Indian-Pioneer Papers, 19: 271–74, Oklahoma Historical Society and Western History Collections, University of Oklahoma. "Moving West," *Christian Recorder*, August 12, 1897. "fastened in the colored group": Toomer, "Book X," quoted in Guterl, *Color of Race*, 158.

31. Woodson, *A Century of Negro Migration*.

32. Jonathan Raban, *Driving Home: An American Journey* (New York: Pantheon, 2010), 9.

33. "lilies": J. Oliphant, interview by author, Wetumka, Oklahoma, November 24, 2005. "ownership of the earth . . .": Du Bois, "Souls of White Folk," 339.

34. Pierre Nora, "Between Memory and History: *Les Lieux de Mémoire*," *Representations* 26 (1989): 7–24. "'black and unknown bards,' historians without portfolio": Robert O'Meally and Geneviève Fabre, "Introduction," in Fabre and O'Meally, eds., *History and Memory in African-American Culture* (New York: Oxford University Press, 1994), 8. James Weldon Johnson's poem "O Black and Unknown Bards," referenced here by O'Meally and Fabre, commemorates the "unknown" composers of African-American spirituals. See James Weldon Johnson,

Lift Every Voice and Sing: Selected Poems by James Weldon Johnson (1935; New York: Penguin, 1993), 25.

35. "without a home . . .": Michael A. Gomez, *Exchanging Our Country Marks: The Transformation of African Identities in the Colonial and Antebellum South* (Chapel Hill: University of North Carolina Press, 1998), 277.

36. "symbols of distant events . . .": Keith Basso, *Wisdom Sits in Places: Landscape and Language among the Western Apache* (Albuquerque: University of New Mexico Press, 1996), xiii, 7 (emphasis original).

1. "Intruder of Color"

1. Thurman Brown (Thomas Jefferson Brown's grandson), interview by author, Okmulgee, Oklahoma, November 24, 2005.

2. On the history of African-descended peoples within the Southeast Indian nations, see Tiya Miles, *Ties That Bind: An Afro-Cherokee Family in Slavery and Freedom* (Berkeley: University of California Press, 2005); Tiya Miles and Sharon Holland, eds., *Crossing Waters, Crossing Worlds: The African Diaspora in Indian Country* (Durham: Duke University Press, 2006); Celia Naylor, *African Cherokees in Indian Territory: From Chattel to Citizens* (Chapel Hill: University of North Carolina Press, 2008); Theda Perdue, *Mixed Blood Indians: Racial Construction in the Early South* (Athens: University of Georgia Press, 2003); Claudio Saunt, *Black, White, and Indian: Race and the Unmaking of an American Family* (New York: Oxford University Press, 2005); Gary Zellar, *African Creeks: Estelvste and the Creek Nation* (Norman: University of Oklahoma Press, 2007); David A. Chang, *The Color of the Land: Race, Nation, and the Politics of Landownership in Oklahoma, 1832–1929* (Chapel Hill: University of North Carolina Press, 2010); Barbara Krauthamer, *Black Slaves, Indian Masters: Slavery, Emancipation, and Citizenship in the Native American South* (Chapel Hill: University of North Carolina Press, 2013). Kevin Mulroy, *The Seminole Freedmen: A History* (Norman: University of Oklahoma Press, 2007); Fay A. Yarbrough, *Race and the Cherokee Nation: Sovereignty in the Nineteenth Century* (Philadelphia: University of Pennsylvania Press, 2007); Circe Sturm, *Blood Politics: Race, Culture, and Identity in the Cherokee Nation of Oklahoma* (Los Angeles: University of California Press, 2002); Daniel Littlefield, *Africans and Creeks: From the Colonial Period to the Civil War* (Westport, CT: Greenwood, 1979). Sarah Deutsch, "Being American in Boley, Oklahoma" in *Beyond Black and White: Race, Ethnicity, and Gender in the U.S. South and Southwest*, ed. Stephanie Cole and Alison M. Parker (College Station: Texas A&M University Press, 2004), 97–122; Christina Snyder, *Slavery in Indian Country: The Changing Face of Captivity in Early America* (Cambridge: Harvard University Press, 2010), 182–212; Ariela Gross, *What Blood Won't Tell: A History of Race on Trial in America* (Cambridge: Harvard University Press, 2008), 140–77. On Brownsville, see "Brown Family," Okmulgee Historical Society and the Heritage

Society of America, comps. and eds., *History of Okmulgee County, Oklahoma*, comp. and ed. Okmulgee Historical Society and the Heritage Society of America (Tulsa, OK: Historical Enterprises, 1985), 1: 587.

3. "full-blooded Irishman": Brown's grandson, Thurman Brown, initially described Brown's mother this way, as an "Irishman." Thurman heard this description from Brown himself. When pressed, he translated to contemporary terms, "a white lady," but his initial choice of "Irishman" illustrates the salience of Irish ancestry and the gradual construction of whiteness in this nineteenth-century setting. On such interracial liaisons in the Civil War era, see Martha Hodes, *White Women, Black Men: Illicit Sex in the Nineteenth-Century South* (New Haven: Yale University Press, 1997). Thurman Brown interview. Harry S. Ashmore, *Arkansas: A Bicentennial History* (New York: Norton, 1978), xiii–xiv; David T. Gleeson, *The Irish in the South, 1815–1877* (Chapel Hill: University of North Carolina Press, 2001), 27, 36.

4. "confusing and troublesome . . . like a slave": Orville W. Taylor, *Negro Slavery in Arkansas* (Durham: Duke University Press, 1958), 253. The number of free African Americans in Arkansas was smaller at every census than in any other slave state. The greatest single concentration was in North Fork Township, Marion County, along the Missouri state line, an agricultural colony on the North Fork of the White River; this may be the area to which the Brown family retreated following the 1859 expulsion. Some historians believe there were a number of slaves in Fort Smith who went unrecorded by the federal census. "a white man": Marzetta Brown Wesley (Thomas Jefferson Brown's granddaughter), interview by author, Okmulgee, Oklahoma, November 22, 2005; *Compendium of the Seventh Census, 1850* (Washington, DC: A.O.P. Nicholson, Public Printer, 1854), 83; 1860 Federal Census Schedule, Slave Population, Town of Helena, Arkansas; Taylor, *Negro Slavery in Arkansas*, 53; 252–53.

5. On Irish labor in the urban South, see Gleeson, *Irish in the South*, chapter 3. 1860 Federal Census, Arkansas (Population), 593; Arkansas (Agriculture), 247. Ashmore, *Arkansas*, 72–73; Taylor, *Negro Slavery in Arkansas*, 53, 240–44, 252–53. 1860 United States Federal Census Schedule, Slave Population, Town of Helena, Arkansas. United States Federal Census of 1860 (Population), xiii.

6. Leo Huff, "Guerrillas, Jayhawkers, and Bushwhackers in Northern Arkansas during the Civil War," *Arkansas Historical Quarterly* 24 (1965): 127–48; "Ku Klux hunted the militia": David Y. Thomas, *Arkansas in War and Reconstruction* (Little Rock: United Daughters of the Confederacy, 1926), 421. "fair-skinned foreigners . . .": Ashmore, *Arkansas*, 96. On postemancipation Arkansas, see Anne J. Bailey and Daniel E. Sutherland, eds., *Beyond Battles and Leaders: Arkansas in the Civil War* (Fayetteville: University of Arkansas Press, 2000). Thurman Brown interview. See "Negro Soldiers," *New York Times*, July 31, 1863. This emigration effort preceded the "exoduster" movement of the late 1870s. See Nell Irvin Painter, *Exodusters:*

Black Migration to Kansas after Reconstruction (1977; New York: Norton, 1992); Randy Finley, *From Slavery to Uncertain Freedom: The Freedmen's Bureau in Arkansas, 1865–1869* (Fayetteville: University of Arkansas Press, 1996), 7. Two decades later, back-to-Africa "fever" took hold in Arkansas in the 1880s and 1890s, drawing on the history of the American Colonization Society in Liberia. More Liberian emigrants left from Arkansas than any other state in the last decades of the nineteenth century. See Kenneth Barnes, *Journey of Hope: The Back-to-Africa Movement in Arkansas in the Late 1800s* (Chapel Hill: University of North Carolina Press, 2004), and Michele Mitchell, *Righteous Propagation: African Americans and the Politics of Racial Destiny after Reconstruction* (Chapel Hill: University of North Carolina Press, 2004), chapter 1.

7. "half Irishman": Thurman Brown interview. "the year of freedom": Creek freedwoman Sweetie Ivery Wagoner, Age 79, Muskogee, Oklahoma, *The WPA Oklahoma Slave Narratives*, ed. T. Lindsay Baker and Julie P. Baker (Norman: University of Oklahoma Press, 1996), 442. "I have this day . . . mother Yellow": Register of Marriages, 1864–1866, Records of the Bureau of Refugees, Freedmen, and Abandoned Lands (Record Group 105) FOR-A, National Archives, Washington, DC, quoted in Finley, *From Slavery to Uncertain Freedom*, 19. "all marriages": General John W. Sprague, March 31, 1866, Circular, Records of the Assistant Commissioner for the State of Arkansas Bureau of Refugees, Freedmen, and Abandoned Lands, 1865–69, vol. 22 (Circulars and Circular Letters Received, May 1865–February 1868), National Archives M-979, quoted in Finley, *From Slavery to Uncertain Freedom*, 38. "sexual violation": *Arkansas Daily Gazette*, December 10, 1868, quoted ibid., 38.

8. "freedmen who consorted": Hodes, *White Women, Black Men*, 158.

9. "tested their freedom": Finley, *From Slavery to Uncertain Freedom*, xiii. "adamantly refused" and Fort Smith barbers: ibid., 44. "African, Ethiopian": Sterling Stuckey, *Slave Culture: Nationalist Theory and the Foundations of Black America* (New York: Oxford University Press, 1987), 200.

10. Marzetta Brown Wesley interview; Tom Brown (Thomas Jefferson Brown's son), interview by author, Okmulgee, Oklahoma, November 23, 2005. Thomas Jefferson Brown's census classification: "Jeff Brown," United States Federal Census, Year: 1920; Census Place: *Yeager, Hughes, Oklahoma*; Roll: T625_1465; Page: 6B; Enumeration District: 79; Image: 1153. "They didn't like . . .": "Mary Peters," George P. Rawick, ed., *The American Slave: A Composite Autobiography, Arkansas Narratives*, vol. 10 (Westport, CT: Greenwood, 1972), 323, 328. On population growth, see Joel Williamson, *New People: Miscegenation and Mulattoes in the United States* (New York: Free Press, 1980), 65. "increasing the color spectrum" Finley, *From Slavery to Uncertain Freedom*, 45.

11. Tom Brown interview. Thurman Brown interview. In the wake of the Civil War, weakened infrastructure lent itself to perceived lawlessness in Indian Territory.

This, in turn, attracted settlers "on the run" from nearby states. The federal government regularly employed black Indians to enforce U.S. law in the Territory. See Art Burton, *Black, Red, and Deadly: Black and Indian Gunfighters in the Indian Territory, 1870–1907* (Austin: Eakin, 1991). On "divorce-seekers," see Daniel F. Littlefield Jr. and Lonnie E. Underhill, "Divorce Seeker's Paradise: Oklahoma Territory, 1890–1897," *Arizona and the West* 17, no. 1 (1975): 21–34.

12. "got on his own . . . interpreted": Thurman Brown interview. See Kent Carter, *The Dawes Commission and the Allotment of the Five Civilized Tribes, 1893–1914* (Orem, UT: Ancestry, 1999).

13. "a very rugged . . .": "An Interview with Mr. E. L. Fisher" and "Legend & Story Form," Interview 8983, October 25, 1937, *Indian-Pioneer Papers*, 30: 73–78, Oklahoma Historical Society and Western History Collections, University of Oklahoma.

14. Ibid.; "An Interview with Fred Brown," Interview 4123, May 20, 1937, *Indian-Pioneer Papers*, 12: 76, Oklahoma Historical Society and Western History Collections, University of Oklahoma. "Life of Polly Barnett," Interview 5510, April 15, 1837, *Indian-Pioneer Papers*, 5: 463, Oklahoma Historical Society and Western History Collections, University of Oklahoma; Thurman Brown interview. "An Interview with Nancy Towery," Interview 12050, December 15, 1937, *Indian-Pioneer Papers*, 91: 451–62, Oklahoma Historical Society and Western History Collections, University of Oklahoma.

15. Interview with Paro Bruner; Interview with Chaney Wallace, "In the matter of the Application of Chaney Wallace née Brown et al. for enrollment as citizen of the Creek Nation," Bixby, Okmulgee, OK, March 26, 1901, Applications for Enrollment of the Commission to the Five Civilized Tribes, 1898–1914, NARA M1301, Record Group 75, Case Number 41.

16. Thurman Brown interview; "Interview with Caesar Simon," reprinted in *Frontier Freedman's Journal*, Spring 2000. On Tecumseh Bruner, see also "An Interview with Robert Johnson of Spendling," Interview 7451, August 31, 1937, *Indian-Pioneer Papers* 48: 350–53; Art T. Burton, *Black Gun, Silver Star: The Life and Legend of Frontier Marshal Bass Reeves* (Lincoln: University of Nebraska Press, 2006), 97. "inescapable economic dimension": Andrés Reséndez, *Changing National Identities at the Frontier: Texas and New Mexico, 1800–1850* (New York: Cambridge University Press, 2005), 129. In the southeast United States, see Perdue, *Mixed Blood Indians*; Richard Godbeer, "Eroticizing the Middle Ground: Anglo-Indian Sexual Relations along the Eighteenth-Century Frontier," in *Sex, Love, Race: Crossing Boundaries in North American History*, ed. Martha Hodes (New York: New York University Press, 1999), 91–111; and Yarbrough, *Race and the Cherokee Nation*.

17. "An Interview with Joseph Bruner" (president of the American Federation of Indians), Interview 13105, February 28, 1938, *Indian-Pioneer Papers*, 12: 318–38,

Oklahoma Historical Society and Western History Collections, University of
Oklahoma; "An Interview with William M. Bruner," Interview 6890, July 20, 1937,
12: 328–33, ibid.; Thurman Brown interview; "since the first Spanish entradas":
Zellar, *African Creeks*, xvii. See Pekka Hämäläinen, *The Comanche Empire* (New
Haven: Yale University Press, 2008), 152–53.

18. On the subject of Indian enslavement in North America, see Snyder, *Slavery in
Indian Country*; Andrés Reséndez, *The Other Slavery: The Uncovered Story of
Indian Enslavement in America* (New York: Houghton Mifflin Harcourt, 2016); and
Alan Gallay, *The Indian Slave Trade: The Rise of the English Empire in the
American South, 1670–1717* (New Haven: Yale University Press, 2003). On the
subject of Native American slaveholding of African-descended people in the U.S.
South, see above, note 2. On African Creek communities during the immediate
postemancipation period, see Zellar, *African Creeks*, 34. See also Miles, *Ties That
Bind*; Naylor, *African Cherokees in Indian Territory*; Krauthamer, *Black Slaves,
Indian Masters*; and Saunt, *Black, White, and Indian*. "captivity operated": Snyder,
Slavery in Indian Country, 7.

19. "my father's people": "An Interview with Joseph Bruner." Recorded spellings
include Paro, Parrow, Pero, and Payro. The "negro towns" mentioned here
included Arkansas Colored, Canadian Colored, and North Fork Colored, all three
established in the 1870s and 1880s before the development of the "all-black" towns.
See Zellar, *African Creeks*, 98, 159.

20. "colored citizen . . . An able argument": *Our Brother in Red* (Cherokee Nation),
April 12, 1890.

21. "the Territory began": "An Interview with Mr. E. L. Fisher" and "Legend & Story
Form," 30: 203–6; Zellar, *African Creeks*, 161–62; Carter, *Dawes Commission*, 33–68.
See also Chang, *Color of the Land*. On parallel developments in New Mexico
Territory, see Pablo Mitchell, *Coyote Nation: Sexuality, Race, and Conquest in
Modernizing New Mexico, 1880–1920* (Chicago: University of Chicago Press, 2005).

22. The Curtis Act of 1898 was an amendment to the Dawes Act of 1887; Carter, *Dawes
Commission*, 34–38. On "intruders," see ibid.; "Records relating to Intruders, 1895–
1909," Record Group 75, Records of the Five Civilized Tribes Agency, Southwest
National Archives, Fort Worth, Texas.

23. Paro Bruner had argued that many "good citizens" were left off the roll because
Dunn had not made the effort to collect names himself and had sent the roll to
Washington before town chiefs were able to collect all names. "one of the issues":
Carter, *Dawes Commission*, 53. "omitted": Bruner, quoted ibid., 46. "failed to get
the names right": Bruner, quoted in Zellar, *African Creeks*, 218.

24. "descriptive," "Surnames are changed": Carter, *Dawes Commission*, 49. "the facts
known": Letters and Documents Concerning Creek Citizenship, October 11,
1874—December 18, 1895 (Records 24947 and 24949, CRN 3), and February 28,
1895—October 25, 1910 (Records 25216, 25411, and 25413, CRN 4), Creek National

Tribal Records, Oklahoma Historical Society, quoted ibid., 202. See also Carter, *Dawes Commission*, 40–49.

25. Interview with Paro Bruner; Interview with Chaney Wallace, "In the matter of the Application of Chaney Wallace née Brown et al. for enrollment as citizen of the Creek Nation."

26. Ibid. On Muskogee office, see Carter, *Dawes Commission*, 138.

27. Writing in 1901, Chaney was urgently concerned with proving the family's presence on the 1867 Dunn roll. This, along with documentation of her mother, Aurelia, on the "Dead Freedmen Rolls," suggests that her mother was in fact listed as a freedwoman of the Creek Nation but may have qualified, too, for "Creek, by Blood." Letter from Chaney Wallas (Wallace) to Rena McNack, Wewoka, Indian Territory, March 29, 1901, transcript (in possession of author).

28. Letter from Chaney Wallas (Wallace) to Rena McNack, Wewoka, Indian Territory, March 29, 1901, transcript (in possession of author). "seeking out bona fide citizens": Zellar, *African Creeks*, 217; and Carter, *Dawes Commission*, 46. Interview with Paro Bruner; Interview with Chaney Wallace, "In the matter of the Application of Chaney Wallace née Brown et al. for enrollment as citizen of the Creek Nation."

29. "blood quantum": Angie Debo, *And Still the Waters Run* (Princeton: Princeton University Press, 1940), 47–49. "the only distinction": Carter, *Dawes Commission*, 49, 387–88. "I have seen many a one": "Lists of Applicants and Docket Books of the Creek Citizenship Commission," 1888–1896, 7RA68, Roll 2, Report of the Commissioner to the Five Civilized Tribes, Record Group 75, Records of the Bureau of Indian Affairs, National Archives, Southwest Region, Fort Worth, TX, quoted in Zellar, *African Creeks*, 202.

30. "The Democrats Carried Oklahoma," *New York Times*, January 2, 1907, 1.

31. This fight to stop allotment was led by Creek Chitto Harjo ("Crazy Snake"). Harjo and his followers were dissatisfied with the 1866 treaties and later laws concerning the Creeks. "Crazy Snake's War," *New York Times*, March 30, 1909. "share equally": "An Interview with Joseph Bruner," Second Interview 6654, "Seven miles Northwest of Sapulpa," July 13 and 23, 1937, *Indian-Pioneer Papers*, 12: 315–17, Oklahoma Historical Society and Western History Collections, University of Oklahoma. See also Kay M. Teall, *Black History in Oklahoma: A Resource Book* (Oklahoma City: Oklahoma City Schools, 1971), 146–47; Carter, *Dawes Commission*, 56; and David Lewis Jr. and Ann T. Jordan, *Creek Indian Medicine Ways: The Enduring Power of Mvskoke Religion* (Albuquerque: University of New Mexico Press, 2002), 19.

32. Thurman refers to "Poppa," his father and Thomas Jefferson Brown's son, Lemuel. Thurman Brown interview by author. On Mekasukey Academy, see Kevin Mulroy, *The Seminole Freedmen: A History* (Norman: University of Oklahoma Press, 2016), 288–89. Thurman Brown, interview by author.

33. "The State of 'Sequoyah,'" *New York Times*, October 5, 1905. On the Negro Protective League of Oklahoma, see Arthur Tolson, "The Negro in Oklahoma

Territory, 1889–1907: A Study in Racial Discrimination," Ph.D. diss., University of
Oklahoma, 1966, 110–44. "for the purpose of": *Oklahoma Guide*, August 31, 1905,
quoted ibid., 110.

34. "observe the usages and customs of each tribe" and matrilineal citizenship: Carter,
Dawes Commission, 45. "See, if your momma was a Creek": Thurman Brown
interview.

35. Thurman Brown interview. Carter, *Dawes Commission*, 45.

36. As part of a local history project, in 1985 Marzetta Wesley wrote and submitted a
short family history of the Browns to Okmulgee County. "some training . . . School
and Church": "Brown Family," 1: 587. "too late": Tom Brown interview.

37. Tom Brown interview; Odevia Brown Field (Thomas Jefferson Brown's
granddaughter), interview by author, Okmulgee, Oklahoma, November 26, 2005.

38. "sufficient land . . .": Dawes Commission *Report*, 1894, 82–87, quoted in Debo, *And
Still the Waters Run*, 32. "wild, speculative, active spirit": Debo, *And Still the
Waters Run*, 88.

39. The Restrictions Bill, as it was known, passed in May of 1908 and "removed the
restrictions from all lands, except homesteads, of citizens of more than half and less
than three-quarters, but it retained restrictions on homesteads of persons, including
minors, with more than half blood and all full-bloods until April 26, 1931." As Angie
Debo noted in 1940, "The Dawes rolls were to be accepted as conclusive in
determining the quantum of Indian blood." Debo, *And Still the Waters Run*, 90;
Carter, *Dawes Commission*, 176; Charles J. Kappler, *Indian Affairs, Laws, and
Treaties* (Washington, DC: Government Printing Office, 1904), 1: 649, 663–64, 764,
772, 788. Further bolstering the protection of "fullbloods," "the so-called McCumber
amendment to the Five Tribes Act of April 26, 1906, extended the inalienability of the
entire allotment of fullbloods for twenty-five years from the passage of the law, and
provided that these restrictions could be removed only by act of Congress." Debo,
And Still the Waters Run, 90. See also Teall, *Black History in Oklahoma*, 137–38.

40. "tells of the nation choosing": Zellar, *African Creeks*, xviii. "White men's
countries": Marilyn Lake and Henry Reynolds, *Drawing the Global Colour Line:
White Men's Countries and the International Challenge of Racial Equality* (New
York: Cambridge University Press, 2008), 6.

41. Marzetta Brown Wesley interview with author.

42. "an island surrounded by land"; *Muskogee Cimeter*, 1904, quoted in Franklin,
Journey toward Hope; Zellar, *African Creeks*, 237. "never rent, lease, or sell":
Okemah Ledger, August 31, 1911, quoted in Crockett, *Black Towns*, 167.

43. William Bittle and Gilbert Geis, *The Longest Way Home: Chief Alfred C. Sam's
Back-to-Africa Movement* (Detroit: Wayne State University Press, 1964), 23.

44. Southwestern Oil and Gas Company Prospectus, c. 1949, in possession of Barbara
(Brown) Player, Reston, Virginia. Barbara (Brown) Player, e-mail message to
author, July 15, 2016.

45. "When you get as much money as Johnny": Quoted in Sigmund Sameth, "Creek Negroes: A Study of Race Relations," M.A. thesis, University of Oklahoma, 1940; Bittle and Geis, *Longest Way Home*, 23.
46. Thurman Brown interview (emphasis added).
47. Ibid.

2. Passing for Black

1. "Grandpa Coleman . . . Monroe": Marzetta Brown Wesley and Odevia Brown Field, interview by author, Okmulgee, Oklahoma, November 22, 2005. "Monroe Coleman," United States Federal Census, Year: 1870; Census Place: Township 15, Chickasaw, Mississippi; Roll: M593_724; Page: 219A; Image: 315478; Family History Library Film: 552223. "Paradise": *Daily Ardmoreite*, November 14, 1902, 1. "white-looking": Wesley and Field interview.
2. On the dissolution of Indian Territory, see especially David A. Chang, *The Color of the Land: Race, Nation, and the Politics and Landownership in Oklahoma, 1832–1929* (Chapel Hill: University of North Carolina Press, 2010). On nineteenth century migrants, see James D. Miller, *South by Southwest: Planter Emigration and Identity in the Slave South* (Charlottesville: University of Virginia Press, 2002), 6.
3. On Kansas "exodus," see Nell Irvin Painter, *Exodusters: Black Migration Kansas after Reconstruction* (1977; New York: Norton, 1992). On emigration "fever" in Arkansas, see Kenneth C. Barnes, *Journey of Hope: The Back-to-Africa Movement in Arkansas in the Late 1800s* (Chapel Hill: University of North Carolina Press, 2004). On the press and nationalism: Benedict Anderson, *Imagined Communities: Reflections on the Origin and Spread of Nationalism* (New York: Verso, 1983), chapter 3. For early historical treatment of Oklahoma's black towns, see, for instance, Arthur Tolson, *The Black Oklahomans: A History, 1541–1972* (New Orleans: Edwards Print, 1974); Norman L. Crockett, *The Black Towns* (Lawrence: Regents Press of Kansas, 1979).
4. "escape" and "came by train": Marzetta Brown Wesley and Odevia Brown Field interview. "new people": Joel Williamson, *New People: Miscegenation and Mulattoes in the United States* (New York: Free Press, 1980). On sexual slavery, reproductive labor, and family formation, see, for instance, Daina Ramey Berry, *Swing the Sickle for the Harvest Is Ripe: Gender and Slavery in Antebellum Georgia* (Urbana: University of Illinois Press, 2007); Nell Painter, *Southern History across the Color Line* (Chapel Hill: University of North Carolina Press, 2002); Bernie D. Jones, *Fathers of Conscience: Mixed-Race Inheritance in the Antebellum South* (Athens: University of Georgia Press, 2009). "racial amalgamation" and "race war": Charles Dew, *Apostles of Disunion: Southern Secession Commissioners and the Causes of the Civil War* (Charlottesville: University of Virginia Press, 2001), 78–79. "whites had invented . . . dire implications . . . rising rage for identity . . . losing the color line": Joel Williamson, *A Rage for Order: Black-White Relations in the American South since Emancipation* (New York:

Oxford University Press, 1986), 33–34. Southern class structure: Martin Ruef and Ben Fletcher, "Legacies of American Slavery: Status Attainment among Southern Blacks after Emancipation," *Social Forces* 82 (2003): 445–80.

5. "revolution": Matthew Pratt Guterl, *The Color of Race in America, 1900–1940* (Cambridge: Harvard University Press, 2001), 156. "the relentless search": Joseph R. Roach, *Cities of the Dead: Circum-Atlantic Performance* (New York: Columbia University Press, 1996), 6.

6. Important exceptions include Williamson, *New People*; Painter, *Southern History across the Color Line*; Jones, *Fathers of Conscience*; Guterl, *Color of Race in America*; David Levering Lewis, *W. E. B. Du Bois: A Biography* (New York: Henry Holt, 2009). On chauvinism, see, for instance, the reception of Lawrence Otis Graham, *Our Kind of People: Inside America's Black Upper Class* (New York: Harper, 1999). See Andrea Lee, "Black Like Us," *New York Times*, February 21, 1999.

7. "Monroe Coleman": 1870 U.S. Census. Marzetta Brown Wesley and Odevia Brown Field interview. "documentation of sex . . .": Martha Hodes, "Racism and the Craft of History," *Reviews in American History* 26 (1998): 510–15, 515.

8. "family trust . . . Wright's name": Anthony Kaye, *Joining Places: Slave Neighborhoods in the Old South* (Chapel Hill: University of North Carolina Press, 2007), 85. Coleman family history: "Oral history with the Honorable J. P. Coleman," former governor of Mississippi and chief judge (ret.), the U.S. Court of Appeals for the Fifth Circuit (1981), Center for Oral History and Cultural Heritage, University of Southern Mississippi.

9. J. P. Coleman, *The Robert Coleman Family from Virginia to Texas, 1652–1965* (Ackerman, MS: James P. Coleman, 1965), 11. Diary of Mrs. Jennie I. Coleman (written in the 1920s), published ibid., 35. "I am much pleased": Alexander Donelson to Andrew Jackson, October 9, 1811, *The Papers of Andrew Jackson*, 6 vols., ed. Harold D. Moser, Sharon McPherson, and Charles F. Bryan, Jr. (Knoxville: University of Tennessee Press, 1980), 2: 266–67, quoted in Adam Rothman, *Slave Country: American Expansion and the Origins of the Deep South* (Cambridge: Harvard University Press, 2007), 45. On Pickens: Hugh C. Bailey, "Israel Pickens, Peoples' Politician," *Alabama Review* 17 (1964): 83–101, quoted in Rothman, *Slave Country*, 165.

10. "indigenous migrations . . .": Rothman, *Slave Country*, 18. "granted passports": "Oral history with the Honorable J. P. Coleman." Greene County: Greene County History, Eutaw Public Library, Eutaw, Alabama. "surrogation": Roach, *Cities of the Dead*, 4.

11. See Thomas Hietala, *Manifest Design: American Exceptionalism and Empire, Revised Edition* (Ithaca, NY: Cornell University Press, 2003), chapter 2. The fiction of the independent white frontiersman depended on the historical erasure of African Americans from the American West. Historian Kenneth Wiggins Porter wrote in 1971, "Historian after historian has in one way or another indicated his belief that the Negro and the frontier were naturally incompatible." See Kenneth

Wiggins Porter, *The Negro on the American Frontier* (New York: Arno, 1971), 3–4; Hietala, *Manifest Design*, chapter 2. "empire for liberty": Reginald Horsman, *Race and Manifest Destiny: The Origins of American Racial Anglo-Saxism* (Cambridge: Harvard University Press, 1981), 105. Rothman, *Slave Country*, 219.

12. "empire for slavery": Ira Berlin, *Generations of Captivity: A History of African-American Slaves* (Cambridge: Belknap Press of Harvard University Press, 2003), 163. See also Rothman, *Slave Country*; Joan E. Cashin, *A Family Venture: Men and Women on the Southern Frontier* (Baltimore: Johns Hopkins University Press, 1994); Randolph B. Campbell, *An Empire for Slavery: The Peculiar Institution in Texas, 1821–1865* (Baton Rouge: Louisiana State University Press, 1991); and, on clearing of fields, Charles S. Syndor, *Slavery in Mississippi* (Gloucester, MA: Peter Smith, 1933). "a Negro boy": Coleman, *Coleman Family*, 67; "Oral history with the Honorable J. P. Coleman." Narrative about Trim (Coleman): "Colemans," in Greene County History, Eutaw Public Library, Eutaw, Alabama, 98. Wiley Coleman et al., Coleman, *Coleman Family*.

13. "Some planters held back": Carl Schurz, *Speeches, Correspondence, and Political Papers of Carl Schurz*, 6 vols., ed. Frederic Bancroft (New York: Putnam, 1913), 6: 17. On racial violence and sexual slavery, see above, note 4.

14. The Mississippi Black Codes, passed by the state legislature at the end of 1865, included apprenticeship laws that obliged freedpeople, "free Negroes," and "mulattoes" under the age of eighteen who were deemed "orphans"—or whose parents were deemed unable to support them—to work for planters without pay. Most significant, the former owners of these minors were given first preference. Eric Foner, *Reconstruction: America's Unfinished Revolution, 1863–1877* (New York: Harper, 1988), 201. Matthew Pratt Guterl notes that the term "apprenticeship" had multiple meanings during this period. "It could refer to a state of legal paternal guardianship or to a period of craft training, or it could be shorthand for 'former slave,' as uttered by former 'masters'—an expression, therefore, of the hope that one could take . . . freedmen and reduce them . . . to some poor measure of their previous existence." Matthew Pratt Guterl, *American Mediterranean: Southern Slaveholders in the Age of Emancipation* (Cambridge: Harvard University Press, 2008), 121. Descendants' recollections: Marzetta Brown Wesley and Odevia Brown Field interview.

15. "Lots and lots": W. E. B. Du Bois, *The Autobiography of W. E. B. Du Bois: A Soliloquy on Viewing My Life from the Last Decade of Its First Century* (New York: International Publishers, 1968), 39. "modishly dressed," "sons and daughters," "conditions close to poverty," "affluent sons . . . set the tone": Lewis, *Du Bois*, 51. Du Bois's recollection of Edmondson: Du Bois, *A Soliloquy*, 111. "mulattoes seemed to be everywhere": Lewis, *Du Bois*, 51. "new people": Charles Chesnutt, *House behind the Cedars* (Boston: Houghton Mifflin, 1901), 57, 83. Williamson, *New People*, xi.

16. On "fancies" and the "fancy girl trade," see, for instance, Brenda Stevenson, *Life in Black and White: Family and Community in the Slave South* (New York: Oxford

University Press, 1996), 180–81; Brenda Stevenson, "What's Love Got to Do with It?: Concubinage and Enslaved Women and Girls in the Antebellum South," *Journal of African American History* 98 (2013): 99–125; Walter Johnson, *Soul by Soul: Life Inside the Antebellum Slave Market* (Cambridge: Harvard University Press, 1999), 113–15; Daina Ramey Berry, *The Price of Their Pound of Flesh: The Value of the Enslaved, from Womb to Grave, in the Building of a Nation* (New York: Beacon, 2017), 18; Edward E. Baptist, "'Cuffy,' 'Fancy Maids,' and 'One-Eyed Men': Rape, Commodification, and the Domestic Slave Trade in the United States," *American Historical Review* 106 (2001): 1619–50. See also Jennifer L. Morgan, *Laboring Women: Reproduction and Gender in New World Slavery* (Philadelphia: University of Pennsylvania Press, 2004). On white anxiety and the growth of the "mulatto" population, see Williamson, *New People*, 24–25; Williamson, *Rage for Order*, 32. "What, after all . . .": Stevenson, *Life in Black and White*, 180–81. "finest specimens . . .": James W.C. Pennington, *The Fugitive Blacksmith; or Events in the History of James W. C. Pennington, Pastor of a Presbyterian Church, New York, Formerly a Slave in the State of Maryland, United States* (London: Charles Gilpin, 1849), v–vi. "Thomas Edmondson," United States Federal Census, Year: 1860; Census Place: Police District 1, Carroll, Mississippi; Roll: M653_578; Page: 846; Family History Library Film: 803578. "not one mulatto in twenty": Williamson, *New People*, 25.

17. "in almost every community . . . casual connections": Williamson, *Rage for Order*, 33.

18. "upbringing . . .": ibid., 33. Samuel Townsend history: ibid., 32–33. "perhaps for two generations . . . mulatto progeny": ibid., 33, 35–36. On legal challenges to "mulatto" heirs, see ibid.; Jones, *Fathers of Conscience*; Ariela Gross, *What Blood Won't Tell: A History of Race on Trial in America* (Cambridge: Harvard University Press, 2008); Painter, *Southern History across the Color Line*.

19. "clear trace": Williamson, *Rage for Order*, 35–36. "Ransom Edmondson," United States Federal Census, Year: 1870; Census Place: Township 20, Range 5, Carroll, Mississippi; Roll: M593_723; Page: 686A; Image: 338958; Family History Library Film: 552222. "Ransom Edmondson," United States Federal Census, Year: 1880; Census Place: Leflore, Mississippi; Roll: 654; Family History Film: 1254654; Page: 259A; Enumeration District: 135. "black harem": Mary Boykin Chesnut, quoted in Williamson, *Rage for Order*, 34. See also Painter, *Southern History across the Color Line*, chapter 2.

20. "there were mulattoes": Williamson, *Rage for Order*, 36. "rising rage" and "a civilization on the make": ibid., 34. "between masters and slaves": ibid. 35. "race mixing": Joel Williamson, *The Crucible of Race: Black-White Relations in the American South since Emancipation* (New York: Oxford University Press, 1984), 40. "race war" and "Racial amalgamation": Dew, *Apostles of Disunion*, 78–79.

21. See W. E. B. Du Bois, *Black Reconstruction in America, 1860–1880* (1935; New York: Free Press, 1998); Foner, *Reconstruction*; Amy Dru Stanley, *From Bondage to Contract: Wage Labor, Marriage, and the Market in the Age of Slave Emancipation*

(New York: Cambridge University Press, 1998); Saidiya Hartman, *Scenes of Subjection: Terror, Slavery, and Self-Making in Nineteenth-Century America* (New York: Oxford University Press, 1997). "real" freedom: Painter, *Exodusters*, 4.

22. On reversals of "redemption," including vagrancy laws, convict labor, etc., see Frederick Douglass, "Southern Barbarism," Speech on the occasion of the Twenty-Fourth Anniversary of Emancipation in the District of Columbia, Washington, DC, April 16, 1886, in *Frederick Douglass: Selected Speeches and Writings*, ed. Philip S. Foner, abridged and adapted by Yuval Taylor (Chicago: Lawrence Hill, 1999), 696–705; Du Bois, *Black Reconstruction*; Ida B. Wells, *Southern Horrors and Other Writings: The Anti-Lynching Campaign of Ida B. Wells, 1892–1900*, ed. Jacqueline Jones Royster (New York: Bedford/St. Martin's, 1996); Foner, *Reconstruction*, chapter 12; David Oshinsky, *"Worse than Slavery": Parchman Farm and the Ordeal of Jim Crow Justice* (New York: Free Press, 1996); Douglas Blackmon, *Slavery by Another Name: The Re-Enslavement of Black Americans from the Civil War to World War II* (New York: Anchor, 2009). Meridian murders: David Blight, *Race and Reunion: The Civil War in American Memory* (Cambridge: Belknap Press of Harvard University Press, 2001), 114; Foner, *Reconstruction*, 396, 428.

23. "suffered gross mistreatment": Hannibal B. Johnson, *Acres of Aspiration: The All-Black Towns in Oklahoma* (Woodway, TX: Eakin, 2002), 15. See also Martha Hodes, *White Women, Black Men: Illicit Sex in the Nineteenth-Century South* (New Haven: Yale University Press, 1999); Oshinsky, *Worse than Slavery*; Blackmon, *Slavery by Another Name*.

24. "Ransom Edmondson," 1870 U.S. Census; "curiously dignified": Du Bois, *Soliloquy*, 111.

25. "Kiziah Miller," United States Federal Census, Year: 1880; Census Place: Beat 5, Clay, Mississippi; Roll: 645; Family History Film: 1254645; Page: 304B; Enumeration District: 046; Image: 0030. "Monroe Coleman," United States Federal Census, Year: 1880; Census Place: Beat 5, Clay, Mississippi; Roll: 645; Family History Film: 1254645; Page: 306A; Enumeration District: 046; Image: 0033. "Monroe Coleman," 1870 U.S. Census.

26. On the construction of race and racial identities in the postemancipation period, see Barbara J. Fields, "Ideology and Race in American History," in *Region, Race, and Reconstruction: Essays in Honor of C. Vann Woodward*, ed. J. Morgan Kousser and James M. McPherson (New York: Oxford University Press, 1982), 143–77; Williamson, *New People*; Martha Hodes, "Fractions and Fictions in the United States Census of 1890," in *Haunted by Empire: Geographies of Intimacy in North American History*, ed. Ann Laura Stoler (Durham: Duke University Press, 2006), 240–70; Gross, *What Blood Won't Tell*, 140–77. On class in the postemancipation era, see also Ruef and Fletcher, "Legacies of American Slavery." Using data from fourteen hundred ex-slaves and free African Americans, sociologists Martin Ruef and Blen Fletcher concluded that "over time, black status attainment became largely decoupled from

the internal hierarchy of slavery." They cite "mediating effects," including "the Freedmen Bureau's educational interventions and the black diaspora," which served "to curtail the reproduction of antebellum status." "Some of my relatives": Lomie (Davis) Reed, conversation with Cecil Cade and Mark A. Phillips, March 22, 1988 (Houston, Texas), audiocassette, Alexander Davis Family Papers, Box 1, Manuscript Collections, Mississippi Department of Archives and History.

27. "moved on the court house . . .": "The Latest Mississippi Massacre," *National Republican*, March 22, 1886, 2. "O God": Ida Wells, diary, March 18, 1886, quoted in Paula J. Giddings, *Ida: A Sword among Lions: Ida B. Wells and the Campaign against Lynching* (New York: Amistad, 2008), 91. "In any other country": Douglass, "Southern Barbarism," 698.

28. For a colonial and indigenous comparison to this event, see Philip Deloria, *Playing Indian* (New Haven: Yale University Press, 1998), chapter 1. "much of the crime . . . white citizen": Douglass, "Southern Barbarism," 699.

29. "data source . . . racial identities . . . black crime statistics" and prison population: Khalil Muhammad, *The Condemnation of Blackness: Race, Crime, and the Making of Modern Urban America* (Cambridge: Harvard University Press, 2011), 4; "refashioned . . . racial category": ibid, 5.

30. "If you ask": Thulani Davis, *My Confederate Kinfolk: A Twenty-First Century Freedwoman Discovers Her Roots* (New York: Basic Civitas, 2011), 9. "racial amalgamation": Dew, *Apostles of Disunion*, 79.

31. On former slaveowning women and "mulatto" children, see Painter, *Southern History across the Color Line*, chapter 2. "the unnamed relative . . . coeds" and "pinhead of privilege": Lewis, *Du Bois*, 51.

32. *Fisk Herald*, August 1886, 6; *Fisk Herald*, February 1888, 12. Edmondson in Galveston: Ransom C. Edmondson, Circular letter from Ransom C. Edmondson to W. E. B. Du Bois, September 28, 1890. W. E. B. Du Bois Papers (MS 312). Special Collections and University Archives, University of Massachusetts Amherst Libraries.

33. "color hierarchies": Michele Mitchell, *Righteous Propagation: African Americans and the Politics of Racial Destiny after Reconstruction* (Chapel Hill: University of North Carolina Press, 2004), 207. "an example of the rapidity . . . race and color": Ralph Ellison, "Going to the Territory," *The Collected Essays of Ralph Ellison*, ed. John Callahan (New York: Modern Library, 2003), 604.

34. "estimates regarding the percentage": Mitchell, *Righteous Propagation*, 212. "of mixed blood": Charles Chesnutt, "What Is a White Man?" *Essays and Speeches*, ed. Joseph McElrath Jr., Robert Leitz III, and Jesse Crisler (Stanford: Stanford University Press, 1999), 73. thirty percent and "Afro-American": T. Thomas Fortune, "Race Absorption," *A.M.E. Church Review* 18, no. 1 (1901): 54–66, esp. 59, quoted in Mitchell, *Righteous Propagation*, 212. *Social Protest Thought in the African Methodist Episcopal Church, 1862–1939*, ed. Stephen Ward Angell and Anthony B. Pinn (Knoxville: University of Tennessee Press, 2000), 56. "no such

thing": Pauline Hopkins, *Contending Forces* (1900; New York: Oxford University Press, 1988), 151. "quite possible" W. E. B. Du Bois, *The Health and Physique of the Negro American* (Atlanta: Atlanta University Press, 1906), 30.

35. "achingly notice[d]": Sophia Cox Johnson, quoted in Mitchell, *Righteous Propagation*, 207. On race and reproduction, see Jennifer Morgan, *Laboring Women: Reproduction and Gender in New World Slavery* (Philadelphia: University of Pennsylvania Press, 2004); Deborah Gray White, *Ar'n't I a Woman? Female Slaves in the Plantation South* (New York: Norton, 1999); Berry, *Swing the Sickle*. "immoral, hierarchical": Mitchell, *Righteous Propagation*, 207.

36. "walking indictments": Lewis, *Du Bois*, 51. "some blacks . . . unity": Williamson, *Rage for Order*, 50. "line of division": ibid., 215.

37. "valuable degree of unity": ibid., 50. "whyte mans children": James Dubose to Coppinger, February 12, 1891, ACS Papers, ser. 1A, container 279, vol. 282, quoted in Mitchell, *Righteous Propagation*, 43. "made no secret . . . 'mission to perform' ": Mitchell, *Righteous Propagation*, 37. See also Edward Wilmot Blyden, "The Call of Providence to the Descendants of Africa in America," in *Liberia's Offering* (New York: John A. Gray, 1862), 67–91. Interracial couples migrating to Liberia: quoted ibid., 42. "I am home bound": Anderson Palmer (Clarksdale, MS) to J. Ormond Wilson, Records of the American Colonization Society, reel 152, 12 March 1911. "wanted to reside" and antebellum precedent: Mitchell, *Righteous Propagation*, 42.

38. "Our mother . . . extended family": Ronne Hartfield, *Another Way Home: The Tangled Roots of Race in One Chicago Family* (Chicago: University of Chicago Press, 2005), xix–xx. "Deprived . . . living colored": ibid., xix.

39. On the development of "racial destiny" in the South and Southwest, see Mitchell, *Righteous Propagation*; Steven Hahn, *A Nation under Our Feet: Black Political Struggles in the Rural South from Slavery to the Great Migration* (Cambridge: Belknap Press of Harvard University Press, 2005). "folk stopped": Davis, *My Confederate Kinfolk*, 9.

40. "The disfranchised . . . deed to power": *National Republican*, March 22, 1886, 2. "most important act . . . to the West": *Chicago Observer*, quoted in *Washington Bee*, August 28, 1886, 1.

41. Memphis lynchings: Ida B. Wells, *Crusade for Justice: The Autobiography of Ida B. Wells* (Chicago: University of Chicago Press, 1991), chapter 6; Giddings, *Ida: A Sword among Lions*, chapter 6; Mia Bay, *To Tell the Truth Freely: The Life of Ida B. Wells* (New York: Hill and Wang, 2010), chapter 3. "what lynching really was . . . down . . . I then began": Wells, *Crusade for Justice*, 64.

42. "for the sake of his wife": Ida B. Wells, "Lynch Law in All Its Phases," address at Boston Tremont Temple, February 13, 1893, published in *Our Day* (Boston: Our Day, 1893), 333–47, reprinted in Ida B. Wells, *The Light of Truth: Writings of an Anti-Lynching Crusader*, ed. Mia Bay (New York: Penguin, 2008), 101. "If you will kill us": *Appeal-Avalanche*, quoted ibid. "The City of Memphis . . . white persons":

Wells, *Free Speech*, quoted in Giddings, *Ida: A Sword among Lions*, 189. See also Ida B. Wells, *Crusade for Justice: The Autobiography of Ida B. Wells*, ed. Alfreda M. Duster (Chicago: University of Chicago Press, 1970), 52. "our first object lesson . . . less than a month": Wells, "Lynch Law," 102. "nation's first . . . movement": Giddings, *Ida: A Sword among Lions*, 189.

43. "hauled him into battle" and "What passed then . . . Jackson was free": Tim Madigan, *The Burning: Massacre, Destruction, and the Tulsa Race Riot of 1921* (New York: St. Martin's, 2003), 12–13.

44. "He thus fortified himself": ibid., 13–14. "became sort of a Colored man": Howell, quoted ibid., xii.

45. "escape from Memphis": Madigan, *The Burning*, 12. Jackson history: Jack Adams, *Autobiography of LTC John (Jack) H. Adams from 1931–2011*, vol. 1 (Bloomington, IN: AuthorHouse, 2012), 30–31. Wilhelmina Guess Howell, quoted in Johnson, *Acres of Aspiration*, xi–xii. *Tulsa Star*, May 30, 1913. "voted with their feet": Leon Litwack, *Trouble in Mind: Black Southerners in the Age of Jim Crow* (New York: Vintage, 1998), 484.

46. James Milton Turner: Arthur Tolson, *Black Oklahomans*, 42. Holcomb letter: Holcomb to S. J. Kirkwood, April 25, 1881, Senate Executive Documents, 47th Cong. Session 1, V (1990), no. 111, p. 2, quoted in Arthur Lincoln Tolson, "The Negro in Oklahoma Territory, 1889–1907: A Study in Racial Discrimination," Ph.D. diss., University of Oklahoma, 1966, 4. Judge J. C. Parker ruling: *The Miscellaneous Documents of the Senate of the United States for the Special Session of the Senate Convened October 10, 1881, and the First Session of the Forty-Seventh Congress* (Washington, DC: Government Printing Office, 1882), 601

47. Eda Ratlaft Lowe ad: *Christian Recorder*, July 5, 1894.

48. On Blair bill: Johnson, *Acres of Aspiration*, 29. "It would afford . . . honored": Murat Halstead, *Junction City Weekly Union*, March 15, 1890, 2, quoted ibid., 30–31. On Eagleson et al., see Jimmie Lewis Franklin, *Journey toward Hope: A History of Blacks in Oklahoma* (Norman: University of Oklahoma Press, 1982), 12. See also ibid., 30–31.

49. On the meeting between Edward McCabe and President Benjamin Harrison, see Kenneth Barnes, *Journey of Hope: The Back-to-Africa Movement in Arkansas in the Late 1800s* (Chapel Hill: University of North Carolina Press, 2004), 85–86. "black state": Tolson, *Black Oklahomans*, 81. "We are here": *Langston City Herald*, April 9, 1890. "We wish to remove": Tolson, *Black Oklahomans*, 78. See also "To Make a Negro State; Western Black Men Organizing in Oklahoma. They Propose to Control That Territory—Equality Demanded—A Race War Threatened," *New York Times*, February 28, 1890; Franklin, *Journey toward Hope*, 40.

50. "on their own": William Cohen, *At Freedom's Edge: Black Mobility and the Southern White Quest for Racial Control, 1861–1915* (Baton Rouge: Louisiana State University Press, 1991), 252. "windswept Oklahoma plains": Johnson, *Acres of Aspiration*, xii.

51. On railroads and appropriation of Indian land, see Chang, *Color of the Land*. "economic motives . . .": Kenneth Marvin Hamilton, *Black Towns and Profit: Promotion and Development in the Trans-Appalachian West, 1877–1915* (Urbana: University of Illinois Press, 1991). On the role of railroads in settlement patterns, see ibid.; Kent Carter, *The Dawes Commission and the Allotment of the Five Civilized Tribes, 1893–1914* (Orem, UT: Ancestry, 1999), 25. "economic motives . . . financial security": Hamilton, *Black Towns and Profit*, 1. See also Richard White and John M. Findlay, *Power and Place in the North American West* (Seattle: University of Washington Press, 2015), 141n44.

52. "Hundreds of letters . . . were started": "To Make a Negro State." "There is nothing . . . emigrate to Oklahoma": *Philadelphia Times*, quoted in *Rochester Democrat and Chronicle*, March 6, 1890.

53. "An official . . . enters the territory": "To Make a Negro State." On "sooners," Murray Wickett, *Contested Territory: Whites, Native Americans, and African Americans in Oklahoma 1865–1907* (Baton Rouge: Louisiana State University Press, 2000), chapter 3.

54. See Claudio Saunt, *Black, White, and Indian: Race and the Unmaking of an American Family* (New York: Oxford University Press, 2006). "six thousand African Americans": Franklin, *Journey toward Hope*, 30–31. Townsend Jackson story: Madigan, *The Burning*, 15–16. "The Choctaws": *Lexington Leader*, November 28, 1891; "white Cappers are running": *Kingfisher Press*, September 24, 1896, quoted in Mozell Hill, "The All-Negro Society in Oklahoma," Ph.D. diss., University of Chicago, 1946, 25. See also Franklin, *Journey toward Hope*.

55. On nineteenth-century black towns in Indian Territory, see Gary Zellar, *African Creeks: Estelvste and the Creek Nation* (Norman: University of Oklahoma Press, 2007), 97–99. Franklin, *Journey toward Hope*, 16–17, 21.

56. The Abe Lincoln Trading Company, and "Once to Every Man": *Lincoln Tribune*, Clearview, Indian Territory, September 17, 1904. "Of the Vastness": "Moving West," *Christian Recorder*, August 12, 1897.

57. Coleman's migration: Marzetta Brown Wesley and Odevia Brown Field interview. "Real estate": E. P. McCabe, "Freedom, Peace, Happiness and Prosperity, Do You Want All These? Then Cast Your Lot with Us and Make Your Home in Langston City," *Langston City Herald*, November 17, 1892, 3.

58. On the role of railroads in settlement patterns, see Hamilton, *Black Towns and Profit*. Carter, *Dawes Commission*. "The next move": *Memphis Scimeter*, reprinted in the *Indianapolis Journal*, September 10, 1894, 2. See also Daniel F. Littlefield Jr. and Lonnie Underhill, "Black Dreams and 'Free' Homes: The Oklahoma Territory, 1891–1893," *Phylon* 34 (1973): 42.

59. On Boley, see especially Sarah Deutsch, "Being American in Boley, Oklahoma," in *Beyond Black and White: Race, Ethnicity, and Gender in the U.S. South and Southwest*, ed. Stephanie Cole and Alison M. Parker (College Station: Texas A&M

University Press, 2004), 97–122; and Melissa Stuckey, "All Men Up: Race, Rights, and Power in the All-Black Town of Boley, Oklahoma, 1903–1939," Ph.D. diss., Yale University, 2009. Like many "all-black" towns in Oklahoma, the town of Boley was founded upon an allotment, in this case that of Creek freedwoman Abigail Barnett. On the "all-black towns," see Kenneth Marvin Hamilton, *Black Towns and Profit: Promotion and Development in the Trans-Appalachian West, 1877–1915* (Urbana: University of Illinois Press, 1991); Norman L. Crockett, *The Black Towns* (Lawrence: Regents Press of Kansas, 1979); Painter, Exodusters; Hannibal B. Johnson, *Acres of Aspiration: The All-Black Towns in Oklahoma* (Woodway, TX: Eakin, 2002); Jimmie Lewis Franklin, *Journey toward Hope: A History of Blacks in Oklahoma* (Norman: University of Oklahoma Press, 1982). Chang, *Color of the Land*, 162 and 162n9.

60. "Beyond the natural yearning . . .": Johnson, *Acres of Aspiration*, xii. "full of mischief": Frederick Douglass, "Why Is the Negro Lynched?" (Bridgwater, UK: J. Whitby and Sons, limited, 1895), 25. Lewis Dolphin origins: Scott L. Malcomson, "Having Their Say," *New Yorker*, April 29, 1996, 138–43, 138.

61. "leaders of this new movement": *New York Times*, February 28, 1890.

62. On southern expansion, see Walter Johnson, *River of Dark Dreams: Slavery and Empire in the Cotton Kingdom* (Cambridge: Belknap Press of Harvard University Press, 2013); Rothman, *Slave Country*; Miller, *South by Southwest*; Dawn Peterson, *Indians in the Family: Adoption and the Politics of Antebellum Expansion* (Cambridge: Harvard University Press, 2017); and Berlin, *Generations of Captivity*. Alexis de Tocqueville, *Democracy in America*, trans. Arthur Goldhammer (1835; New York: Library Company of America, 2004), 324. "pioneers who owned . . .": Miller, *South by Southwest*, 6.

63. On Townsend Jackson: Madigan, *The Burning*, 15–16. On Johnson Whittaker: Ralph Ellison, address given September 19, 1979, at the Ralph Ellison Festival at Brown University, printed in *Carleton Miscellany*, Winter 1980, reprinted as "Portrait of Inman Page: A Dedication Speech," in Callahan, *Collected Essays of Ellison*, 606.

64. On Whittaker and "unknown history": Ellison, "Going to the Territory," 605–7. Jackson: Madigan, *The Burning*, 15–16.

65. On related transformations prior to emancipation, see Michael Gomez, *Exchanging Our Country Marks*, and Sterling Stuckey, *Slave Culture*. "golden age of black nationalism": Wilson Moses, *The Golden Age of Black Nationalism, 1850–1925* (New York: Oxford University Press, 1988), 6. "the reaction of a formerly disunited group to a sense of mutual oppression": ibid., 16. "centrifugal energies . . . uplift of 'the race' ": Guterl, *Color of Race*, 159.

66. "no-nation": Lewis, *Du Bois*, 155. "children of white fathers . . . troubled whiteness": ibid. "redrawn with a heightened emphasis . . .": Guterl, *Color of Race*, 155.

67. "almost half a million . . . intervening decade": Lewis, *Du Bois*, 442. "Ransom Edmondson," United States Federal Census, Year: 1920; Census Place: Washington, Washington, District of Columbia; Roll: T625_211; Page: 15A; Enumeration District: 206; Image: 474. "Men who, by and by": Charles Johnson, "The Vanishing Mulatto," *Opportunity*, October 1925, 291. R. C. Edmondson to Fayette Avery McKenzie, Correspondence with Alumni, Papers 1915–1926, Box 1 and 2, Fayette Avery McKenzie Papers, Tennessee Archives and Records Services Division, Nashville. Hartfield, *Another Way Home*, 52. "to speak of race": Guterl, *Color of Race*, 102. "the advent of bi-racialism was a revolution of sorts": ibid., 156.

68. Day Shepherd: Hartfield, *Another Way Home*, 42. "the immorality": Marshall Hall, *The Two-Fold Slavery of the United States, With a Project of Self-Emancipation* (London: Adam Scott, 1854), 29. "an absence of kin . . . kinless outsiders": Dylan Penningroth, *The Claims of Kinfolk: African American Property and Community in the Nineteenth-Century South* (Chapel Hill: University of North Carolina Press, 2003), 13. "If, in the Anglo world": Tiya Miles, *Ties That Bind: The Story of an Afro-Cherokee Family in Slavery and Freedom* (Berkeley: University of California Press, 2006), 51. "opposite of slavery . . . modern Western ideas about freedom": Christina Snyder, *Slavery in Indian Country: The Changing Face of Captivity in Early America* (Cambridge: Harvard University Press, 2012), 5.

69. "Black nationalism": Moses, *Golden Age* 19–20. "linchpin of race and empire": George Hutchinson, "End of the Family Romance," in *Race, Nation, and Empire in American History*, ed. James T. Campbell, Matthew Pratt Guterl, and Robert G. Lee (Chapel Hill: University of North Carolina Press, 2007), 55–74, 55.

3. "He Dreamed of Africa"

1. "Some of my relatives": Lomie (Davis) Reed, conversation with Cecil Cade and Mark A. Phillips, March 22, 1988 (Houston, Texas), audiocassette, Alexander Davis Family Papers, Box 1, Manuscript Collections, Mississippi Department of Archives and History. Lomie (Davis) Reed, conversation with Cecil Cade and Mark A. Phillips, March 22, 1988 (Houston, Texas), transcript (in possession of the author), 7 and Appendix A.

2. "getting blacks to go vote": Reed conversation, 7 and Appendix A. "potential black space": Tiya Miles and Sharon Holland, eds., *Crossing Waters, Crossing Worlds: The African Diaspora in Indian Country* (Durham: Duke University Press, 2006), 4.

3. Sturgis exodus: Steven Hahn, *A Nation under Our Feet: Black Political Struggles in the Rural South from Slavery to the Great Migration* (Cambridge: Belknap Press of Harvard University Press, 2005), 454. "difficult, if not impossible": ibid., 453. "no less than two million": J. H. Harris to J. Ormond Wilson, July 14, 1892, Records of the American Colonization Society, quoted ibid.

4. On labor and transnational migration in the late nineteenth century, see Marilyn Lake and Henry Reynolds, *Drawing the Global Colour Line: White Men's Countries and the International Challenge of Racial Equality* (New York: Cambridge University Press, 2008), and Dirk Hoerder, *Migrations and Belongings, 1870–1945* (Cambridge: Harvard University Press, 2012). On African-American emigration and nationalism, see Hahn, *A Nation under Our Feet*, chapter 7, and Michele Mitchell, *Righteous Propagation: African Americans and the Politics of Racial Destiny after Reconstruction* (Chapel Hill: University of North Carolina Press, 2004), chapter 1. On revised periodization of the Great Migration, see Sarah Jane Mathieu, "The African American Great Migration Reconsidered," *OAH Magazine of History* 23, no. 4, North American Migrations (2009): 19–23. "great age" and "economic liberalism . . . everywhere in revolt": Lake and Reynolds, *Drawing the Global Colour Line*, 23. "most intensive period": Patrick Manning, quoted ibid., 23.

5. Robin Kelley and Tiffany Patterson, "Unfinished Migrations: Reflections on the African Diaspora and the Making of the Modern World," *African Studies Review* 43 (2000): 19–20. "the reaction of": Wilson Moses, *The Golden Age of Black Nationalism, 1850–1925* (New York: Oxford University Press, 1988), 16.

6. "negro nationality": Henry McNeal Turner, *Christian Recorder*, quoted in *Respect Black: The Writings and Speeches of Henry McNeal Turner*, comp. and ed. Edwin S. Redkey (New York: Arno and the *New York Times*, 1971), 52–57. On racial identification in the antebellum era, see Michael A. Gomez, *Exchanging Our Country Marks: The Transformation of African Identities in the Colonial and Antebellum South* (Chapel Hill: University of North Carolina Press, 1998). "great age": Lake and Reynolds, *Drawing the Global Colour Line*, 23. Wilson Moses, *The Golden Age of Black Nationalism* (New York: Oxford University Press, 1988), 6.

7. On the complexities of legalized marriage after emancipation, see, for instance, Tera Hunter, *Bound in Wedlock: Slave and Free Black Marriage in the Nineteenth Century* (Cambridge: Harvard University Press, 2017), chapter 6; Thavolia Glymph, *Out of the House of Bondage: The Transformation of the Plantation Household* (New York: Cambridge University Press, 2008). Clay County Marriage Records, 1882. Cade and Phillips, transcript of Reed conversation, 45.

8. "opposite of slavery": Christina Snyder, *Slavery in Indian Country: The Changing Face of Captivity in Early America* (Cambridge: Harvard University Press, 2010), 5. "move about": Heather Williams, *Help Me to Find My People: The African American Search for Family Lost in Slavery* (Chapel Hill: University of North Carolina Press, 2012), 100.

9. The family appears to have migrated before 1860, the time of the second child's birth. Two generations later, Lomie (Davis) Reed, saw a lady in Waco, Texas, who she said resembled her mother's relatives. Lomie introduced herself and learned that the woman was a daughter of one of Rebecca's sisters. "old enough": Reed

conversation, 41. "sold south": David Hackett Fischer and James C. Kelly, *Bound Away: Virginia and the Westward Movement* (Charlottesville: University of Virginia Press, 2000), 231.

10. On enslaved women and girls and the domestic slave trade, see, for instance, Deborah Gray White, *Ar'n't I a Woman? Female Slaves in the Plantation South* (New York: Norton, 1999); Daina Ramey Berry, *Price for Their Pound of Flesh: The Value of the Enslaved, from Womb to Grave, in the Building of a Nation* (New York: Beacon, 2017); Johnson, *Soul by Soul.* "Rebecca was holding": Reed conversation, transcript, 41. R. Coleman, conversation with author, Montpelier, Mississippi, October 2007. "negro fever": Walter Johnson, *River of Dark Dreams: Slavery and Empire in the Cotton Kingdom* (Cambridge: Belknap Press of Harvard University Press, 2013), 374. "They didn't always marry": Reed conversation, A-1; Cade and Phillips, transcript ibid., 41. Censuses of 1870, 1880, and 1910 are consistent with Lomie (Davis) Reed's recollection of South Carolina, though she sometimes referred to North Carolina. Reed (Rebecca Watkins's granddaughter) conversation.

11. On southern expansion, see Johnson, *River of Dark Dreams*; Adam Rothman, *Slave Country: American Expansion and the Origins of the Deep South* (Cambridge: Harvard University Press, 2005); and Charles Sydnor, *Slavery in Mississippi* (Gloucester, MA: Peter Smith, 1933). "Thos Davis," United States Federal Census, 1830; Census Place: Pickens, Alabama; Series: M19; Roll: 2; Page: 112; Family History Library Film: 0002329. "Thomas Davis," United States Federal Census, Year: 1840; Census Place: Oktibbeha, Mississippi; Roll: 218; Page: 121; Image: 246; Family History Library Film: 0014842. "Thomas Davis," 1850 U.S. Federal Census—Slave Schedules [database online]. Provo, UT: Ancestry.com Operations Inc, 2004.

12. "sold to someone": Reed conversation, 7 and Appendix A. On apprenticeship: Matthew Pratt Guterl, *American Mediterranean: Southern Slaveholders in the Age of Emancipation* (Cambridge: Harvard University Press, 2008), 121.

13. Reed conversation, 1.

14. Ibid., 7 and Appendix A (emphasis Reed's). "native schools": John W. Alvord, *First Semi-Annual Report on Schools and Finances of Freedmen, January 1, 1866* (Washington, DC: Government Printing Office, 1868), 9–10, quoted in Heather Andrea Williams, *Self-Taught: African American Education in Slavery and Freedom* (Chapel Hill: University of North Carolina Press, 2005), 92.

15. Reed conversation, 7 and Appendix A.

16. On the *Azor* and the Liberia Exodus Joint Steamship Company, see James Campbell, *Middle Passages: African American Journeys to Africa, 1787–2005* (New York: Penguin, 2007), 109–13. Exodus for Kansas: Nell Irvin Painter, *Exodusters: Black Migration to Kansas after Reconstruction* (1977; New York: Norton, 1992).

17. Historian Thavolia Glymph illustrates how "freedom was made in spaces where women dominated," and especially within the plantation household. Glymph

documents the ways in which "freed and becoming-free domestic servants," such as Della, rejected "political and social conventions of the past" and urged "the transformation of the plantation household and the making of new and free homes, black and white, and of new women, black and white." Glymph, *Out of the House of Bondage*, 135.

18. "petty accumulations": Hahn, *A Nation under Our Feet*, 460. "forlorn and forsaken": W. E. B. Du Bois, *The Souls of Black Folk* (Chicago: A. C. McClurg, 1903), 443–45, 448–49, 458–74, quoted in Hahn, *A Nation under Our Feet*, 460. Elic and three of his four siblings were all living on farms in Clay County in 1880. "Lomie says that 25 or 30 years ago [1957–62], her brother Thad returned to the Maben farm," finding only one little storage house still standing. Cade and Phillips, transcript of Reed conversation, 7.

19. *Huntsville Gazette*, September 23, 1882, quoted in Hahn, *A Nation under Our Feet*, 393, 364. "This was the world": ibid., 393.

20. "reversing the action of the government": Frederick Douglass, *The Life and Times of Frederick Douglass* (Boston: De Wolfe and Fiske, 1892), 395. "Della Davis," United States Federal Census, Year: 1900; Census Place: Beat 3, Oktibbeha, Mississippi; Roll: 823; Page: 2B; Enumeration District: 0090; FHL microfilm: 1240823.

21. "claim service and allegiance . . .": Frederick Douglass, "The Civil Rights Case, speech at the Civil Rights Mass-Meeting held at Lincoln Hall, Washington, DC, October 22, 1883," in *Frederick Douglass: Selected Speeches and Writings*, ed. Phillip S. Foner and Yuval Taylor (Chicago: Lawrence Hill, 1999), 685–92, 688. "more muted tones": Hahn, *A Nation under Our Feet*, 428. Ibid., 461, 462n87: Julius E. Thompson, *The Black Press in Mississippi, 1865–1985: A Directory* (West Cornwall, CT: Locust Hill, 1988).

22. On the circulation of the *African Repository* in the U.S. South, see Hahn, *A Nation under Our Feet*, 326–27. Eli Morrow to William Coppinger, August 4, 1877, American Colonization Society, roll 116A, quoted ibid., 326–27.

23. "To those of my race": Booker T. Washington, "Speech to the Atlanta Cotton States and International Exposition," September 18, 1895, in *The Booker T. Washington Papers*, 14 vols., ed. Louis R. Harlan and Raymond W. Smock (Urbana: University of Illinois Press, 1974), 3: 583–87. "saw their survival": Hahn, *A Nation under Our Feet*, 452.

24. "Negro rural communities . . . had a chance": Booker T. Washington, "The Rural Negro Community," *Annals of the American Academy of Political and Social Science*, vol. 40, *Country Life* (1912): 81–89, 81, 82, 89.

25. On the transition to cotton production in the delta: Rothman, *Slave Country*, 45–47. "with an additional": Norman L. Crockett, *The Black Towns* (Lawrence: Regents Press of Kansas, 1979), 15. See also Kenneth Marvin Hamilton, *Black Towns and Profit: Promotion and Development in the Trans-Appalachian West, 1877–1915* (Urbana: University of Illinois Press, 1991).

26. For early black town literature, for instance, Arthur Tolson, *The Black Oklahomans: A History, 1541–1972* (New Orleans: Edwards, 1974); and Norman L. Crockett, *The Black Towns* (Lawrence: Regents Press of Kansas, 1979). "cheap land prices": Cade and Phillips, transcript of Reed conversation, 9. Vernon Lane Wharton, *The Negro in Mississippi, 1865–1890* (Chapel Hill: University of North Carolina Press, 1947), 110, chapter 7; Reed conversation, 9. While Elic and Della worked as sharecroppers for most of their time in the delta, the Davis interview transcript is vague as to whether they ever legally owned a farm or a house during this period. Cade and Phillips, transcript of Reed conversation, 9. Town was recorded here as "Merogold" in original transcript, but in most other cases as Merigold, in keeping with present-day spelling. Reed conversation, 9.

27. "not necessarily Washingtonian": Hahn, *A Nation under Our Feet*, 452.

28. On generational change, see Leon Litwack, *Trouble in Mind: Black Southerners in the Age of Jim Crow* (New York: Vintage, 1998), 252. See also Joel Williamson, *The Crucible of Race: Black-White Relations in the American South since Emancipation* (New York: Oxford University Press, 1984).

29. Reed conversation, 9. "news that land . . . dawning of freedom": Julie Saville, *The Work of Reconstruction: From Slave to Wage Labor in South Carolina, 1860–1870* (New York: Cambridge University Press, 1994), 20, 194–95.

30. "many of them . . . someone": Williams, *Help Me to Find My People*, 192–93.

31. Reed conversation, A-2. On African-American women's sartorial performance after emancipation, see Hunter, *To 'Joy My Freedom*, and Stephanie M. H. Camp, *Closer to Freedom: Enslaved Women and Everyday Resistance in the Plantation South* (Chapel Hill: University of North Carolina Press, 2004).

32. "we raised cotton . . . skim off": Reed conversation, A-2.

33. "I liked to work" and "smart person": ibid., A-3. See Glymph, *Out of the House of Bondage*; Sharon Ann Holt, *Making Freedom Pay: North Carolina Freedpeople Working for Themselves, 1865–2000* (Athens: University of Georgia Press, 2000). "the possibility of . . .": Schwalm, *Hard Fight for We*, 235.

34. On landownership and Reconstruction, see W. E. B. Du Bois, *Black Reconstruction in America, 1860–1880* (1935; New York: Free Press, 1998). Eric Foner, *Nothing but Freedom: Emancipation and Its Legacy* (Baton Rouge: Louisiana State University Press, 1983). On gender, labor, and politics during and after the Civil War and Reconstruction era, see Glymph, *Out of the House of Bondage*; Camp, *Closer to Freedom*; Deborah Gray White, *Ar'n't I a Woman? Female Slaves in the Plantation South* (New York: Norton, 1999); Jacqueline Jones, *Labor of Love, Labor of Sorrow: Black Women, Work, and the Family, from Slavery to the Present* (New York: Basic, 1985); Hunter, *To 'Joy My Freedom*; Sarah Haley, *No Mercy Here: Gender, Punishment, and the Making of Jim Crow Modernity* (Chapel Hill: University of North Carolina Press, 2016); Talitha L. LeFlouria, *Chained in Silence: Black Women and Convict Labor in the New South* (Chapel Hill: University of North

Carolina Press, 2016); Schwalm, *Hard Fight for We*; and Amy Dru Stanley, *From Bondage to Contract: Wage Labor, Marriage, and the Market in the Age of Slave Emancipation* (New York: Cambridge University Press, 1998). "little prospect," "back in those days," and "big white house": Reed conversation, A-2. "his little place": ibid.

35. Gerald David Jaynes, *Branches without Roots: Genesis of the Black Working Class in the American South, 1862–1882* (New York: Oxford University Press, 1986), 10, 15. "no law forbidding . . . auction sale": Frederick Douglass, "Southern Barbarism," Speech on the occasion of the Twenty-Fourth Anniversary of Emancipation in the District of Columbia, Washington, DC, April 16, 1886, in *Frederick Douglass: Selected Speeches and Writings, ed.* Philip S. Foner, abridged and adapted by Yuval Taylor (Chicago: Lawrence Hill, 1999), 696–705, 700.

36. "One time . . . on his place": Reed conversation, A-3. "self-employment": Saville, *Work of Reconstruction*, 26. See also Jaynes, *Branches without Roots*, 15; Du Bois, *Black Reconstruction*; Eric Foner, *Reconstruction: America's Unfinished Revolution, 1863–1877* (1988; New York: Perennial Classics, 2002); Demetrious L. Eudell, *The Political Languages of Emancipation in the British Caribbean and the U.S. South* (Chapel Hill: University of North Carolina Press, 2002); and Saidiya Hartman, *Scenes of Subjection: Terror, Slavery, and Self-Making in Nineteenth-Century America* (New York: Oxford University Press, 1997).

37. "fowl, stock . . . casualties of free labor": Saville, *Work of Reconstruction*, 27. "down in the delta": Reed conversation, A-3. "My mother got those cows. . . . All of the cotton": Lomie (Davis) Reed, conversation with Cecil Cade and Mark A. Phillips, March 22, 1988 (Houston, Texas), audiocassette, Alexander Davis Family Papers, Box 1, Manuscript Collections, Mississippi Department of Archives and History (emphasis Reed's). Dylan Penningroth has highlighted enslaved people's customary use and ownership of land in the antebellum era. Dylan Penningroth, *The Claims of Kinfolk: African American Property and Community in the Nineteenth-Century South* (Chapel Hill: University of North Carolina Press, 2003). "out of the category of property": ibid., 134, "eyes wide open": ibid., 111. Food and clothing: ibid., 56. "The tendency was": Testimony of Sam'l B. Smith, Esq., before the American Freedmen's Inquiry Commission, November 19, 1863, filed with O-328 1863, Letters Received, ser. 12, RG 94 [K-90], quoted in *Freedom: A Documentary History of Emancipation, 1861–1867*, ed. Ira Berlin, Thavolia Glymph, Steven F. Miller, Joseph P. Reidy, Leslie S. Rowland, and Julie Saville, series I, vol. 3. See also *The Wartime Genesis of Free Labor: The Lower South* (New York: Cambridge University Press, 1990), 751.

38. "I believe": Reed conversation, A-4. "Left us high and dry": ibid. (emphasis Reed's). "They kept everything": ibid., 9, A-3. On Mound Bayou, see Hamilton, *Black Towns and Profit*. Reed Conversation, A-3 and A-4 (emphasis original).

39. "It seems like . . . nothing between them": Reed conversation, A-1.

40. Ibid., A-3.
41. On convict labor after the Civil War, see Haley, *No Mercy Here*; LeFlouria, *Chained in Silence*; David M. Oshinsky, *"Worse than Slavery": Parchman Farm and the Ordeal of Jim Crow Justice* (New York: Free Press, 1996); Douglas Blackmon, *Slavery by Another Name: The Re-Enslavement of Black Americans from the Civil War to World War II* (New York: Anchor, 2009). Vardaman campaign slogan: Eugene White, "Anti-Racial Agitation in Politics: James Kimble Vardaman in the Mississippi Gubernatorial Campaign of 1903," *Journal of Mississippi History* 7 (1945): 105, quoted in Oshinsky, *Worse than Slavery*, 90. "vigorous campaign": Governor James K. Vardaman, "To the Officers of the Counties, Cities, Towns, and Villages of Mississippi," Mississippi Department of Archives and History, quoted ibid., 91–92. See also William Gillette, *Retreat from Reconstruction, 1869–1879* (Baton Rouge: Louisiana State University Press, 1980), 163; Frank E. Smith, *The Yazoo River* (New York: Rinehart, 1954), chapter 18; William Sallis, "The Color Line in Mississippi Politics, 1865–1915," Ph.D. diss., University of Kentucky, 1967, 236; Albert D. Kirwan, *Revolt of the Rednecks: Mississippi Politics, 1876–1925* (New York: Harper and Row, 1965), 146.
42. "In the Southern States": Douglass, "Southern Barbarism," 700–701. "time to move on": Reed conversation, 11. "First, he left": ibid., A-4.
43. "flight from Mississippi . . . your land": ibid., 11.
44. "dad was trying": ibid., A-4 (emphasis added). "You couldn't buy anything": Lomie (Davis) Reed, ibid., A-5 (emphasis Reed's). "I remember they made": ibid. (emphasis Reed's).
45. "he worked . . . come to Oklahoma": ibid. (emphasis Reed's). "everything was different": ibid., A-4, 13.
46. On shifting relations between black Indians and newcomers, see Chang, *Color of the Land*, 160–63. Constitution of the State of Oklahoma, 1907, sec. 2, art. 23, and sec. 35, art. 6; [Robert Lee Williams], untitled manuscript, n.d., folder 4, box 1, Robert Lee Williams Collection, Oklahoma Historical Society. "the provision defined": David A. Chang, *The Color of the Land: Race, Nation, and the Politics of Landownership in Oklahoma, 1832–1929* (Chapel Hill: University of North Carolina Press, 2010), 160–61. See also Gary Zellar, *African Creeks: Estelvste and the Creek Nation* (Norman: University of Oklahoma Press, 2007), 194.
47. "The Democrats carried Oklahoma": "Give Roosevelt No Chance," ibid., January 2, 1907, 1. See also "Oklahoma Negro Issue Put up to Roosevelt," ibid., February 2, 1907, 4; "Grandfather's Clause," ibid., October 27, 1910.
48. James Garden: *New York Times*, December 25, 1907. On racial violence and disfranchisement after Oklahoma statehood, see Chang, *Color of the Land*; Claudio Saunt, *Black, White, and Indian: Race and the Unmaking of an American Family* (New York: Oxford University Press, 2005); and Melissa Stuckey, "All Men Up: Race, Rights, and Power in the All-Black Town of Boley, Oklahoma,

1903–1939," Ph.D. diss., Yale University, 2009; *Crisis*, February 1914, 175. Painter, *Exodusters*, 7; William Bittle and Gilbert Geis, *The Longest Way Home: Chief Alfred C. Sam's Back-to-Africa Movement* (Detroit: Wayne State University Press, 1964), 54, 56–57. "never rent, lease, or sell": *Okemah Ledger*, August 31, 1911, quoted in Crockett, *Black Towns*, 167.

49. "suckling babe": *Muskogee Cimeter*, quoted in *Crisis*, July 1911, 100. On the meeting between Edward McCabe and President Benjamin Harrison, see Kenneth Barnes, *Journey of Hope: The Back-to-Africa Movement in Arkansas in the Late 1800s* (Chapel Hill: University of North Carolina Press, 2004), 85–86.

50. On socialism in Oklahoma, see James Green, *Grass-Roots Socialism: Radical Movements in the Southwest, 1895–1943* (Baton Rouge: Louisiana State University Press, 1978), chapter 3; Chang, *Color of the Land*, 181; H. L. Meredith, "Agrarian Socialism and the Negro in Oklahoma, 1900–1918," *Labor History* 11, no. 3 (1970): 277–84. "Practically all the rich": "Robbery," *Professional World*, excerpted in *Crisis*, February 1914, 175. "vehicle for . . . politics": Chang, *Color of the Land*, 180.

51. "went to the meetingplace . . . a new way" and "If Elic had expected": Reed conversation, 13.

52. Several hundred African-American Oklahomans migrated to the Canadian Plains, including the provinces of Alberta and Saskatchewan. Monroe Coleman had a brother in Mississippi, James Coleman, who stopped in Oklahoma before moving on to Canada around 1910. On the migration to Canada, see Sarah-Jane Mathieu, *North of the Color Line: Migration and Black Resistance in Canada, 1870–1955* (Chapel Hill: University of North Carolina Press, 2010); R. Bruce Shepard, "The Origins of the Oklahoma Black Migration to the Canadian Plains," *Canadian Journal of History/Annales Canadiennes d'Histoire* 23 (1988): 1–23; S. Grow, "The Blacks of Amber Valley: Negro Pioneering in Northern Alberta," *Canadian Ethnic Studies* 6 (1974), 17–38; R. Bruce Shepard, "Diplomatic Racism: The Canadian Government and Black Migration from Oklahoma, 1905–1912," *Great Plains Quarterly* 3 (1983): 5–16; R. Bruce Shepard, "Plain Racism: The Reaction against Oklahoma Black Immigration to the Canadian Plains," *Prairie Forum* 10 (1985): 365–82. "visited bustling . . . his family": Reed, paraphrased by Cade and Phillips, 13. "we have no home": Mary J. Evans (Muldrow, IT) to Coppinger, Dec 31 1891, Records of the American Colonization Society, ser. 1A, container 282, vol. 285. Library of Congress, Manuscripts Division.

53. There was a Zion Hill in Mississippi; it is possible that Reed interchanged memories of Oklahomas and Mississippi. "full-time preacher . . . and visit": Reed conversation, 45.

54. "dreamed of Africa . . . on his own": ibid., 13.

55. On "racial destiny," see Mitchell, *Righteous Propagation*. "potential black space": Miles and Holland, *Crossing Waters, Crossing Worlds*, 4 "geographical state . . . racial heritage and destiny": Moses, *Golden Age*, 20.

56. "didn't get around much . . . he should be": Reed conversation, 40. "community and family ties": Penningroth, *Claims of Kinfolk*, 176.
57. On the unresolved question African-American citizenship, see Robin D. G. Kelley, "'But a Local Phase of a World Problem': Black History's Global Vision, 1883–1950," *Journal of American History* 86 (1999): 1045–77, 1049; and Robin D. G. Kelley, *Freedom Dreams: The Black Radical Imagination* (New York: Beacon, 2003), 18. "As paradoxical": Campbell, *Middle Passages*, xxiv.

4. "No Such Thing as Stand Still"

1. Lomie (Davis) Reed, conversation with Cecil Cade and Mark A. Phillips, March 22, 1988 (Houston, Texas), transcript (in possession of author), A-5, 13, 15.
2. Carter Godwin Woodson, *A Century of Negro Migration* (Washington, DC: Association for the Study of Negro Life and History, 1918).
3. On the development of "bi-racialism" (termed by eugenicist Lothrop Stoddard) see Matthew Pratt Guterl, *The Color of Race in America, 1900–1940* (Cambridge: Harvard University Press, 2001), 6, 154–83.
4. William E. Bittle and Gilbert L. Geis wrote the only book-length work on the subject, *The Longest Way Home: Chief Alfred C. Sam's Back-to-Africa Movement* (Detroit: Wayne State University Press, 1964), arguing that the movement illustrated the migrants' "desperate hopes" (2) and "the final and extreme . . . rejection of an American residency" (14). J. Ayo Langley used the Sam movement to explore African nationalism and racial consciousness in West Africa; Hill situated Sam within a "steady flow of West African trader-nationalists" and the intersection between economics and politics in pan-African nationalism. Robert Hill and James Anquandah reconstructed Sam's family tree and biographical detail. See "Chief Alfred Sam" in *The Marcus Garvey and UNIA Papers*, vol. 1, *1826–August 1919*, ed. Robert A. Hill and Carol A. Rudisell (Berkeley: University of California Press, 1983), 536–47, 483–84; Robert Hill, "Before Garvey: Chief Alfred Sam and the African Movement, 1912–1916," in *Pan-African Biography*, ed. Robert Hill (Los Angeles: University of California Press, 1987), 57; J. Ayo Langley, "Chief Sam's African Movement and Race Consciousness in West Africa," *Phylon* 32 (1971): 164–78; Moses Nathaniel Moore, *Orishatukeh Faduma: Liberal Theology and Evangelical Pan-Africanism, 1857–1946* (Evanston, IL: Scarecrow, 1996), chapter 4; David A. Y. O. Chang, "Where Will the Nation Be at Home? Race, Nationalisms, and Emigration Movements in the Creek Nation," in *Crossing Waters, Crossing Worlds: The African Diaspora in Indian Country*, ed. Tiya Miles and Sharon Holland, (Durham: Duke University Press, 2006), 80–99; and Kendra Field and Ebony Coletu, "The Chief Sam Movement, A Century Later: Public Histories, Private Stories, and the African Diaspora," *Transition* 114 (July 2014). On antebellum emigration and colonization in Africa, Mexico, and Canada, see especially James Campbell, *Middle Passages:*

African American Journeys to Africa, 1787–2005 (New York: Penguin, 2006); Wilson J. Moses, *Afrotopia: The Roots of African American Popular History* (New York: Cambridge University Press, 1998); Bell Wiley, *Slaves No More: Letters from Liberia, 1833–1869* (Lexington: University of Kentucky Press, 1980); Bruce Allen Dorsey, "A Gendered History of African Colonization in the Antebellum United States," *Journal of Social History* 34 (2000): 77–103; Sarah Cornell, "Citizens of Nowhere: Fugitive Slaves and Free African Americans in Mexico, 1833–1857," *Journal of American History* 100 (2013): 351–74; Robin Winks, *The Blacks in Canada: A History* (New Haven: Yale University Press, 1971). "utterly desperate . . . ephemeral flash": Bittle and Geis, *Longest Way Home*, 2, 12. "early rumblings": Steven Hahn, *A Nation under Our Feet: Black Political Struggles in the Rural South, from Slavery to the Great Migration* (Cambridge: Belknap Press of Harvard University Press, 2005), 455.

5. On "geopolitical" peoplehood and literacy, see Wilson Moses, *Afrotopia: The Roots of African American Popular History* (New York: Cambridge University Press, 1998), 26; Phillip Troutman, "Grapevine in the Slave Market: African American Geopolitical Literacy and the 1841 *Creole* Revolt," in *The Chattel Principle: Internal Slave Trades in the Americas*, ed. Walter Johnson (New Haven: Yale University Press, 2008), 203–33; Hahn, *A Nation under Our Feet*, chapters 7, 9; Michele Mitchell, *Righteous Propagation: African Americans and the Politics of Racial Destiny after Reconstruction* (Chapel Hill: University of North Carolina Press, 2004), chapter 1.

6. Cade and Phillips, transcript of Reed conversation, 13. "disposed of their property": "African Delegation Meets; Final Call before Sailing, Is It Providential?" *Wewoka and Lima Courier*, December 5, 1913, 1. "American Negroes and the Gold Coast (From an American Correspondent)," "born farmers": *African Mail*, May 29, 1914, 351. "shivered through": J. P. Owens, *Clearview* (Okemah, OK: J. P. Owens, 1995), 23. "There are hundreds": "Ship of African Pioneers Has Not Sailed," *Wewoka and Lima Courier*, January 30, 1914, 1. It appears there were two camps, North Gold Coast and South Gold Coast. Owens, *Clearview*, 23.

7. On gathering at First Baptist: "EDUCATIONAL. A Meeting of African Delegates," *Wewoka and Lima Courier*, October 31, 1913, 1. "American Negroes and the Gold Coast."

8. On postemancipation "Liberia fever," see Campbell, *Middle Passages*; Edwin S. Redkey, *Black Exodus: Black Nationalist and Back-to-Africa Movements, 1890–1910* (New Haven: Yale University Press, 1969); Mitchell, *Righteous Propagation*; Hahn, *A Nation under Our Feet*; and Kenneth Barnes, *Journey of Hope: The Back-to-Africa Movement in Arkansas in the Late 1800s* (Chapel Hill: University of North Carolina Press, 2004). Moses, *Afrotopia*, 25–26. See also Robin D. G. Kelley, "'But a Local Phase of a World Problem': Black History's Global Vision, 1883–1950," *Journal of American History* 86 (1999), 1045–77; Brent Edwards, *The Practice of Diaspora: Literature, Translation, and the Rise of Black Internationalism* (Cambridge: Harvard University Press, 2003); Hahn, *A Nation under Our Feet*, 453–54; and Redkey, *Black*

Exodus, 73–149. "Forty Negroes Off for Africa with Sam," *Sun*, February 11, 1914, 9. Letter from L. T. Michell (Holdenville, Oklahoma) to J. Ormond Wilson, Records of American Colonization Society, September 6, 1910, 1. Letter from P. M. Eckals (Wewoka, Indian Territory) to American Colonization Society, Records of the American Colonization Society, February 11, 1901. Letter from J. M. Miller (Ackerman, Mississippi) to American Colonization Society, Records of American Colonization Society, September 1, 1903, 1. *African Repository* 67, no. 2 (1891): 36. Incoming Correspondence, Records of American Colonization Society, reels 151 (1906–8), 152 (1908–12). Eckals letter.

9. On Turner and the *African League*, see Frederick Starr, *Liberia: History, Description, Problems* (Chicago, 1913). Dorman's letter to Sam: Orishatukeh Faduma, "The African Movement," *African Mail*, November 20, 1914, 73.

10. On Chief Sam's biography, see "Chief Alfred Sam," in Hill and Rudisell, *Marcus Garvey and UNIA Papers*, 1: 536–47, 483–84; Hill, "Before Garvey." On the British Gold Coast and mining economy during the period, see Raymond Dumett, *El Dorado in West Africa: The Gold Mining Frontier, African Labor, and Colonial Capitalism in the Gold Coast, 1875–1900* (Athens: Ohio University Press, 1998). On Sam and the Shiloh colony, see Shirley Nelson, *Fair, Clear, and Terrible: The Story of Shiloh, Maine* (Eugene, OR: Wipf and Stock, 2009), and William Charles Hiss, "Shiloh: Frank W. Sandford and the Kingdom, 1893–1948," Ph.D. diss., Tufts University, 1978, 505–13, esp. 507n1. "African 'Paradise' Lure for Negroes," *New York Times*, February 11, 1914, 5. "American Negroes and the Gold Coast." Henry McNeal Turner, quoted in Redkey, *Black Exodus*, 266.

11. The "American correspondent" listed as author of the May 29, 1914, article may have been Orishatukeh Faduma. "American Negroes and the Gold Coast." Faduma, "The African Movement." See also Moore, *Orishatukeh Faduma*, 140. "Back to Africa under Auspices of a Black Chief," *World*, March 8, 1914, 7.

12. On the Tulsa burning, see Alfred L. Brophy, *Reconstructing the Dreamland the Tulsa Riot of 1921: Race, Reparations, and Reconciliation* (New York: Oxford University Press, 2002); Scott Ellsworth, *Death in a Promised Land: The Tulsa Race Riot of 1921* (Baton Rouge: Louisiana State University Press, 1992); and Hannibal Johnson, *Black Wall Street: From Riot to Renaissance in Tulsa* (Austin: Eakin, 2007). Faduma, "The African Movement." "At Last!": *Gold Coast Leader*, January 23, 1915. "EDUCATIONAL: A Meeting of African Delegates." "African Delegation Meets," *Wewoka and Lima Courier*, November 21, 1913. See Moore, *Orishatukeh Faduma*, 140.

13. "Forty Negroes Off for Africa with Sam." M. A. Sorrell, *African Pioneer*, excerpted ibid. "African 'Paradise' Lure for Negroes."

14. "Forty Negroes Off for Africa with Sam." Sorrell, *African Pioneer*. "African 'Paradise' Lure for Negroes." "African Delegates," *Wewoka and Lima Courier*, November 7, 1913. "African Delegation Meets" (November 21, 1913). On departure plans, see also "African Delegation Meets" (December 5, 1913); "Delegates Gone to New York," *Wewoka and Lima Courier*, January 23, 1914, p. 1; "Ship of African Pioneers," 1.

15. On the movement's "delegates," see "At Last!" See also "The African Movement," *African Mail*, November 27, 1914, 82.

16. On labor and transnational migration in the late nineteenth century, see Marilyn Lake and Henry Reynolds, *Drawing the Global Colour Line: White Men's Countries and the International Challenge of Racial Equality* (New York: Cambridge University Press, 2008), and Dirk Hoerder, *Migrations and Belongings, 1870–1945* (Cambridge: Belknap Press of Harvard University Press, 2014). Hahn, *Nation under Our Feet*, 331. Mitchell, *Righteous Propagation*, 17–19.

17. On the history of African-descended peoples within the Creek nation, see David A. Chang, *The Color of the Land: Race, Nation, and the Politics of Landownership in Oklahoma, 1832–1929* (Chapel Hill: University of North Carolina Press, 2010); Claudio Saunt, *Black, White, and Indian: Race and the Unmaking of an American Family* (New York: Oxford University Press, 2005); Gary Zellar, *African Creeks: Estelvste and the Creek Nation* (Norman: University of Oklahoma Press, 2007); Daniel Littlefield, *Africans and Creeks: From the Colonial Period to the Civil War* (Westport, CT: Greenwood, 1979). See Mozell C. Hill, "The All Negro Communities of Oklahoma," *Journal of Negro History* 31 (1946): 254–68, 256. "black space": Miles and Holland, *Crossing Waters, Crossing Worlds*, 4.

18. "open and even marginal space . . .": Miles and Holland, *Crossing Waters, Crossing Worlds*, 9, 7, 10. "searched outside": Kelley, "'But a Local Phase,'" 1049.

19. "homeseekers and colored capitalists": Inaugural editorial, Boley *Progress*, March 9, 1905. "Stay in the South," *Boley Progress*, February 1, 1906, 1. Booker T. Washington, "Boley: A Negro Town in the West," *Outlook* 88 (1908), 31, 30. "transformed Indians": Miles and Holland, *Crossing Waters, Crossing Worlds*, 7. "response to white racism": William Katz, *The Black West: A Documentary and Pictorial History of the African American Role in the Westward Expansion of the United States* (New York: Touchstone, 1996), 249. "at home": Chang, "Where Will the Nation Be at Home?" 98. On nation-building, see above, note 5. On the coalescence of African-American freedom movement and imperial projects at the turn of the century, see Mitchell, *Righteous Propagation*, and Gerald Horne, *Black and Brown: African Americans and the Mexican Revolution, 1910–1920* (New York: New York University Press, 2005). On Oklahoma's black towns, see Kenneth Marvin Hamilton, *Black Towns and Profit: Promotion and Development in the Trans-Appalachian West, 1877–1915* (Urbana: University of Illinois Press, 1991); Jimmie Lee Franklin, *Journey toward Hope: A History of Blacks in Oklahoma* (Norman: University of Oklahoma Press, 1982); Norman L. Crockett, *The Black Towns* (Lawrence: Regents Press of Kansas, 1979); Hill, "The All Negro Communities of Oklahoma," 254–68; and Bittle and Geis, *Longest Way Home*, 18–39. See also Bonnie Lynn-Sherow, *Red Earth: Race and Agriculture in Oklahoma Territory* (Lawrence: University Press of Kansas, 2004), 43 and note 6. On relations with Native Americans as black transnationalism, see Kelley, "'But a Local Phase,'"; and Miles and Holland, *Crossing Waters, Crossing Worlds*, 1–23.

20. "gained their liberty . . .": Claude Clegg, *The Price of Liberty: African Americans the Making of Liberia* (Chapel Hill: University of North Carolina Press, 2004), 162. "demonstrate their fitness": Miles and Holland, *Crossing Waters, Crossing Worlds*, 7. "Literary Society," *Boley Progress*, March 9, 1915, 4. "Uncle Jesse": "Boley Recalled in Song," *Boley Progress*, October 16, 1905, 3, quoted in Katz, *Black West*, 251. "A. G. Belton to William Coppinger," July 22, 1891, Records of the American Colonization Society, Manuscript Division, Library of Congress, Washington, DC, as quoted in Redkey, *Black Exodus*, 9. "the life of pioneers": Orishatukeh Faduma, "What the African Movement Stands For," *African Mail*, September 25, 1914, 521–22. See also Sarah Deutsch, "Being American in Boley, Oklahoma," in *Beyond Black and White: Race, Ethnicity, and Gender in the U.S. South and Southwest*, ed. Stephanie Cole and Alison M. Parker (College Station: Texas A&M University Press, 2004) 97–122; William Bittle and Gilbert Geis, "Racial Self-Fulfillment and the Rise of an All-Negro Community in Oklahoma," *Phylon* 18 (1957): 247–60.

21. "relentless search": Joseph R. Roach, *Cities of the Dead: Circum-Atlantic Performance* (New York: Columbia University Press, 1996), 6.

22. On African-American migration to Canada, see Chapter 3, note 52. On African Americans in Mexico, see Horne, *Black and Brown*; Sarah Cornell, "Americans in the U.S. South and Mexico: A Transnational History of Race, Slavery, and Freedom, 1810–1910," Ph.D. diss., New York University, 2008; Arnold Shankman, "The Image of Mexico and the Mexican-American in the Black Press, 1890–1935," *Journal of Ethnic Studies* 3 (1975): 43–56; and Rosalie Schwartz, *Across the Rio to Freedom: U.S. Negroes in Mexico* (El Paso: Texas Western Press, 1975). See also George Junne Jr., ed., *Blacks in the American West and Beyond—America, Canada, and Mexico: A Selectively Annotated Bibliography* (Westport, CT: Greenwood, 2000). Katz, *Black West*, 252. "ripe audience . . . ships for Africa": ibid., 252, 254.

23. "become pioneers": Orishatukeh Faduma, "What the African Movement Stands For," *African Mail*, October 2, 1914, 3. "in plain language": "EDUCATIONAL. A Meeting of African Delegates." "Christlike": see Sorrel quoted in "Forty Negroes Off for Africa with Sam." "nine miles": Faduma, "The African Movement."

24. "has a power": "EDUCATIONAL. A Meeting of African Delegates." "lay aside factions": "Ship of African Pioneers," 1 (emphasis added).

25. "Ship of African Pioneers," 1. Anderson Palmer (Clarksdale, MS) to J. Ormond Wilson, Records of the American Colonization Society, reel 152, 12 March 1911. "EDUCATIONAL," 1. Toomer, "Book X" (final draft), quoted in Guterl, *Color of Race*, 158.

26. On South Gold Coast, see Owens, *Clearview*, 23. Letter from Tom Johnson to Booker T. Washington, February 27, 1914, in *The Booker T. Washington Papers*, 14 vols., ed. Louis R. Harlan and Raymond W. Smock (Urbana: University of Illinois Press, 1982), 12 (1912–14): 453.

27. Harlan and Smock, *Booker T. Washington Papers*, 12: xviii. "To Tom Johnson," March 5, 1914, ibid., 12: 468.

28. "Migration," *Crisis*, February 1914, 190.

29. On apparently fraudulent movements in the late nineteenth century, see Redkey, *Black Exodus*; Barnes, *Journey of Hope*; and Campbell, *Middle Passages*. Campbell, *Middle Passages*, 124. On "Edward Blyden," see [W. W. Meingault] to Coppinger, 12, 13, July 1891, Records of the American Colonization Society, August 13, 1891, reel 137.

30. "318 foot steamship": "Forty Negroes off for Africa with Sam." "personal interview" and "raison d'etre": "The African Movement" (November 27, 1914). "open and above board": Okfuskee County Attorney Tom Hazelwood to Governor Lee Cruce, December 1913, Cruce Papers, Oklahoma Historical Society.

31. On local reception, Mrs. W. H. Lewis, whose husband died from scurvy en route, maintained, "The promised reception in Africa had not been arranged." Conversely, Ghanaian testimonies of firsthand witnesses speak to a generous welcome in which local residents contributed supplies and helped to support the American migrants in the initial months. "Chief Sam in Consul's Trap," *New York Sun*, February 26, 1914. "Breakers Ahead for African Colonists," *New York Sun*, February 14, 1914, 4. "African Delegation Will Meet," *Wewoka and Lima Courier*, November 28, 1913. See also Field and Coletu, "The Chief Sam Movement."

32. "At Last!"; Mitchell, *Righteous Propagation*, 19; Guterl, *Color of Race*, 166; David Levering Lewis, *W. E. B. Du Bois, 1868–1919: Biography of a Race* (New York: Holt Paperbacks, 1994), 99.

33. "Rev. A. Davis" on board the *Curityba*: George Wesley Harris to Booker T. Washington, February 12, 1914, in *The Booker T. Washington Papers*, 14 vols., ed. Louis R. Harlan and Raymond W. Smock (Urbana: University of Illinois Press, 1982), 12 (1912–14): 437–39. Bittle and Geis, *Longest Way Home*, 2; "Forty Negroes off for Africa with Sam"; "Migration," *Crisis*, February 1914, p. 190. "British Warning for 'Chief Sam,'" *New York Times*, February 26, 1914, 7; Harlan and Smock, *Booker T. Washington Papers*, 12: 437–38. "'Back to Africa' Ship Arrives with Chief Sam," *Galveston Daily News*, June 19, 1914. "Chief Sam's Ship Will Be Christened Saturday," *Galveston Daily News*, July 10, 1914. Letter from A. Davis, M. Sorrell, and Dr. P. J. Dorman to Vice Consular, May 18, 1914, "Negroes in West Africa," nos. 36–73, FO 115/1804, National Archives of the UK (TNA). "next trip:" Reed conversation, 13.

34. The *Progress* reported based on letters received from migrants requesting support to return. George V. Perry, "Sam's Bunch Starving!" *Boley Progress*, July 16, 1915, 1. See also "Chief Sam's Followers Are Starving to Death!" *Tulsa Star*, May 1, 1915, 1. Telegram from Chief Sam to British Ambassador, May 4, 1914, "Negroes in West Africa," nos. 36–73, FO 115/1804, National Archives of the UK (TNA). Nana Kurantsi III, chief of Saltpond, interview by James Anquandah, 1977, transcript and notes (in James Anquandah's possession, University of Ghana, Legon), 21–23, 39–40. Reporting on departure, arrival, and the movement: "At Last!"; "The African Movement" (November 27, 1914); "Forty Negroes off for Africa with Sam"; Faduma, "The African Movement." "British Warning for 'Chief Sam.'"

35. Report, June 21, 1915, Commission of the Central Province of the Gold Coast, "Public Records and Archives Administration Department, ADM 12/3/21, not paginated. See also letter "From Alfred Charles Sam" to Booker T. Washington, February 1915, in Harlan and Smock, *Booker T. Washington Papers*, 13: 246–47.
36. Ibid.
37. Ibid.
38. Reed conversation, 45n6, 13. "Alexander Davis," Passport Application, Harris County, Texas, December 2, 1916, Ancestry.com. U.S. Passport Applications, 1795–1925 [online database]. Lehi, UT: Ancestry.com Operations, Inc., 2007.
39. The *Brooklyn Eagle* story was reprinted in the *Kansas City Sun*. "The Latest from King Sam," *Kansas City Sun*, December 30, 1916, 4.
40. Ibid. "Delegates Gone to New York." Mitchell, *Righteous Propagation*, 9. "Migration," *Crisis*, February 1914, p. 190; "Chicago Negroes Now Turn Eyes on Africa; Chief Sam's Venture Makes Many Anxious to Join Colonization Trip 'Back Home,' " *Washington Herald*, February 22, 1914. Letter from W. E. B. Du Bois to A. Muldavin, September 23, 1931. W. E. B. Du Bois Papers (MS 312), Special Collections and University Archives, University of Massachusetts Amherst Libraries.
41. Letter from Booker T. Washington to Isaiah T. Montgomery, Jan. 25, 1915, in Harlan and Smock, *Booker T. Washington Papers*, 13 (1914–15): 233. August Meier, "Booker T. Washington and the Town of Mound Bayou," *Phylon* 15 (1954): 396. Booker T. Washington, "The Rural Negro Community," *Annals of the American Academy of Political and Social Science* 40 (1912): 81. "Negroes Eagerly Await 'Back to Africa' Ship," *Galveston Daily News*, June 4, 1914, 1; Letter from O. Faduma to Booker T. Washington, December 12, 1913, Booker T. Washington papers, Manuscript Division, Library of Congress, Washington, DC, quoted in Moore, *Orishatukeh Faduma*, 141–43. Letter from Tom Johnson to Booker T. Washington, February 27, 1914, Harlan and Smock, *Booker T. Washington Papers*, 12: 453. On the "separatist impulse," see also Rina Okonwo, "Orishatukeh Faduma: A Man of Two Worlds," *Journal of Negro History* 68 (1983), 27; Hahn, *A Nation under Our Feet*, 453–54; and Redkey, *Black Exodus*, 73–149.
42. Alfred M. Green, *Letters and Discussion of the Formation of Colored Regiments, and the Duty of the Colored People in Regards to the Great Slaveholders' Rebellion, in the United States of America* (Philadelphia: Ringwalt and Brown, 1862), 29–30.

Epilogue

1. "the desperate hopes": William E. Bittle and Gilbert L. Geis, *The Longest Way Home: Chief Alfred C. Sam's Back-to-Africa Movement* (Detroit: Wayne State University Press, 1964), 2, 14.

2. "many children": J. P. Owens, *Clearview* (Okemah, OK: J. P. Owens, 1995), 23. "There are hundreds": "Ship of African Pioneers Has Not Sailed," *Wewoka and Lima Courier*, January 30, 1914, 1.

3. See Owens, *Clearview*.

4. In fact, the U.S. government may have deliberately conflated Garvey with Sam, in order to undermine the UNIA's organizing efforts. In August 1919, an anonymous writer counseled the U.S. attorney general to "issue releases to the Negro press warning Negroes against bogus schemes of African repatriation and Negro Steamship Corp." and to give "the example of the Chief Sam fiasco." National Archives, D, RG 65, File 198940-2, quoted in Robert Hill, "Before Garvey: Chief Alfred Sam and the African Movement, 1912–1916," in *Pan-African Biography*, ed. Robert Hill (Los Angeles: University of California Press, 1987), 57. On the UNIA in Oklahoma, see Robert A. Hill, Emory J. Tolbert, and Deborah Forczek, eds., *The Marcus Garvey and UNIA Papers*, vol. 3, 1920–1921 (Berkeley: University of California Press, 1984), 470nn1,2; "Okmulgee U.N.I.A. Holds Monster Meeting," *Negro World*, March 19, 1921. On Weleetka and the UNIA, see Robert A. Hill, Tevvy Ball, Erika A. Blum, et al., eds., *The Marcus Garvey and UNIA Papers*, vol. 9, *Africa for the Africans, 1921–1922* (Berkeley: University of California Press, 1995), 316n1. On Garveyism in the rural South, see Steven Hahn, *A Nation under Our Feet: Black Political Struggles in the Rural South, from Slavery to the Great Migration* (Cambridge: Belknap Press of Harvard University Press, 2005), epilogue; and Mary G. Rolinson, *Grassroots Garveyism: The University Negro Improvement Association in the Rural South, 1920–1927* (Chapel Hill: University of North Carolina Press, 2007). See also Tony Martin, *Race First: The Ideological and Organizational Struggles of Marcus Garvey and the Universal Negro Improvement Association* (Westport, CT: Majority, 1976).

5. "U.S. Born citizens": Ship Manifest, Adriatic, Liverpool to New York City, October 28, 1915.

6. "family architecture": Suzannah Lessard, *The Architect of Desire: Beauty and Danger in the Stanford White Family* (New York: Delta, 1997), 5. "the first generation out of bondage": Thulani Davis, *My Confederate Kinfolk: A Twenty-First Century Freedwoman Discovers Her Roots* (New York: Basic Civitas, 2011), 5–6. See also Robert F. Engs, *Freedom's First Generation: Black Hampton, Virginia, 1861–1890* (Philadelphia: University of Pennsylvania Press, 1979).

7. Michel-Rolph Trouillot, *Silencing the Past: Power and the Production of History* (Boston: Beacon, 1995), 72–73, 82.

8. Rayford Whittingham Logan, *The Negro in American Life and Thought: The Nadir, 1877–1901* (New York: Dial, 1954), 52. W. E. B. Du Bois, *Black Reconstruction in America, 1860–1880* (1935; New York: Free Press, 1998), 30.

9. "deeply held beliefs": Trouillot, *Silencing the Past*, 72.

INDEX

Page numbers in *italics* indicate illustrations